CHURCH AND SOCIETY IN THE LAST
CENTURIES OF BYZANTIUM

Church and society in the last centuries of Byzantium

THE BIRKBECK LECTURES, 1977

DONALD M. NICOL

Koraës Professor of Modern Greek and
Byzantine History, Language and
Literature, University of London, King's College

CAMBRIDGE UNIVERSITY PRESS

CAMBRIDGE

LONDON · NEW YORK · MELBOURNE

Published by the Syndics of the Cambridge University Press
The Pitt Building, Trumpington Street, Cambridge CB2 1RP
Bentley House, 200 Euston Road, London NW1 2DB
32 East 57th Street, New York, NY 10022, USA
296 Beaconsfield Parade, Middle Park, Melbourne 3206, Austrialia

First published 1979

Printed in Great Britain at the
University Press, Cambridge

Library of Congress Cataloguing in Publication Data

Nicol, Donald MacGillivray.
Church and society in the last centuries of Byzantium.

(The Birkbeck lectures; 1977)
Bibliography: p.
Includes index.
1. Byzantine Empire – Civilization. 2. Byzantine
Empire – History. I. Title. II. Series.
DF531.N5   949.5'04   78-72092
ISBN 0 521 22438 1

CONTENTS

PREFACE

In 1977 I had the honour to deliver the Birkbeck Lectures at Cambridge. A singular honour it was since, as Professor Walter Ullmann observed when introducing me to my audience, the lectures had not been devoted to a Byzantine theme since the late Fr Francis Dvornik gave them in 1948. Byzantine studies have not received much encouragement from the University of Cambridge for all the precedent set by J. B. Bury and Sir Steven Runciman. I am therefore all the more grateful to the Master and Fellows of Trinity College for honouring me by their invitation to be their Birkbeck Lecturer and for their kindness to me in making the ordeal as painless as possible.

The chapters of this book are substantially the texts of those lectures with certain modifications, additions and amendments. In 1972 I published a book entitled *The Last Centuries of Byzantium, 1261–1453*. It was intended to serve as a textbook for students of a period of history which is notoriously complicated and which was not covered by any similar work in the English language. As a bare narrative of the political, ecclesiastical and military events of the declining years of the Byzantine Empire that book may have its uses. But I had always hoped to delve deeper into the nature of a society which had at the same time such a tragic propensity for collapse and such a remarkable talent for cultural and spiritual regeneration. The Birkbeck Lectures gave me the opportunity to arrange some of my thoughts on the matter. My debt to greater scholars in this field is, I hope, amply expressed in the bibliography and notes to the text. But it is a field which is still only partially ploughed by modern historians; and I have tried to draw most of my material direct from the original sources. Those sources which I have consulted (and the list is of necessity selective) may also be found in the bibliography.

The Byzantine Empire ended in 1453. Its inhabitants were therefore denied the experiences of material change and technological advance which were to transform western European society in the following century. They had no printing presses; they never knew of the existence of America; they had no Reformation; and their first and last bitter taste of heavy artillery warfare was at the final siege of their City by the Turks. They were the survivors and upholders of the last of the great pre-technological civilisations. They would probably have been out of sympathy with most of the developments, innovations and inventions of later years. The Byzantines of the last centuries were the nearest of their kind in time to our own age. They were nearer still to the Italians of the Renaissance; and they were uncomfortably near to the emerging civilisation of the Ottomans which was in the end to engulf them. Yet they retained an identity which kept them apart in religion, culture, language and outlook. This book may be described as an attempt to explore that identity, a series of reflexions on the Byzantine character.

In the transliteration of Greek words consistency is almost impossible without pedantry. English gentlemen of a bygone age, bred on the Classics, liked to refer to Cicero as Tully and Pompeius as Pompey because it gave them a pleasing illusion that the great men of antiquity had belonged to the same club as themselves. They fostered a similar conceit of familiarity with the ancient Hellenes by turning their names into Latin form. I have never felt inclined to perpetuate this practice of pretending to some familiarity with people who were so different from our English-speaking selves. It is moreover a practice particularly insulting to the memory of the last Byzantines, most of whom were proud to be distinct from the Latins or Franks of the western world. I would not go so far in the matter of literal transliteration of Greek names and words as the late Arnold Toynbee; but I prefer to render them in the form nearest to their Greek sound and spelling, except in cases where there is a generally accepted English equivalent.

My thanks are due to Dr Philip Sherrard, who read and made valuable comments on a first draft of this book while it was still in lecture form, and to Miss Catherine Blade, who patiently typed and retyped parts of a well-worked manuscript. Finally I must express my gratitude to the Cambridge University Press.

King's College, London   D.M.N.
July 1978

ABBREVIATIONS

The following abbreviations are used for periodicals, collections of sources and reference works:

AB   *Analecta Bollandiana*
B   *Byzantion*
BHG³   *Bibliotheca Hagiographica Graeca*, 3rd edn
BNJ   *Byzantinisch-neugriechische Jahrbücher*
BS   *Byzantinoslavica*
BZ   *Byzantinische Zeitschrift*
CFHB   *Corpus Fontium Historiae Byzantinae*
CSHB   *Corpus Scriptorum Historiae Byzantinae*
DHGE   *Dictionnaire d'histoire et de géographie ecclésiastique*
DIEE   *Δελτίον τῆς ἱστορικῆς καὶ ἐθνολογικῆς ἑταιρείας τῆς Ἑλλάδος*
DOP   *Dumbarton Oaks Papers*
DR   Dölger, F., *Regesten der Kaiserurkunden des oströmischen Reiches*
DTC   *Dictionnaire de théologie catholique*
EEBS   *Ἐπετηρὶς Ἑταιρείας Βυζαντινῶν Σπουδῶν*
EO   *Echos d'Orient*
JÖBG   *Jahrbuch der österreichischen byzantinischen Gesellschaft*
JÖB   *Jahrbuch der österreichischen Byzantinistik*
MM   Miklosich, F. and Müller, J., *Acta et Diplomata graeca medii aevi sacra et profana*
MPG   Migne, J. P., *Patrologiae cursus completus. Series graeco-latina*
NH   *Νέος Ἑλληνομνήμων*
OCA   *Orientalia Christiana Analecta*
OCP   *Orientalia Christiana Periodica*
REB   *Revue des études byzantines*
SBN   *Studi Bizantini e Neoellenici*
VV   *Vizantijskij Vremennik*
ZRVI   *Zbornik Radova Vizantološkog Instituta*

I

The background: the theocratic Empire

Opinions may vary about when the Byzantine, as distinct from the Roman or Late Roman Empire began. But about its end there can be no doubt whatever. The Byzantine Empire as a social and political institution ended on 29 May 1453. It was a Tuesday. The fall of Constantinople on that day completed the process of transition from a Christian Roman Empire to a Muslim Ottoman Empire. It had been a long process. It may be said to have begun almost exactly a hundred years before, in 1354. On 2 March of that year Gallipoli was destroyed by earthquake. The Osmanlis (or Ottomans) at once sailed over the Hellespont from Asia Minor to settle in the ruins. At Gallipoli they established their first permanent bridgehead on the soil of Europe. Forty years later almost the whole of the Balkans, Northern Greece, Macedonia, Serbia and Bulgaria were under Turkish rule. The ancient Greco-Roman cities in Asia Minor – Nicaea, Nikomedia, Ephesos and others – had succumbed even before 1354. But now the way into Europe was open to the infidel, the way that had been kept closed to the Arabs and the Seljuqs. The hope of reaching an entente between Christians and Muslims as European and Asiatic powers, which had been in the mind of at least one Byzantine emperor, was doomed. There were really only two cities left in the Empire – Thessalonica and Constantinople. The former was to have its first taste of Turkish conquest in 1387. The latter was to become the capital of an Ottoman Empire already in other respects well established on that fateful Tuesday in 1453.

The fall of Constantinople marked the end of the
century-long process which had begun with the Turkish
occupation of Gallipoli in 1354. Nearly a hundred years
before that event the Byzantines had made a brave show
of inaugurating a new era for their ancient Empire. They
had weathered the storm of the Fourth Crusade and in
1261 recovered their capital city from the westerners who
had stolen it. It has become fashionable to imply that the
Byzantines by their ineptitude and isolationism brought
the Fourth Crusade upon themselves. There may be some
truth in this. But neither they nor the crusaders can have
foreseen the consequences of that dreadful deed: a ruined,
burnt and pillaged city, a diaspora of refugees to east and
west, the setting-up of three rival Byzantine states in exile,
and the French or Italian occupation of most of Greece and
the Greek islands. (One forgets, for example, that Athens,
conquered by Burgundian adventurers in 1204, was not
again a Greek city until 1833.) The Latin régime in
Constantinople ended in 1261 when the Emperor in exile
at Nicaea, Michael VIII Palaiologos, entered the city in
triumph as the 'new Constantine', the second founder of
the Christian Roman Empire. It was from him that all the
emperors of the last centuries of that Empire, with one
notable exception, were descended. The year 1261 was
therefore the beginning, the year 1354 the middle, and the
year 1453 the end of these last centuries of Byzantium, the
end of the world.[1]

In that world, the Byzantine world, the distinction
between things spiritual and things temporal was often
blurred and seldom defined. Church and Empire were seen
as the two elements of one society, the soul and the body.
In the fourth century Eusebius of Caesarea had declared

---

1 General historical surveys of the period in English may be found in the
   following works: A. A. Vasiliev, *History of the Byzantine Empire, 324–1453*
   (Madison, 1952), pp. 580–722; G. Ostrogorsky, *History of the Byzantine
   State* (Oxford, 1968), pp. 444–572; *Cambridge Medieval History,* IV: *The
   Byzantine Empire,* Part 1: *Byzantium and its Neighbours* (Cambridge, 1966),
   pp. 331–87 (G. Ostrogorsky); D. M. Nicol, *The Last Centuries of Byzantium, 1261–1453* (London, 1972).

that the Christian Roman Empire was the earthly reflexion of the Kingdom of Heaven. Just as there was only one God in heaven so there could only be one ruler on earth, and that was the Emperor of the Romans. The emperor was God's regent on earth, the visible head of church and state, because the two were interdependent.[2] This theory sometimes left room for doubt as to where *imperium* ended and *sacerdotium* began. The ideal, as expressed by the Patriarch Photios in the ninth century, was that the emperor and the Patriarch of Constantinople worked in harmony, the one having care of the bodies, the other the souls of the people.[3] This happy state of psychosomatic co-operation was liable to be upset by extremists; for some emperors and some patriarchs too overstepped the limits of their jurisdiction. But in general it was agreed that there was something very special, something holy, about the office of emperor; and its holder, who was after all sometimes described as 'the thirteenth apostle', was very near to being a priest. A Byzantine canonist of the thirteenth century ruled that: 'The emperor has all the prerogatives of a priest except the right of administering the sacraments.'[4] Rightly so, for the emperor was the God-crowned ruler and protector of the Christian world.

It is significant that there is no Greek word for 'Christ-

2 On this fundamental tenet of Byzantine political thought, see especially N. H. Baynes, 'The Byzantine state', and 'Eusebius and the Christian Empire', in Baynes, *Byzantine Studies and Other Essays* (London, 1955), pp. 47–50, 168–72; F. Dvornik, *Early Christian and Byzantine Political Philosophy* (Dumbarton Oaks Studies, IX: Washington, D.C., 1966), II, pp. 611ff.; and S. Runciman, *The Byzantine Theocracy* (Cambridge, 1977), chs. 1 and 2, esp. pp. 22–5.

3 The views of Photios are expressed in the *Epanagoge*, composed about 880: J. and P. Zepos, *Jus Graecoromanum*, II (Athens, 1931), pp. 236–368, Tituli II and III, pp. 240–3; English trans. in E. Barker, *Social and Political Thought in Byzantium from Justinina I to the last Palaelogus* (Oxford, 1957), pp. 89–93. Cf. Runciman, *Byzantine Theocracy*, pp. 94–5. See also the texts collected in O. Mazal, *Die Prooimien der byzantinischen Patriarchenurkunden* (Byzantina Vindobonensia, VII: Vienna, 1974), pp. 145–57.

4 Demetrios Chomatianos, *Letter to Constantine Kabasilas*, ed. J. B. Pitra, *Analecta Sacra et Classica Spicilegio Solesmensi Parata*, VI (Rome, 1891), cols. 631–2.

endom', no Byzantine equivalent for the Latin term *christianitas*. The word that would have sprung to a Byzantine mind is *oikoumene*, or *basileia* – the Empire. The 'Christ-named people' ($\chi\rho\iota\sigma\tau\acute{\omega}\nu\nu\mu\sigma\varsigma$ $\lambda\alpha\acute{o}\varsigma$) who formed the great Christian society were the privileged inhabitants of the oecumenical Empire, whose visible head was the *basileus*, the God-protected ruler, defender of the faith and order ($\dot{\epsilon}\pi\iota\sigma\tau\eta\mu\sigma\nu\acute{\alpha}\rho\chi\eta\varsigma$) of the Church.[5] This idea persisted to the very last days of Byzantium. In 1393 the Grand Duke of Moscow, Basil I, suggested that things had reached such a sorry pass in Constantinople that, although the Church was seen to be surviving, there was no longer any very evident emperor to lead society: 'We have a Church but no emperor.' The Byzantine reply to this rude outburst by a Russian prince was composed by the Patriarch of Constantinople, Antonios IV. It is a justly celebrated document. In summary terms, the Patriarch pointed out, first, that, even though the Turks were hammering at the gates of the city, there was still an emperor on the throne, and second, that to talk of a Church without an emperor was an absurdity. The oecumenical Church, of which Russia was a part, postulated an oecumenical emperor. The one could not exist

5 For the term *epistemonarches*, signifying 'defender of the faith and regulator of order in the Church', see George Pachymeres, *De Michaele Palaeologo*, ed. I. Bekker (*CSHB*, 1835), p. 261 line 3; Demetrios Chomatianos, *Letter to Constantine Kabasilas*, col. 631. For other examples of the use of the term see DuCange, *Glossarium ad scriptores mediae et infimae graecitatis* (Lyons, 1688), col. 427. Cf. A. Michel, *Die Kaisermacht in der Ostkirche (843–1204)* (Darmstadt, 1959), pp. 47, 77. The Patriarch Athanasios I (on whom see below) applied the title to his emperor. Alice-Mary M. Talbot (ed.), *The Correspondence of Athanasius I Patriarch of Constantinople. Letters to the Emperor Andronicus II, Members of the Imperial Family, and Officials* (Dumbarton Oaks Texts, III [= *CFHB*, VII]: Washington, D.C., 1975), no. 61 line 48; no. 95 line 21. Athanasios's views on *imperium* and *sacerdotium* are clearly expressed in letter no. 104, addressed to the emperor about 1309 (ed. Talbot, p. 264 lines 25–8): 'For priesthood was not granted to Christian people for the sake of empire, but empire for the sake of priesthood, so that if the empire in a manner pleasing to God supported the Church with the secular arm and honored and protected Her, the empire in turn would be supported and protected and increased by God.' Cf. letter no. 61, p. 139.

without the other.[6] The same view was expressed by the
monks of Constantinople in the thirteenth century when
they were being persecuted by the Emperor Michael VIII.
The historian of the time tells us that the monks counted
the days till they should be rid not of their emperor but
of their miseries; for they could no more live without an
emperor than a body can live without a head.[7]

Some Orthodox theologians of today have deplored
this Byzantine identification of Church and society.
Alexander Schmemann writes: 'The tragedy of the Byzantine Church consisted precisely in the fact that it became
merely the *Byzantine* Church, that it merged itself with
the Empire not so much administratively as, above all,
psychologically, in its own self-awareness. The Empire
became for it the absolute and supreme value, unques-
tioned, inviolable, and self-evident.'[8] Perhaps this was a
tragedy. But at least until 1453 it was a fact of Byzantine
life.

The Church on earth, which implied the Empire on
earth, was a reflexion of the Church in heaven. The
Byzantines therefore lived in constant communication
with the other world, in constant expectation of miracle
or supernatural intervention in their material affairs. The
interplay of time and eternity was always real to them.
The Church on earth provided the links, the channels of
grace between this world and the other. The sacraments
or 'mysteries' were the regular means of communication.
But there were other channels: tangible ones like icons or
relics; living ones like monks or holy men. Society within
the Empire was under the special protection of God. But

---

6 The text of the Patriarch's letter is in *MM*, II, pp. 188–92. Partial English
trans. in E. Barker, *Social and Political Thought*, pp. 194–6. For discussion
of its significance see S. Runciman, *The Great Church in Captivity. A Study
of the Patriarchate of Constantinople from the Eve of the Turkish Conquest to
the Greek War of Independence* (Cambridge, 1968), pp. 71–6; Ostrogorsky,
History of the Byzantine State, pp. 553–4; D. Obolensky, *The Byzantine
Commonwealth. Eastern Europe, 500–1453* (London, 1971), pp. 264–6.

7 Pachymeres, *De Michaele Palaeologo*, p. 490.

8 A. Schmemann, *The Historical Road of Eastern Orthodoxy* (London, 1963),
pp. 222–3.

God would remove his protection if his people drifted into sin or lapsed into heresy. The Byzantines studied and wrote treatises about the 'art of war'. They knew that God helps those who help themselves. But they truly believed that ultimately the safety of their city depended as much on the strength and purity of their faith as on armed defence. Time and again Constantinople was saved from its enemies by the intervention of the Virgin. Time and again Thessalonica was saved from Arabs, Slavs or Bulgars by the intervention of its Saint Demetrios.[9] Such matters were beyond reason and above politics. Theology too, in its proper sense of the knowledge of God, was held to be beyond reason. Byzantine theologians distrusted the subtleties of syllogism and dialectic as aids towards the understanding of God. Only a mystic or a saint could come to the fullness of that understanding. Yet, because Byzantine society was so permeated by religious feeling, theology in some sense was seldom far from men's minds. If the ancient Greek was, as Aristotle said, 'a political animal', the Byzantine was a theological animal. In the absolute monarchy under which he lived religion was almost the only form of politics available to him. Rival emperors or pretenders might fight for possession of the throne, but their motives were seldom political in the modern sense. They were personal, they were dynastic; but the warring factions were not intent on changing the existing order of society or the institutions of government. The order of society was in any case divinely ordained; and the orthodoxy of an emperor's theology was held to be more significant for the maintenance of that order than his 'politics'. There was indeed one political upheaval in the fourteenth century which had nothing to do with theology or the Church. But it is unique. When Byzantine society was divided the division was usually on ecclesiastical or theological grounds. The christological debates of the fourth to sixth centuries, the iconoclastic controversy

9 See N. H. Baynes, 'The Supernatural Defenders of Constantinople', in Baynes, *Byzantine Studies and Other Essays*, pp. 248–60.

of the eighth and ninth centuries, the passionate arguments about the rights and wrongs of union with the Roman Church in the last centuries – all these were matters of life and death. The issues were basically theological. But they divided families, divided society, divided the Empire.

In the last centuries of Byzantium there were three great debates of this nature: the Arsenite schism, the hesychast controversy and the question of union with the Roman Church. Each one of them demonstrates the extent to which religion was the politics of the Byzantine people. The so-called Arsenite schism, which divided church and society in the thirteenth century, began with the crime of an emperor and with a conflict of loyalties among his subjects.[10] The Emperor Michael VIII Palaiologos, who had chased the Latins out of Constantinople in 1261 and restored the city to its proper owners, had imprudently inaugurated the new era by blinding the boy Emperor John IV, whom many believed to be the lawful heir to the throne. Like the United Kingdom the Byzantine Empire had no written constitution. Its monarchy was, in principle if seldom in practice, elective and not hereditary. Emperors had blinded or even murdered their rivals before Michael VIII. But many people felt that the victim in 1261 had a prescriptive right at least to share the *imperium* which his fathers had saved from extinction after the Fourth Crusade. For the young John IV was the last of the line of the dynasty of Laskaris, which had ruled the Empire in exile at Nicaea for over fifty years. Michael VIII's treatment of him was criminal, a crime against humanity and against the Church. The Patriarch of Constantinople, Arsenios, very properly excommunicated him. As soon as he could find a pretext, the Emperor deposed his patriarch.

10 On the Arsenite schism, see especially L. Petit, 'Arsène Autorianus et les Arsénites', *DTC*, I, ii, cols. 1991–4; I. Sykoutris, Περὶ τὸ σχίσμα τῶν Ἀρσενιατῶν, *Hellenika*, II (1929), pp. 267–332; III (1930), pp. 15–44; V. Laurent, 'Les grandes crises religieuses à Byzance. La fin du schisme arsénite', *Académie Roumaine. Bulletin de la section historique*, XXVI (Bucharest, 1945), pp. 225–313. Cf. Nicol, *Last Centuries*, pp. 50, 67, 102–5, 110–11, 131–3.

But such was the feeling in the Church that it was another
two years before Michael could persuade a substitute
patriarch to absolve him and receive him back into the
fold.

The deposed Patriarch Arsenios promptly became a
martyr. A faction of bishops, priests, monks and laymen
broke away from the rest of the Church. They called
themselves the Arsenites and refused to recognise the
authority of any subsequent patriarchs. They remained
loyal to the memory of Arsenios who had had the courage
to condemn the Emperor as a criminal. Not all of them
perhaps were motivated by such lofty principles. As so
often in Byzantium, the trouble was partly about the
extent to which the emperor had the right to interfere in
the affairs of the Church. This, as has already been
suggested, was a perennial problem and one to which no
Byzantine canonist had ever provided a definitive answer,
merely a series of interpretations and recommendations.
Here again, the Empire could perhaps have done with a
written constitution; the Church could have done with an
army of canon lawyers. But in either eventuality the
Empire, and the Church, would have ceased to have that
specific quality which we call 'Byzantine'. There were
plenty of precedents for an emperor to disembarrass
himself of a troublesome patriarch. But that did not mean
that such action was right or acceptable to the Church.
'Caesaropapism' is now rightly a somewhat discredited
word.[11] But it should be remembered that Byzantine
emperors who overstepped the invisible line between the
preserves of the *imperium* and the preserves of the
sacerdotium were frequently given hell by their bishops in
this world, whatever happened to them in the next.

The Arsenites were also encouraged by the emotional
hostility towards Michael VIII of the large number of

11 See D. J. Geanakoplos, 'Church and State in the Byzantine Empire: A
   reconsideration of the problem of Caesaropapism', in Geanakoplos,
   *Byzantine East and Latin West: Two Worlds of Christendom in Middle Ages
   and Renaissance* (Oxford, 1966), pp. 55–83.

supporters of the disprised and blinded Emperor John Laskaris. They were most numerous and most loyal in Asia Minor, where the Laskarid dynasty had earned its fame and its following. The Arsenite schism therefore represents very well the amalgam of ideals, of politics and of religion which constituted an opposition party in Byzantium. It was always difficult to tell where religion ended and politics began. The schism was not officially resolved until 1310, long after Michael VIII and Arsenios were dead and gone, when circumstances had changed, memories had faded and passions cooled.[12]

The second great debate that divided Church and society in the last centuries of Byzantium concerned the precepts and practices of certain monks who came to be known as the hesychasts; or rather it was about the theological implications of the mystical experience which the accomplished hesychast claimed to enjoy. This was on a much higher and more rarefied plane than the conflict waged by the Arsenites. The most eloquent champion of the hesychasts and indeed a major formulator of their theology was Gregory Palamas, a monk with a great following on Mount Athos. Councils of bishops were convened and reconvened to determine the truth or the falsehood of Palamite theology. The Church was rent by controversy. Society was divided into Palamites and anti-Palamites, hesychasts and anti-hesychasts.[13]

Put in its simplest form the argument was about the nature of the divine light of the Transfiguration. Nothing

---

12 Nicol, *Last Centuries*, pp. 110–11.
13 On Hesychasm, see esp. J. Meyendorff, *Introduction à l'étude de Grégoire Palamas* (Paris, 1959) (English trans., *A Study of Gregory Palamas*, by G. Lawrence (London, 1964)); J. M. Hussey and T. A. Hart, in *Cambridge Medieval History*, IV, 2 (Cambridge, 1967), pp. 198–205; Runciman, *Great Church*, pp. 128–58; J. Meyendorff, *Byzantine Hesychasm: historical, theological and social problems. Collected Studies* (Variorum: London, 1974); Meyendorff, *Byzantine Theology. Historical Trends and Doctrinal Themes* (New York, 1974), pp. 76–8, 107–9; Meyendorff 'Spiritual trends in Byzantium in the late thirteenth and early fourteenth centuries', in P. A. Underwood (ed.), *The Kariye Djami*, IV (New York, 1975), pp. 93–106. See also Ch. 2.

could seem further above the sordid world of politics. But
the controversy coincided with the outbreak of a civil war,
or rather a dynastic war, following the death of the
Emperor Andronikos III in 1341. Andronikos left an infant
son, John V, as his successor. The bone of contention was
the regency and guardianship of this heir to the throne in
Constantinople. The Grand Domestic John Cantacuzene
had been the late emperor's chief minister and friend and
had every right to expect the regency as his reward. But
his claim was disputed by the Patriarch of Constantinople,
John Kalekas, and by the Grand Duke Alexios Apokaukos.
Both men owed their positions to Cantacuzene. But both
posed as champions of the legitimate heir, John V, and of
his mother, the Empress Anne of Savoy; and she was
persuaded that it was the Patriarch who should act as
regent. Cantacuzene and his supporters went to war to
right this wrong.[14] These were the circumstances in which
the hesychast dispute arose. The Patriarch, who was in fact
no great theologian, convinced himself that Gregory
Palamas and his hesychast monks had gone too far and
were guilty of heresy. He had them condemned by his
synod. Palamas was imprisoned and then excommunicated. Those who believed, as did the pretender John
Cantacuzene, that hesychast doctrine was perfectly
orthodox therefore tended to take the other side in the war
over the regency. Cantacuzene was thus able to count on
the overwhelming and invaluable support of the monks,
especially on Mount Athos. This was not mere political
opportunism on his part. His own memoirs and theological
writings, which he composed later in his life, show that

14 The circumstances of the civil war of 1341–7 are outlined by Nicol, *Last
Centuries*, pp. 191ff., and Nicol, *The Byzantine Family of Kantakouzenos
(Cantacuzenus) ca. 1100–1460. A genealogical and prosopographical study*
(Dumbarton Oaks Studies, XI: Washington, D.C., 1968), pp. 44–63. Cf.
P. Charanis, 'Internal strife in Byzantium during the fourteenth century',
B, XV (1940–1), pp. 208–30; G. Weiss, *Joannes Kantakuzenos – Aristokrat,
Staatsmann, Kaiser und Mönch – in der Gesellschaftsentwicklung von Byzanz
im 14. Jahrhundert* (Wiesbaden, 1969); K. P. Matschke, *Fortschritt und
Reaktion in Byzanz im 14. Jahrhundert* (Berlin, 1971).

Cantacuzene was no amateur theologian. He had thought his way to his own convictions.

The political undertones of the hesychast controversy have probably been overstated by some modern historians. It is possible, for example, to name certain parties who at the time ought, by reason of their social and political affinities, to have been Palamites but were not; and vice versa. The violently anti-Palamite scholar and theologian Nikephoros Gregoras is an outstanding case. As an old personal friend and admirer of John Cantacuzene, Gregoras had no doubts about the justice of his claim to the regency or to the throne. But his own deep thought on the matter of Hesychasm led him to denounce his friend as a deviationist in theology and therefore not fit to be emperor.[15] It is possible too that, without the circumstances of civil war, the hesychast dispute would not have divided society in the way that it did. The political victory in that war went, in the end, to John Cantacuzene in 1347. He had already been emperor in name for six years; he was now emperor in fact and master of Constantinople. As such it was his right and his duty to bring the warring factions in his Church and society into harmony. In 1351 he summoned a council of bishops and laymen to the palace. There Gregory Palamas and the theology and practice of Hesychasm were vindicated and their opponents condemned as heretical. Palamas became Metropolitan of Thessalonica in 1350 and died in 1359. Soon afterwards he was canonised by the Orthodox Church.[16]

The hesychast movement was one of the manifestations of a general revival of spirituality in Byzantine society in the early fourteenth century. The same age witnessed a remarkable revival of scholarship and secular learning.[17]

15 A very large part of the third volume of the printed text of *Byzantina Historia* of Nikephoros Gregoras (ed. L. Schopen [*CSHB*, 1855]) is devoted to polemics against Palamas and the hesychasts. Cf. R. Guilland, *Essai sur Nicéphore Grégoras. L'homme et l'œuvre* (Paris, 1926), esp. pp. 23–54.
16 Meyendorff, *Introduction*, pp. 141–53; Nicol, *Last Centuries*, pp. 239–41.
17 See S. Runciman, *The Last Byzantine Renaissance* (Cambridge, 1970), and below, Ch. 2.

Some may have felt like retreating to monasteries or to libraries rather than facing the harsh facts of a fading Empire and a crumbling world. But mere escapism is not enough to explain this renewed concern with the way of the mystic and the pursuits of the scholar. A lead in the revival of spirituality had been given some forty years before the hesychast controversy began. In 1289 a monk called Athanasios, who was famed for his sanctity and austerity, had been persuaded to leave the comfort of his cell to become Patriarch of Constantinople. The letters that Athanasios wrote to the Emperor and to other dignitaries survive. They reveal much about Byzantine society of the time, not least about its shortcomings in the way of piety and morality.[18] John Knox would have admired the Patriarch Athanasios: he was a stern puritan and rigorous ascetic who expected everyone to live up to his own high standards of unhappiness.

The evils in his society which Athanasios repeatedly denounced were all in his view attributable to the depravity and lawlessness of lapsed Christians. The unseemly wealth of the Church and the monasteries, the avarice of the clergy, the sharp practices of businessmen and black marketeers, the fearful poverty and near starvation of the poor, even the alarming success and progress of the infidel Turks – all these things were the direct consequence of godlessness and immorality. The only remedy was a return to the sober God-fearing life. It is to the credit of the Patriarch Athanasios that he practised what he preached. He relieved the monasteries of some of their wealth and spent the proceeds on setting up soup kitchens for the poor and hungry in Constantinople. He bullied the Emperor into taking steps to beat the black market and regulate the

18 One hundred and fifteen of the patriarch's letters have been edited, with an English translation and commentary, by Alice-Mary Maffry Talbot, *The Correspondence of Athanasius I* [see n. 5: cited hereafter as *Letters of Athanasios*, ed. Talbot]. On the patriarch's life and career see also Talbot, 'The Patriarch Athanasius (1289–1293; 1303–1309) and the Church', *DOP*, XXVII (1973), pp. 11–28, where the earlier literature is cited. See also below, Ch. 2.

supply of food.[19] He advised him to keep the army well supplied and fed; for no good would come of looking for military aid from the heretical Christians of western Europe. Byzantium must stand on its own feet, reform its ways, repent and earn forgiveness and the help of God.[20]

The emperor who had appointed Athanasios was Andronikos II, the son of Michael VIII. It was at his court that the scholars of the age, such as Gregoras, gathered to read their learned papers. He was the patron of the new learning, but at the same time pious to a fault. He was mesmerised by the Patriarch Athanasios, who rather disapproved of scholarship. Somebody is said to have drawn a cartoon of the Emperor Andronikos with a bit in his mouth being led along like a horse by his patriarch.[21] But the methods that the patriarch employed to enforce his high ideals made him many enemies. He was obliged to resign in 1293. Ten years later he sent a message to the palace predicting the imminent wrath of God against the impious people of Constantinople. That very night there was a small earthquake, followed two days later by a large one. A procession led by the Emperor made its way to the monastery where Athanasios was living and on bended knees implored the great prophet to return as their patriarch.[22] His second term of office lasted six years. They were critical years, in which the wrath of heaven was clearly seen to be visited on the Byzantines. The Turks were carrying all before them in Asia Minor. The heartland of the Empire was all but lost; and thousands of refugees

---

19 See esp. *Letters of Athanasios*, ed. Talbot, nos. 22, 72–4, 78, 93, 100, 102, 106; and Angeliki E. Laiou, 'The provisioning of Constantinople during the winter of 1306–1307', *B*, xxxvii (1967), pp. 91–113.

20 *Letters of Athanasios*, ed. Talbot, no. 37, p. 78 lines 12–15: '. . . do not think that we shall prevail by means of armed attacks . . . even if the whole West, if it were possible, were to join to help us. What then is the solution? Turning toward God and repentance to the utmost of our ability, for which he is patiently waiting.' Cf. no. 84, p. 224 lines 73–7.

21 Gregoras, I, pp. 258–9.

22 Pachymeres, *De Andronico Palaeologo*, pp. 359–77, 379–84; Gregoras, I, pp. 215–16. *Letters of Athanasios*, ed. Talbot, pp. xix–xxiii; Nicol, *Last Centuries*, pp. 109–10.

with dreadful tales to tell were daily crowding into the capital from across the water. Many people agreed that the only hope of salvation lay in repentance. But they objected to having repentance thrust upon them by a tyrant patriarch. In 1309 Athanasios concluded that he was a prophet without honour in his own country. He resigned for a second time and went back to his monastic cell.[23]

One of the dangers that Athanasios had foreseen was that his people might be driven to seek help from the western world. He himself had observed what a mixed blessing even an army of mercenaries from the west could be; for he and his emperor had had to contend with the greed and depredations of the so-called Catalan Company whose soldiers, hired as mercenaries in a fit of imperial optimism, in the end did rather more damage to the Empire than to the Turks.[24] But what the Patriarch had in the back of his mind was the awful prospect that the Byzantines might become so desperate that they would again take to bargaining with the Pope in order to qualify for a crusade from the west.[25] This brings us to the third great debate that divided Byzantine society – the question of the rights and wrongs of union with the Roman Church. On this issue the division was far from being an equal one. Those in favour of union were always a small minority. Most Byzantines, even in the dark twilight of their Empire, firmly believed that their survival depended on preserving the integrity of their Orthodox faith. No threat to their material existence could make them willingly commit the sin of uniting with the western Church. A sin it was, since the westerners, apart from the damage

23 Gregoras, I, pp. 258–9. *Letters of Athanasios*, ed. Talbot, pp. xxiv–xxvi.
24 For the activities of the Catalans see now Angeliki E. Laiou, *Constantinople and the Latins. The Foreign Policy of Andronicus II 1282–1328* (Cambridge, Mass., 1972), pp. 127–242; K. M. Setton, 'The Catalans in Greece, 1311–1380', in Setton (ed.), *A History of the Crusades*, III: *The Fourteenth and Fifteenth Centuries*, ed. H. W. Hazard (Madison, 1975), pp. 167–224.
25 For the patriarch's anti-Latin sentiments, cf. Talbot, 'The Patriarch Athanasius', pp. 19–20; Laiou, *Constantinople and the Latins*, pp. 198–9.

which they had done to Byzantium, were in schism and in heresy. Two thirteenth-century writers may be quoted to state this case, the first one of the minority who tried to bring the union into being, the second a fervent anti-unionist. 'What can one say', writes the unionist, 'when women and children still in the nursery, when men whose knowledge is limited to farming or manual labour, all cry criminal to anyone who so much as whispers about the union of the churches?'[26] 'Those who unrepentantly take communion with the Italians', writes the anti-unionist, 'defile their souls no less than those who commune with heretics and will suffer the same punishments on the day of judgment.'[27]

Nevertheless, there were individual cases of Orthodox Byzantines being converted to the Roman faith; and on two occasions union of a kind was proclaimed if not achieved between the churches collectively – first at the Council of Lyons in 1274, second at the Council of Florence in 1439. The Union of Lyons was arranged to forestall the imminent danger of a repetition of the Fourth Crusade, to be led by Charles of Anjou, brother of Louis IX of France. It served its purpose for a few years. But the hostility to it in Byzantium was so violent and prolonged that even the popes could see that this was no union of hearts and minds. And in the end it was they who broke it off and dignified the Christian enemies of Byzantium with the status of crusaders. The popes were always liable to think that if the Greeks stubbornly refused to admit the error of their ways then they deserved to be brought back to the fold of Rome by force. Charles of Anjou would most certainly have launched his armada against Constantinople with the full blessing of the Pope,

26 John Bekkos (Beccus), *De Injustitia* (or *De Depositione Sua Orationes*), I, *MPG*, CXLIII, col. 984.
27 Meletios Homologetes (Confessor), (Λόγος τρίτος) Κατ' Ἰταλῶν, ed. V. Laurent and J. Darrouzès, *Dossier grec de l'Union de Lyon (1273–1277)* (Archives de l'Orient Chrétien, 16: Paris, 1976), p. 563 lines 257–61.

had not his plans and ambitions been wrecked by the
revolt known as the Sicilian Vespers in 1282.[28]

The Union of Florence in the fifteenth century was a
different matter. Times had changed. By then the danger
to Constantinople came not from the Christian west but
from the Muslim east; and since the Turks were already
masters of a large part of eastern Europe the anxiety was
felt by western Christendom as well. Common fear of the
Turks, and the need to take common action on a material
level, were factors propitious to the progress of union on
a spiritual plane. That union was proclaimed, after months
of wrangling, at Florence in 1439.[29] But once again the
reaction in Byzantium was violently hostile. It was
commonly said that the Orthodox bishops at Florence had
signed the death warrant of their Church and Empire. Far
from saving the day by ensuring the promise of western
aid, they had betrayed their souls and made it certain that
God would now withdraw his favour and leave the
Byzantines to their own devices. The hope of a miracle
had been snuffed out. Seventeen years before, in 1422,
when the Turks had laid siege to Constantinople, their
efforts had been thwarted by the intervention of the Virgin
Mary.[30] After the scandal of the Union of Florence the

28 The Greek documents relating to the Union of Lyons are collected by
    Laurent and Darrouzès, *Dossier grec*. On the circumstances of the Union
    and the Byzantine reaction to it, see B. Roberg, *Die Union zwischen der
    griechischen und der lateinischen Kirche auf dem II. Konzil von Lyon (1274)*
    (Bonn, 1964); S. Runciman, *The Sicilian Vespers. A History of the
    Mediterranean World in the Late Thirteenth Century* (Cambridge, 1958);
    D. J. Geanakoplos, *Emperor Michael Palaeologus and the West, 1258–1282. A
    Study in Byzantine-Latin Relations* (Cambridge, Mass., 1959); D. M. Nicol,
    'The Byzantine reaction to the Second Council of Lyons, 1274', *Studies
    in Church History*, VII, ed. G. J. Cuming and D. Baker (Cambridge, 1971),
    pp. 113–46 (reprinted in Nicol, *Byzantium: its ecclesiastical history and
    relations with the western world. Collected Studies* [Variorum: London, 1972],
    no. VI).
29 J. Gill, *The Council of Florence* (Cambridge, 1959); D. J. Geanakoplos,
    'The Council of Florence (1438–39) and the problem of union between
    the Byzantine and Latin Churches', in Geanakoplos, *Byzantine East and
    Latin West*, pp. 84–111; Runciman, *Great Church*, pp. 104–9.
30 The Turkish siege of Constantinople in 1422 was described by John
    Kananos (Cananus): *De Constantinopoli oppugnata (1422)*, ed. I. Bekker, in

Virgin would not intervene again. The Byzantines would have to go it alone – unless they repented without delay and renounced the shameful deed. An oracle had foretold that the end would come when there would be an emperor and a patriarch whose names began with the same letter. The oracle had now been fulfilled. The Emperor John and the Patriarch Joseph had accomplished the ruin of the Church at Florence, and the ruin of the Church would surely be followed by the ruin of the Empire.[31]

It is true that at the end the sound of Turkish guns beyond the walls of Constantinople proved more persuasive than all the theologians. In a moment of panic many Byzantines were terrorised into accepting the submission required of them by the Latins. In December 1452, at a solemn liturgy in the Great Church of St Sophia, the names of the Pope and the Patriarch were commemorated together and the decrees of the Union of Florence were read out. But only the most optimistic of the unionists can have believed that this was more than a gesture inspired by despair and fear; and most of the population refused thereafter, in the last months of their freedom, to worship in their cathedral. They preferred to receive the sacraments in churches whose priests had not been defiled by association with the Latins.[32]

Right to the last it was assumed that Church and society were one. If you believed, as most Byzantines did, that the purity of your faith had been contaminated by the errors of the Latins, then it followed that society too was

(S)Phrantzes (*CSHB*, 1838), pp. 457–79. Cf. Nicol, *Last Centuries*, pp. 347–8.

31 The oracle is recorded by the later Patriarch Gennadios (George Scholarios): *Oeuvres complètes de Gennade Scholarios*, ed. L. Petit, X. A. Siderides, M. Jugie, IV (Paris, 1935), p. 511. The Greek letters ἰώ (as in Ἰωάννης, Ἰωσήφ) meant 'alas' or 'woe'.

32 Gill, *Council of Florence*, pp. 383–7; S. Runciman, *The Fall of Constantinople 1453* (Cambridge, 1965), pp. 69–72. For the supposed corruption of Greek priests by Latins, see Doukas (Ducas), *Istoria Turco-Bizantina (1341–1462)*, ed. V. Grecu (Bucharest, 1958), p. 319. Cf. I. Ševčenko, 'Intellectual repercussions of the Council of Florence', *Church History*, XXIV (1955), esp. pp. 296–300.

contaminated, or at least those members of it who had
supped with the heretics. The contamination was physical
as well as spiritual. When the cathedral of St Sophia was
recovered from the Latins in 1261 its altar had to be
ritually cleansed from the pollution before it was fit for
Orthodox use. The same purifying procedure had to be
undertaken again in 1282, after the cathedral had been for
some years the seat of a unionist patriarch, even though
he was a Greek. The prayers for the dedication of a new
church were recited; the naves, narthex, walls, columns
and sacred icons were sprinkled with holy water; and the
abomination of the 'scandal' was thus purged.[33] The
Emperor Michael VIII, who was held responsible for that
scandal, and who had quite literally saved his people from
invasion by the Latins as a result, was denied the last rites
befitting an emperor when he died in 1282. He had saved
the body of his Empire but at the expense of its immortal
soul. The 'new Constantine' died in heresy, an outcast
from his own Church and society. Even his corpse was
thought to be contaminated. It was laid on a mountain side
and covered with a mound of earth. No grave was dug,
no burial service was read. His widow was advised to
abandon any hope for the rest or salvation of her husband's
soul and to promise that she would never ask that he be
properly buried.[34]

Thus deeply was Byzantine society affected by any
attempt to tamper with the Orthodoxy of its religious
beliefs. To enforce his policy of union with Rome Michael
VIII had been driven to persecuting and imprisoning his
opponents in large numbers. The charge against them
was treason. By no means all of them were monks or
churchmen. They included several of his own relatives,
officers in the army and ministers of state. As soon as
Michael was dead, his son and successor Andronikos II
hastened to proclaim the end of the scandal and the

33 Pachymeres, *De Andronico Palaeologo*, pp. 19–20.
34 Pachymeres, *De Andronico Palaeologo*, pp. 16, 55; Gregoras, I, pp. 150–5.
   Nicol, 'The Byzantine reaction', pp. 137–8, 140–1.

restoration of Orthodoxy. The prisoners were released and became the heroes of the hour. It is doubtful whether the Roman Church gained much from the making and breaking of the Union of Lyons. But the Orthodox Church gained immensely from the reaction against that union. It emerged stronger than ever before as the guardian of the true Byzantine conscience. Its members were far from being united. The Arsenite schism remained to be healed. The unrepentant unionists and their fellow travellers had still to be convicted. But its quarrels and debates were of its own making and demonstrated the freedom of the Church, whether from imperial or foreign interference. People looked more and more to their monks and bishops and patriarchs and less to their emperors for assurance and comfort as their Empire crumbled around them. By the end of the fourteenth century there was not much of that Empire left. The emperors themselves had meekly and perforce accepted the status of vassals of the Ottoman Sultans. But by contrast the Church had grown in prestige and confidence; and the See of Constantinople had successfully reimposed its moral authority over most of the once-independent Orthodox churches of eastern Europe.

The greatest Patriarchs of Constantinople in the four-teenth century were monks brought up in the hard school of Mount Athos, the 'factory of virtue' as it was sometimes called.[35] As the flourishing monastic settlements in Asia Minor were overrun by the Turks, the Holy Mountain of Athos became still more important as the greatest surviving spiritual powerhouse of the Empire. Since the tenth century its monasteries had been under the juris-diction of the emperors. In 1312 it was decreed that they should henceforth be under the direct authority of the Patriarch of Constantinople.[36] The role of the emperor in

35 For Athos as the ἐργαστήριον ἀρετῆς, see, e.g., the *Testament* of Isidore, in *MM*, ɪ, p. 288.
36 Text in Ph. Meyer, *Die Haupturkunden für die Geschichte der Athos-Klöster* (Leipzig, 1894), pp. 190–4; F. Dölger, *Aus den Schatzkammern des Heiligen Berges* (Munich, 1948), ɪ, No. 5.

Church and society was changing. He was still the
vice-gerent of God on earth, God-guarded and God-
crowned. He was still indispensable in the theocratic
society. But even in the ceremony of his coronation a
subtle innovation had occurred. The emperors of the late
thirteenth century and after were not merely crowned by
their patriarchs. They were also anointed with the chrism
of confirmation. This was a new development in the
Byzantine coronation rite. It signified that the Church
quite literally set its seal of confirmation upon the emperors
at the moment of their accession.[37]

This is not to say that the last Byzantine emperors were
the tools of their patriarchs or the slaves of their Church.
They had minds of their own; and they were still
committed, with the help of the Church, to upholding the
divine order of things as the divinely ordained rulers of
Christian society. They were not oblivious of the plight
of the poor and the refugees in their midst, nor of the gap
between the very rich and the very poor. Constantinople
and Thessalonica were never short of orphanages and old
people's homes endowed by imperial or private funds and
attached to monasteries. Philanthropy was one of the
required virtues of an emperor, applauded by every court
poet and orator.[38] And within their limitations most of
the late Byzantine emperors were philanthropic and well
intentioned. But it is the limitations that matter. The
rudest affront ever offered to the political ideology of
Byzantium was the so-called Zealot revolution in Thessalonica in the 1340s.[39] It took its most dramatic form in

37 D. M. Nicol, '*Kaisersalbung*. The unction of emperors in late Byzantine
   coronation ritual', *Byzantine and Modern Greek Studies*, II (1976), pp. 37–52.
38 See D. J. Constantelos, *Byzantine Philanthropy and Social Welfare* (New
   Brunswick, N.J., 1968); H. Hunger, 'Philanthropia. Eine griechische
   Wortprägung auf ihrem Wege von Aischylos bis Theodoros Metochites',
   Anzeiger phil.-hist. Klasse Österreichische Akademie der Wissenschaften, Nr.
   100 (Graz-Vienna-Cologne, 1963), pp. 1–20 (reprinted in Hunger, *Byzantinische Grundlagenforschung. Gesammelte Aufsaetze* [Variorum: London,
   1973], no. XIII).
39 There is a wealth of literature on the Zealot revolution. See Nicol, *Last
   Centuries*, p. 215 n. 16, to which should now be added: G. L. Kurbatov

Thessalonica, although the revolutionary fervour gripped all the towns of Thrace at about the same time. So far as we can judge from the meagre evidence, this was a movement of protest against the prevailing social and political system – a movement without precedent or parallel in Byzantine history. When, for a second time in one generation, the people of Thrace saw their country-side about to become a battlefield in a struggle for power between rival factions of their ruling class, they registered their objection by taking the law into their own hands. In the city of Adrianople, for instance, rioting broke out, crowds rampaged through the streets plundering and destroying the houses of the rich, the aristocracy were arrested and their property was confiscated. The city was taken over by a revolutionary régime.

The example set by Adrianople was quickly followed in other towns. But in Thessalonica the movement seems to have been more highly organised. A faction or junta calling themselves the Zealots controlled the revolution and, when the dust of rioting had settled, set up an administration which ruled the city as a virtually inde-pendent commune for nearly eight years, from 1342–50. The Zealots had their ups and downs; they squabbled among themselves; and latterly they retained their power only by gross violence and hideous massacres. But one assumes that in Thessalonica as elsewhere the support for rebellion was at first widespread and fervent. One can do no more than assume this: the evidence is so disappoint-ingly sparse and so highly debatable. Historians, Marxist and other, are still arguing about the true significance of this movement in fourteenth-century Byzantine society;

and V. I. Rutenburg, 'Ziloti i Ciompi', *VV*, xxx (1969), pp. 3–37; J. W. Barker, 'The "monody" of Demetrios Kydones on the Zealot rising of 1345 in Thessaloniki', Μελετήματα στὴ μνήμη B. Λαούρδα (Thessalonike, 1975), pp. 285–300; P. Charanis, 'Observations on the "Anti-Zealot" Discourse of Cabasilas', *Revue des études sud-est européennes*, ix (1971), pp. 369–76; E. Werner, 'Gesellschaft und Kultur im XIV. Jahrhundert: Sozial-ökonomischen Fragen', *Actes du XIVe Congrès International des Etudes Byzantines*, i (Bucharest, 1974), pp. 93–110.

and they are likely to go on doing so unless some new documentary evidence is found. The circumstances which sparked the fire of revolution are clear enough. The second civil war, or struggle for power, broke out, as we have seen, in 1341. The contestants were the regency in Constantinople and the commander-in-chief John Cantacuzene. He made his headquarters at Didymoteichon in Thrace; and it was against him and everything that he stood for as a millionaire and landowning aristocrat that the people rose up. 'Cantacuzenism' became their war cry, the slogan of their discontent. It is therefore unfortunate that our prime sources for what happened should be John Cantacuzene himself, in his memoirs, and his old friend and political sympathiser, Nikephoros Gregoras. The Zealots and their sympathisers left no records, or none that was allowed to survive; and our only other witnesses are the victims of their régime, such as Demetrios Kydones, whose family suffered greatly in Thessalonica and who later became the prime minister of the victorious Cantacuzene.

This is unfortunate, but it is also instructive, because it is clear that the Byzantine ruling class, of which Cantacuzene was an outstanding member, did not understand the social and political tensions within its own society any better than we do. Philanthropy and charity were indeed Christian virtues to which they paid more than lip service. But the idea of eliminating some of the need for charity by social change was beyond them. The intellectuals of the day turned out elegant Greek essays on the subjects of society and government, comparing the merits of monarchy, oligarchy and democracy. They predictably concluded that monarchy was the system favoured by God and that democracy was the work of the devil and synonymous with anarchy.[40] The Greek word *monarchia*

---

40 See, e.g., Theodore Metochites, *Miscellanea philosophica et historica*, ed. C. G. Müller and T. Kiessling (Leipzig, 1821), pp. 604–42. Cf. G. I. Bratianu, 'Empire et "démocratie" à Byzance', *BZ*, xxxvii (1937), pp. 86–111; Bratianu, ' "Démocratie" dans la lexique byzantin à l'époque des Paléologues', *Mémorial Louis Petit* (Bucharest, 1948), pp. 32–40; B.

was of course not one that they normally used to describe their own system of government. Nor was the concept of *demokratia* one with which they were familiar. But prize essays in Byzantium, like prose compositions today, had to be written in what was thought to be Attic Greek. Reflexions on the state of contemporary society when couched in such archaic language were always at least one stage removed from reality.[41]

One has always to bear this in mind when reading Byzantine texts, especially of the later period. Writers schooled in ancient rhetoric and the second sophistic made a virtue of veiling their meaning in the obscurity of a dead or at least an artificial language. For example, when the Black Death struck Constantinople in 1347 the casualties must have been appalling. Again one has to assume that this was so in default of factual evidence. The city had more than its share of educated, literate observers who might have described the nature and the horror of the plague and recorded the number of its victims. But the only detailed account which we have is that in the memoirs of John Cantacuzene, written long after the event. He was there; he lost a son in the epidemic. But like the good Byzantine he was, he knew that the fair copy for an account of a plague was that given by Thucydides about the plague at Athens in the time of Pericles. No Greek author could improve on that. He therefore transcribed it, with minor variations, into his own history – with the result that we are not much the wiser about the Black Death in Constantinople in 1347.[42]

Tatakis, *La philosophie byzantine* (Paris, 1959), p. 255; I. P. Medvedev, *Vizantijskij Gumanism XIV–XV vv.* [Byzantine Humanism, fourteenth–fifteenth centuries] (Leningrad, 1976), pp. 132–8.

41 Gregoras, II, pp. 795–6, describes the Zealot régime in purely archaic terms: 'neither an aristocracy, of the type which Lycurgus gave to the Lacedaemonians, nor a democracy like the first constitution of the Athenians established by Cleisthenes, nor such as Zaleucus devised for the Epizephyrian Locrians or Charondas of Catana in Sicily . . . but a kind of strange ochlocracy'.

42 John Cantacuzenus (Kantakouzenos), *Historiae*, ed. L. Schopen (*CSHB*), III, pp. 49–53. Cf. H. Hunger, 'Thukydides bei Johannes Kantakouzenos. Beobachtungen zur Mimesis', *JÖB*, xxv (1976), pp. 181–93; T. S. Miller,

Cantacuzene's descriptions of the revolutions in Thrace and Thessalonica are indeed more vivid and informative than that. But again they are shrouded in archaic language.[43] Each uprising is defined as *stasis*, the ancient Greek word for political faction or sedition. The rebels are collectively termed the *demos*, with no attempt to distinguish their social and economic groupings, except for a maddeningly imprecise allusion to something called the 'middle class';[44] and the kind of régime that they set up is contemptuously defined as *ochlokratia*, or mob-rule – a word found in Polybios and Plutarch.[45] The relationship between governing and governed is reflected in a general use by all writers of the terms *dynatoi* and *penetes* – the powerful and the poor – or, better, the 'privileged' and the 'under-privileged', since 'poor' did not mean destitute. But the moral implications of this distinction passed them by; and it did not occur to them to examine the underlying causes of social unrest or revolt, or to see whether the mob, the 'sweepings of the gutter', had any

'The Plague in John VI Cantacuzenus and Thucydides', *Greek, Roman and Byzantine Studies*, XVIII (1976), pp. 385–95. See, in more general terms, H. Hunger, 'On the imitation (mimesis) of Antiquity in Byzantine literature', *DOP*, XXIII/XXIV (1969–70), pp. 17–38 (reprinted in Hunger, *Byzantinische Grundlagenforschung* (London, 1973], no. XV); Hunger, 'Klassizistische Tendènzen in der byzantinischen Literatur des 14. Jh.', *Acte du XIVe Congrès International des Etudes Byzantines*, I (Bucharest, 1974), pp. 139–51.

43 The difficulties of reaching the truth in Byzantine rhetorical texts are well illustrated by the so-called 'Anti-Zealot Discourse' of Nicholas Kabasilas. This text, which for years was used as a basic source for the policy of the Zealots in Thessalonica, has now been shown to refer to a totally different set of events. I. Ševčenko, 'Nicolas Cabasilas' "Anti-Zealot" Discourse: a reinterpretation', in *DOP*, XI (1957), pp. 79–171, XIV (1960), pp. 181–201, and XVI (1962), pp. 403–8.

44 In the revolution (στάσις) at Adrianople, for example, the middle class (μέσοι τῶν πολιτῶν) suffered because they did not know whether to side with the ruling class (ἄριστοι or δυνατοί) or with the *demos* (Kantakouzenos, II, p. 179). In Thessalonica, once the revolutionary régime had gained control, the Zealots won over the middle class (τοὺς μέσους τῶν πολιτῶν) and forced them to acquiesce (*ibid.* II, p. 235; cf. *ibid.* II, p. 393, and see below, n. 50, for Alexios Makrembolites).

45 The term ὀχλοκρατία is used not by Kantakouzenos but by the more pedantic Gregoras, II, p. 796 lines 11–12.

justification for their violent action in Thessalonica and elsewhere. One way of showing your superiority was by unearthing such a rare Greek word as συρφετώδης, or 'refuse', to denounce the Zealots.[46] It proved that you had read your Polybios, Plutarch or Lucian – or at worst the lexicographers.

There are grounds for thinking that some of the leaders of the Church had a better understanding of the social inequalities and injustices that might lead to revolution. But they were quicker to condemn the excesses of violence against the existing order committed by the Zealots than to propose changes in that order. Gregory Palamas, for example, who became Bishop of Thessalonica in 1350 when the Zealot régime had been crushed, delivered a sermon there just after his arrival.[47] He denounced the defeated rebel leaders as wild beasts who had made Thessalonica like an enemy-occupied city, who had plundered houses and property and insulted and murdered its citizens without pity or humanity. To his credit he called upon the victims and survivors not to seek their revenge but to work for peace and concord. But the concord (ὁμόνοια) which he recommended was really a return to a social and political order which he and most of his contemporaries believed to be ordained by God – the order of a theocratic society under the co-operative rule of a God-crowned emperor and a God-fearing patriarch. This was, and always had been, the 'divine order' of the Christian Roman Empire. The *pax Byzantina* rested upon the acceptance of order (*taxis*) as something sacred, personified in the institution of the emperor.[48] It was permissible to make gradual adaptations to changing

46 The word is used in connexion with the Zealots by Gregoras, II, p. 674 line 5, who, having defined the 'sweepings of the gutter' as a third stratum in society in addition to the 'rich' and the 'poor', then with characteristic imprecision refers to them as 'this *demos*'. The word is also used by the Patriarch Philotheos in his brief account of the Zealot revolution (see n. 49).

47 Gregory Palamas, *Homilies*, I, in *MPG*, CLI, col. 12.

48 Hélène Ahrweiler, *L'idéologie politique de l'empire byzantin* (Paris, 1975), esp. pp. 129–47.

circumstances but not to make sudden innovations. The former could be achieved by compromise or 'economy' (*oikonomia*), but innovations went against the order of things. It is noteworthy that one of the normal Byzantine words for 'heresy' was 'innovation' or 'novelty' (*kainotomia*). The commonest words for social or political disturbance are *ataxia* and *synchysis* – disorder and confusion. The terms speak for themselves. The Patriarch Philotheos writing of the Zealot revolution says: 'The present disorder and confusion in the world are far removed from the ancient state and custom of the city of Thessalonica; nor is it the work of the best or even of the middle class of its citizens, but of a mob swept from the gutter – and these not of our own people but of barbarians from afar and from the surrounding islands driven here as refugees, men full of blood and murder, an ochlocracy, who have made this city once famous for its goodness famous for its evil.' It is interesting that Philotheos blames 'barbarians' or foreigners for the trouble. Would that he had been more precise.[49]

There appears to be only one Byzantine writer of this age who presents the notion that the ordinary, underprivileged people have any positive role to play in the running of society. His name was Alexios Makrembolites. Among other works he wrote (about 1343) a *Dialogue between the Rich and the Poor*, which is the closest thing to a sociological document to come out of fourteenth-century Byzantium.[50] Makrembolites condemns his rulers and leaders, especially those of the Church, for the way in which they 'eat up' the people. The exploitation of the

49 Philotheos, *Life of Sabas*, ed. A. Papadopoulos-Kerameus, Ἀνάλεκτα Ἱεροσολυμιτικῆς Σταχυολογίας, v (St Petersburg, 1888), p. 194.
50 I. Ševčenko, 'Alexios Makrembolites and his "Dialogue between the Rich and the Poor"', *ZRVI*, vi (1960), pp. 187–228 (Greek text and English trans., pp. 203–28). Cf. M. A. Poljakova, 'Alexios Makremvolites, Razgovor bogatych i bednych', *VV*, xxiii (1972), pp. 278–85; M. A. Poljakovskaja, 'K voprosu o socialnych protivorečijach v posdnevizantijskom gorode (po Alekseju Makremvolitu)', *Antičnaja drevnost' i srednie veka*, viii (Sverdlovsk, 1972), pp. 95–107.

poor by the rich he sees as one of the main causes of the Empire's desperate plight. But the 'rich' of his *Dialogue* are really the 'middle class'. They are not the *dynatoi*, the fabulously wealthy landowning aristocracy. And his 'poor' are not 'the sweepings of the gutter of Constantinople'. They are rather those who like himself wanted the opportunity to better their condition and to rise in the social scale. They do not really question the fact that great social differences exist; they do not advocate basic changes in the order of things. The message of the *Dialogue* is that the disparity between rich and poor has become too great because everyone has abandoned Christian standards of morality and forgotten the divine order of society. This then is no revolutionary manifesto and, as its editor says, 'the *Dialogue* will be disappointing to those who examine late Byzantine texts for evidence of *articulate* revolutionary thinking – a thing which in my opinion did not exist'.[51]

The Zealot revolution was prompted by the selfish antics of the ruling class in Byzantium. The Church was of course identified with that ruling class in so far as its interests ran *pari passu* with those of the Empire. The monasteries were great and wealthy landowners like the *dynatoi*, with their own armies of dependent peasants and manual labourers.[52] But there is little to support the view that the disturbances in Thessalonica and Thrace in the 1340s were in the nature of peasant revolts. Nor is there any evidence that the Zealots did much calculated violence to churches or church property. Minor acts of sacrilege are reported to have been committed in the excitement of revolt.[53] But the Zealot leaders consistently claimed to

---

51 Ševčenko, 'Alexios Makrembolites', p. 202.
52 P. Charanis, 'The monastic properties and the state in the Byzantine Empire', *DOP*, IV (1948), pp. 51–118; Charanis, 'The monk as an element in Byzantine society', *DOP*, XXV (1971), pp. 61–84 (reprinted in Charanis, *Social, Economic and Political Life in the Byzantine Empire. Collected Studies* [Variorum: London, 1973], nos. I and II.
53 Kantakouzenos, II, pp. 570–1, reports such things as mock baptisms and burlesquing of other Christian sacraments by the Zealots in the streets of Thessalonica, which in fact incensed the *demos* against them.

be loyal to the Patriarch, who was acting as regent in Constantinople. If there was a confrontation between the Church and society it was the work of the wealthy landowners and military aristocracy, who repeatedly tried to lay their hands on the estates of the monasteries; and in this they often had the support of their emperor, who excused his Caesaropapism in this respect by pleading the necessities of defence.[54] The Church was always on its guard against imperial attempts to sequester its property for military purposes. It might have been better for the defence and survival of the Empire if the Church had been more realistic and flexible in this matter. But at least it was consistent.

After two destructive civil wars in the 1320s and 1340s the emperors who emerged triumphant from the wreckage could hardly expect the imperial image to be untarnished. The civil wars, like the anarchy of revolution, could be put down to the sins and wickedness of mankind. The concept of the divine order did not change. But the feeling grew that the guardianship of that order was now less in the hands of the emperors and more in those of the patriarchs. The Church, united in the restoration of Orthodoxy and invigorated by the fresh winds of hesychast spirituality, was seen to be a more enduring and purposeful institution than the state. It was also a richer institution. The Church had contrived to make sound investments in this world as well as in the next; and its monasteries on Athos and elsewhere were handsomely endowed and supported by the rulers of Orthodox countries which had long since ceased to acknowledge any

---

54 The 'Anti-Zealot Discourse' of Nicholas Kabasilas (see n. 43) has much to say about the secularisation of Church property, but the culprits are not the Zealots. See Ševčenko's comments in *DOP*, XI (1957), pp. 153–60. See also Charanis, 'The monastic properties and the state'; G. Ostrogorsky, *Pour l'histoire de la féodalité byzantine* (Brussels, 1954), esp. pp. 155ff.; G. T. Dennis, *The Reign of Manuel II Palaeologus in Thessalonica, 1382–1387* (OCA, 159: Rome, 1960), pp. 90–1; Laiou, *Constantinople and the Latins*, pp. 119–20; and Nicol, *Last Centuries*, pp. 135, 280–1, 287.

material dependence upon the Byzantine Empire. Its leaders were not afraid to offend or to defy their emperors. Of the twenty-six Patriarchs of Constantinople between 1261 and 1453, thirteen resigned or were deposed for what might be called political reasons. It was still the case, as the historian George Akropolites had observed in the thirteenth century, that emperors preferred their patriarchs to be submissive and obedient.[55] But in the last hundred years it was the emperors and not the patriarchs who sank their pride by obediently submitting to the moral and political pressures of foreign powers, Christian and Muslim. The Church to the end retained a different set of priorities. It is no accident that for a generation after the vindication of Palamas, from 1347 to 1376, the Church was controlled by patriarchs of strongly monastic and hesychast inclination.[56] The fanatical Athanasios, himself a product of the powerhouse of Athos, must, for all his faults, be honoured as the first of a line of late Byzantine Patriarchs of Constantinople who almost supplanted the emperors in the lead that they gave to society.[57]

By a delicious irony the mortal remains of Athanasios are now to be found in Venice. They were taken there from Constantinople, where they had been venerated for a hundred years and more, in 1454, in the mistaken belief that they were the relics of the great fourth-century Athanasios of Alexandria. They are housed in the Church of San Zaccaria, where they are much admired as a

---

55 George Akropolites, *Historia*, i, ed. A. Heisenberg (Leipzig, 1903), p. 72 lines 2–7; p. 106 line 22–p. 107 line 3: ταπεινοτέρους γὰρ καὶ μετρίους εἶναι τὸ φρόνημα τοὺς πατριαρχεύοντας οἱ κρατοῦντες ἐθέλουσι καὶ προσπίπτειν εὐχερῶς τοῖς σφῶν αὐτῶν βουλήμασιν ὡς προστάγμασι.

56 Isidore I (1347–50), Kallistos I (1350–3), Philotheos Kokkinos (1353–4), Kallistos (again: 1355–63), Philotheos (again: 1364–76).

57 See Meyendorff, 'Spiritual trends', p. 99. The career of the Patriarch Matthew I (1397–1410) reveals the extraordinary industry and authority of such monastic prelates. See H. Hunger, 'Das Testament des Patriarchen Matthaios I (1397–1410)', *BZ*, LI (1958), pp. 288–309; Hunger, *Reich der neuen Mitte. Der christliche Geist der byzantinischen Kultur* (Graz–Vienna–Cologne, 1965), p. 276.

supposed symbol of oecumenism during the Week of
Unity celebrations.[58] It is a strange end for the relics of
a wildly Orthodox anti-unionist Byzantine patriarch who
loathed all Latins and who once described Italy as 'a
foreign land inhabited by barbarians and by an utterly
insolent nation which has lost all sense'.[59]

58 D. Stiernon, 'Le quartier du Xérolophos à Constantinople et les reliques
    vénitiennes du Saint Athanase', *REB*, xix (1961), pp. 165–88. *Letters of
    Athanasios*, ed. Talbot, p. xxvii.
59 *Letters of Athanasios*, ed. Talbot, no. 84, p. 222 lines 44–6.

2

Saints and scholars: the 'inner' and the 'outer' wisdom

The Patriarch Athanasios fancied himself as a voice crying in the wilderness of Constantinople. 'I am consumed by anxiety', he wrote about 1303, 'to find a man who would worthily proclaim the road to repentance to our adulterous and all but faithless generation, either by shouting something strange and stentorian, or by sounding the trumpet in a terrifying manner, just as the angel of God at the end of the world . . . since we need a strange sound, bowed down as we are by our sensual and bestial behaviour, to make us look up, if only for a while, toward heaven . . . and to make us lament and beat our breasts.'[1]

Was the society of Constantinople at the beginning of the fourteenth century so utterly corrupt and bestial? It is hard to believe it when one stands in the Church of the Saviour in Chora (Kariye Djami), with its exquisite mosaics and dramatic frescoes, or in the Church of the Virgin Pammakaristos (Fetiye Djami).[2] Both of these monastic churches stand within the walls of Constantinople, and both were restored and decorated by private benefactors within or just after the lifetime of Athanasios. The list could be extended; at least seven other such pious foundations in the city can be dated to much the same period.[3] It was an age of patronage, both imperial and

1 Letters of Athanasios, ed. Talbot, no. 43, p. 88 line 19; p. 90 line 76.
2 *The Kariye Djami*, ed. P. A. Underwood, 4 vols. (Bollingen Series, LXX, New York, 1966–75); H. Belting, C. Mango, Doula Mouriki, *The Mosaics and Frescoes of St Mary Pammakaristos (Fethiye Camii) at Istanbul* (Dumbarton Oaks Studies, XV: Washington, D.C., 1978).
3 I. Sevčenko, 'Society and intellectual life in the fourteenth century', *Actes du XIVe Congrès International des Etudes Byzantines*, I (Bucharest, 1974), pp.

31

private. The patron of the Church of the Chora was
Theodore Metochites, one of the most cultured men of
his time. He was also one of the wealthiest; and while we
can be sure that his wealth was not all honestly acquired,
he was in theory a man of high ideals and Christian
principles.[4] Metochites was a statesman and a diplomat
who rose to become Grand Logothete of the Emperor
Andronikos II. But above all he was a scholar, an
antiquarian, a philosopher, a bibliophile and a teacher. His
written works run to nearly 1,900 folios in manuscript.[5]
His learning was encyclopaedic and his contemporaries
described him as 'a living library'.[6] His most distinguished
and no less erudite pupil was Nikephoros Gregoras, who,
among many other learned works, found time to write
the history of his age. Neither of these remarkable men
was particularly corrupt; neither of them was in any way
bestial. There were many more of the same scholarly
stamp. They were the luminaries of that limited enlightenment which has been called the last Byzantine
renaissance.[7] Renaissance is perhaps too generous a word.
The phenomenon might more justly be described as a
reappraisal of the legacy of Antiquity by a bookish and

69–92, esp. p. 80 n. 32, for lists of the monasteries founded or restored
by imperial or aristocratic patrons in the thirteenth and fourteenth
centuries.

4 On Metochites, see esp.: H.-G. Beck, *Theodoros Metochites. Die Krise des
byzantinischen Weltbildes im 14. Jahrhundert* (Munich, 1952); H. Hunger,
'Theodoros Metochites als Vorläufer des Humanismus in Byzanz', *BZ*,
LV (1952), pp. 4–19 (reprinted in Hunger, *Byzantinische Grundlagenfor-
schung*, no. XXI); I. Ševčenko, *Etudes sur la polémique entre Théodore
Métochite et Nicéphore Choumnos. La vie intellectuelle et politique à Byzance
sous les premiers Paléologues* (Brussels, 1962); Ševčenko, 'Theodore Meto-
chites, the Chora, and the intellectual trends of his time', in *The Kariye
Djami*, IV, pp. 17–91; M. Gigante, 'Per l'interpretazione di Teodoro
Metochites quale umanista bizantino', *SBN*, NS IV (XIV) (1967), pp. 11–25.

5 Ševčenko, 'Theodore Metochites', p. 37.

6 Gregoras, I, p. 273 line 3.

7 S. Runciman, *Last Byzantine Renaissance*; D. M. Nicol, 'The Byzantine
Church and Hellenic learning in the fourteenth century', *Studies in Church
History*, V, ed. G. J. Cuming (Leiden, 1969), pp. 23–57 (reprinted in Nicol,
Byzantium...Collected Studies, no. XII); I. P. Medvedev, *Vizantijskij
Gumanism XIV–XV vv.* [Byzantine Humanism, fourteenth–fifteenth
centuries] (Leningrad, 1976).

rather pretentious élite in the first half of the fourteenth century.[8]

It is tempting but dangerous to make analogies between developments in Byzantium and in the west at this time. It is fascinating to think that Giotto was painting the Arena chapel at Padua at precisely the same moment that the masters of the Chora were at work in Constantinople; that Eckhart and Tauler were the exact contemporaries of Gregory of Sinai and Gregory Palamas. But they lived in societies between which there was little understanding and practically no intellectual contact. Furthermore, in Byzantine society the élite had always been brought up on the Classics. They were heirs to an unbroken tradition of scholarship and literacy among the laity as well as the clergy. That tradition had been maintained, even reinvigorated, during the years of exile after the Fourth Crusade, and it was intensified after the recovery of Constantinople in 1261. It has been calculated that Byzantium produced ninety-one writers in the fourteenth century, or one to every two or three thousand of the population of the capital city. Forty-five per cent of these were laymen, two being emperors, one a prince and one a princess. Most of them had evidently read at least two books of the Iliad, Hesiod, some Pindar, selections of the tragedians and of Aristophanes, a little Theocritus, some Demosthenes and Aelius Aristides, and Gregory Nazianzene's Eulogy of St Basil.[9] They were not reawakening to their classical heritage after a long sleep. They shared a basic literary background, and they conversed with each other, often through virtually meaningless but painfully contrived correspondence, in a shared literary language of unbelievable preciosity.

It has often been said that the Byzantines were the

8 See, e.g., the remarks of I. Ševčenko, 'Theodore Metochites', in *The Kariye Djami*, IV, p. 40f. and n. 166; J. Meyendorff, 'Spiritual trends in Byzantium in the late thirteenth and early fourteenth centuries', *ibid*. p. 101 ('The Byzantine "renaissance" produced slight changes in taste and outlook, but the medieval patterns of mind were never really abandoned'); and cf. *ibid*. p. 106.

9 Ševčenko, 'Society and intellectual life', pp. 69ff., esp. p. 89 n. 69.

librarians of the Middle Ages. Certainly the world would
be a poorer place without the work of their scribes and
scriptoria. But one of the most important developments
in late Byzantine scholarship was a revived interest in
philology and textual criticism. Even modern classicists,
who are often rather unkind about Byzantium, grudgingly
admit that scholars like Maximos Planoudes and Demetrios
Triklinios did some good for the transmission of texts.[10]
Their efforts helped to reintroduce into circulation some
works of Antiquity which had been neglected – among
them, for example, Plutarch. Theodore Metochites had
read his Plutarch with attentive admiration; but he could
hardly have done so had not Planoudes prepared editions
of the text.[11] Metochites and Gregoras were also proud
to have revived the sciences of mathematics and astronomy
through studying neglected texts of Euclid, Ptolemy,
Diophantos and Cleomedes.

   This intellectual movement was deliberately fostered by
imperial patronage. The court of Andronikos II was
compared by contemporaries to the Stoa and the Lyceum
of Antiquity.[12] Yet it was the same Emperor Andronikos
who appointed and lived under the spell of the fanatical
Patriarch Athanasios, who openly professed to despise
scholarship. Gregoras once unkindly described Athanasios
as 'an ignoramus with unwashed feet'; for the Patriarch
was in the habit of walking the streets in hairshirt and
sandals.[13] At the same time he half admired the Patriarch
as a holy man. We are here in sight of a peculiarly
Byzantine paradox. It is well illustrated in a double

10 H. Hunger, 'Von Wissenschaft und Kunst der frühen Palaiologenzeit. Mit
   einem Exkurs über die Kosmike Delosis Theodoros' II. Dukas Laskaris',
   JÖBG, VIII (1959), pp. 123–55, esp. pp. 139ff. (reprinted in Hunger,
   Byzantinische Grundlagenforschung, no. XX); L. D. Reynolds and N. G.
   Wilson, *Scribes and Scholars. A Guide to the Transmission of Greek and Latin
   Literature*, 2nd edn (Oxford, 1974), pp. 64–9.
11 Ševčenko, 'Theodore Metochites', pp. 41–2.
12 Gregoras, I, pp. 327, 334–5.
13 Gregoras, I, p. 180 lines 18–23. Cf. Pachymeres, *De Andronico Palaeologo*,
   p. 140. *Letters of Athanasios*, ed. Talbot, pp. xxviii–xxxi [on the educational
   background and literary style of Athanasios].

portrait preserved in a most beautiful manuscript in Paris. The portrait is that of the Emperor John Cantacuzene, who abdicated in 1354 and entered a monastery. It shows him robed as an emperor on the left of the picture and as a monk on the right, as it were beside himself with spirituality.[14] John Cantacuzene was a soldier, a statesman and a theologian all at once. But when the soldier and statesman in him failed and the theologian in him took over, then he translated himself to the higher estate of monasticism.

Byzantine society recognised two estates – that of the world and that of the spirit, the cosmic and the pneumatic, or monadic. There were no orders of monks such as the Benedictines, Dominicans and Franciscans. But the monastic estate – μοναδικὴ πολιτεία – was a well-defined and respected higher order of society. The importance of the monks in Byzantine life can hardly be over-emphasised.[15] The great monasteries of the Empire, even in its decline, were wealthy, populous and influential. But they served a different purpose from monasteries in the west. Byzantine monks had never been called upon to be the great educators of society like western monks in the Dark Ages. Literacy had never been a monopoly of the Church in Byzantium. Monks were not always associated with learning, although more of them took to scholarship in the later period. But they were thought to be learned in the wisdom that went with their calling, the higher or 'inner' wisdom of the spirit. The required reading for the acquisition of such wisdom was not Plato or Aristotle or Plutarch, but the Scriptures and the Fathers. Ancient Greek literature and philosophy were known in monastic circles as the 'outer' wisdom, the learning 'outside the

14 Cod. Paris. B.N. gr. 124, fol. 123. Colour reproduction in A. Grabar, *Byzantine Painting* (Geneva, 1953), p. 184. See most recently I. Spatharakis, *The Portrait in Byzantine Illuminated Manuscripts* (Leiden, 1976), p. 135 and figs. 87–9.
15 See, e.g., D. Savramis, *Zur Soziologie des byzantinischen Mönchtums* (Leiden, 1962); P. Charanis, 'The monk as an element in Byzantine society', *DOP*, xxv (1971), pp. 61–84.

door', the wisdom of 'the Hellenes'.[16] They could
provide a preparation or an introduction to the truth. But
beyond a certain point in the development of the inner
wisdom no form of human vocabulary was adequate. The
true theology or knowledge of God sought by the
hesychast came as a direct and personal experience uncircumscribable in human terms. The goal was no less than
theosis or the deification of man through an apprehension
of the divine light.

Monks had been known as hesychasts from quite early
times. *Hesychia* meant the state of holy peace and tranquillity, of solitude and *ataraxia*, conducive to meditation.
But in the fourteenth century the word hesychast came
to acquire a special significance. It was the name given
to those monks, mainly on Mount Athos, who had perfected a particular technique of prayer and contemplation,
through which they claimed to be able to perceive the
divine light with mortal eyes – to experience an illumination of the soul which transfigured their whole being.
The illumination was said to be of the same nature and
quality as the light which transfigured Christ and blinded
the apostles on Mount Tabor, the uncreated Light of the
Transfiguration or Metamorphosis. In other words, the
hesychast had a direct experience of the deification of man
by divine grace, involving the body as well as the soul.
He could never claim to see God in His 'essence'; but he
could and did claim to experience God through His
'energies' or 'operations'. It was this claim and its
theological implications which prompted some to accuse
the hesychasts of presumption or of error and started a
controversy that was to divide the Empire.[17]

16 Runciman, *Last Byzantine Renaissance*, pp. 28ff.; G. Podskalsky, *Theologie
und Philosophie in Byzanz. Der Streit um die theologische Methodik in
der spätbyzantinischen Geistesgeschichte (14./15. Jh.), seine systematischen
Grundlagen und seine historische Entwicklung* (Byzantinisches Archiv, 15:
Munich, 1977), esp. pp. 16ff.
17 On Hesychasm, see refs. at Ch. 1 n. 13. There are useful bibliographical
surveys of the subject by D. Stiernon, 'Bulletin sur le palamisme', *REB*,
XXX (1972), pp. 231–341, and by I. Medvedev, 'Sovremennaja bibliografia
isichastich sporov v Vizantii XIV v.', *Antičnaja drevnost' i srednie veka*, X
(Sverdlovsk, 1973), pp. 270–4.

The 'divine light' that can illuminate the soul of the mystic and the potential deification of man were clearly not new ideas that burst upon the Byzantine Church in the fourteenth century. They were concepts firmly rooted in the long tradition of Byzantine mystical practice and speculation. Such expressions, and all the theology which they imply, are to be found in the writings of the Greek Fathers, Gregory of Nyssa and the Pseudo-Dionysios. The themes were developed by such men as John Klimax and notably Symeon the New Theologian, about the year 1000. In his *Catecheses* Symeon insists on the possibility and the necessity of an actual perception of Christ and an actual union with Christ. The only real truth comes through illumination by the divine light.[18] *Hesychia* is the condition in which this perception, this participation (or μέθεξις) in the divine can be attained.

The hesychasts of the fourteenth century were directly in the tradition of Symeon. They derived their immediate inspiration from the teaching and example of a saint called Gregory of Sinai, who had come to Mount Athos by way of Crete.[19] Their major advance on earlier mystical practice was the formulation of a method of prayer designed to induce the state of receptivity into which the divine light might shine. This was to be attained by *nepsis*, or 'vigilance' – a preparation of the body as well as the mind. The technique had been described by a monk on Athos called Nikephoros the Hesychast at least thirty years before it became a matter of controversy, in a treatise on *Vigilance and the Guardianship of the Heart*.[20] Another

18 See, e.g., *Syméon le Nouveau Théologien, Catéchèses*, ed. B. Krivocheine, II (Sources chrétiennes, 104: Paris, 1964), no. XVI, pp. 236–53. Cf. J. Meyendorff, *Byzantine Theology*, pp. 73–5.

19 On Gregory of Sinai, see H.-G. Beck, *Kirche und theologische Literatur im byzantinischen Reich* (Munich, 1959), pp. 694–5; K. Ware, 'The Jesus Prayer in St Gregory of Sinai', *Eastern Churches Review*, IV (1972), pp. 3–22. His Life was written by the later Patriarch Kallistos; ed. I. Pomjalovskij, *Žitie iže vo svjatych otsa našego Grigorija Sinaita* (St Petersburg, 1894). Cf. *BHG³*, I, p. 235.

20 Nikephoros the Hesychast, Περὶ νήψεως καὶ φυλακῆς καρδίας, in *MPG*, CXLVII, cols. 945–66. French trans. *Petite philocalie de la prière du cœur*, by J. Gouillard, 2nd edn (Paris, 1968), pp. 138–53; English trans. (from the

anonymous treatise on *The Method of Holy Vigilance*
recommended that: 'In the solitude of his cell the monk
must sit with chin resting on his breast and eyes fixed upon
his navel. Then, while carefully regulating his breathing,
he must constantly say over the Jesus-Prayer.'[21] The fixity
of physical posture combined with the mechanical repetition of the same words were to induce a receptive
state in which the mind was evacuated. It is easy to make
fun of such spiritual extravagances. Edward Gibbon did
so with great gusto. The inner light of the hesychasts he
describes as 'the production of a distempered fancy, the
creature of an empty stomach and an empty brain'.
Hesychasm for Gibbon 'consummates the religious follies
of the Greeks'.[22]

But the first to ridicule the hesychasts was a Greek monk
from South Italy, Barlaam of Calabria. Barlaam had been
educated in Rome and was something of a scholar. He
arrived in Constantinople on a visit about 1330. He was
invited to give a course of lectures on philosophy. To
begin with he was a great success; but then he fell out with
some of his Orthodox acquaintances who suspected his
rather western views on the uses of philosophical argument
in theology. It was then that Barlaam vented his spleen
by picking on the hesychast monks of Athos. He accused
them of being absurd, of being *omphalopsychoi*, or men
who keep their souls in their navels; but worse still he
attacked them as heretics.[23]

Russian version), *Writings from the Philokalia on Prayer of the Heart*, by E.
Kadloubovsky and G. E. H. Palmer (London, 1951), pp. 22–34. Cf. Beck,
Kirche, p. 693; Meyendorff, *Introduction à l'étude de Grégoire Palamas*, pp.
201–2, 210–11; Runciman, *Great Church*, p. 137.

21 Ed. I. Hausherr, *La méthode d'oraison hésychaste* (*Orientalia Christiana*, IX,
2: Rome, 1927). Cf. J. Meyendorff, 'Le thème du "retour en soi" dans
la doctrine palamite du XIVe siècle', *Revue de l'histoire des religions*, CXLV
(1954), pp. 188–206, esp. pp. 191–2 (reprinted in Meyendorff, *Byzantine
Hesychasm*, no. XII).

22 E. Gibbon, *Decline and Fall of the Roman Empire*, ed. J. B. Bury, VI
(London, 1898), p. 506.

23 Meyendorff, *Introduction*, pp. 65ff.; Meyendorff, 'Spiritual trends', pp.
101–3; Tatakis, *Philosophie byzantine*, pp. 263–6, 272–4; Runciman, *Great
Church*, pp. 138–44.

This was how the controversy began. The man who took up the challenge of Barlaam of Calabria was the monk Gregory Palamas, himself a leading hesychast on Mount Athos, who had already crossed swords with him on the matter of theology. Palamas rushed to the defence of his fellow monks with a manifesto which most of them signed. Barlaam was denounced and went back to Italy. In later years he tried, without much success, to teach Greek to Petrarch; and in due course he went over to the Roman Church, reverting, as the Byzantine historian puts it, to the customs and dogmas of the Latins in which he had been reared.[24] The historian who makes this offensive remark was Nikephoros Gregoras. Like most true Byzantines Gregoras disapproved of westerners, especially when they claimed, as Barlaam had done, to know more about Orthodoxy than the Orthodox themselves. Gregoras had no hesitation about joining in the denunciation of Barlaam. But when he began to look more closely into the theology of Hesychasm as expounded by Palamas he began to have serious doubts. He was not alone among contemporary philosophers and theologians, although he was the most outspoken among the laity. He was encouraged by the support of the monk Gregory Akindynos, a friend and pupil of Palamas, who had turned against his master; and there were others in the Church who had honest doubts about Hesychasm. In the end, however, the Orthodoxy of Palamas and of hesychast theology were upheld by the bishops in council under the presidency of the Emperor John Cantacuzene, in 1351.[25] The anti-Palamites and anti-hesychasts, principally Barlaam and

---

24 Gregoras, II, p. 559. The Athonite manifesto (*Tomos Hagioreitikos*) is printed in *MPG*, CL, cols. 1225–36. See Meyendorff, *Introduction*, pp. 350–1.
25 See above, p. 11 and n. 16. For the Council of 1351 and its decisions, see Meyendorff, *Introduction*, pp. 141–53. The theology of Hesychasm was formulated by Gregory Palamas, with special reference to the attacks of Barlaam, in his *Triads* in defence of the holy hesychasts: ed. J. Meyendorff, *Grégoire Palamas, Défense des saints hésychastes*, 2 vols. (Spicilegium Sacrum Lovaniense, 30, 31: Louvain, 1959; 2nd edn, 1973); also in Palamas, Γρηγορίου τοῦ Παλαμᾶ Συγγράμματα, ed. P. K. Chrestou, I (Thessalonike, 1962), pp. 359–694.

Akindynos, were condemned as heretics. Many of their followers took refuge in Cyprus, which was then under French rule, or in the Latin west. Gregoras continued to make a martyr of himself in Constantinople and died, still protesting, nine years later. But the truth was that Hesychasm came as a natural development in the train of Orthodox spirituality; and as such it was easily and quickly absorbed into the generally accepted canon of Orthodox doctrine and belief in Bulgaria, Russia and elsewhere by the end of the fourteenth century.[26]

Hesychasm was essentially a monastic movement. The Byzantines never lost sight of the real meaning of the word *monachos* – a solitary. The basic training of the hesychast had of necessity to be done in a monastic community or at least under the personal guidance of a *pneumatikos*, or spiritual father. It was a training not in reading books or copying manuscripts but in the long discipline or *askesis* of mind and body, through fasting, repentance and tears. But the community or *koinobion* was for many simply the undergraduate school of monasticism at which the monk might qualify to enter the graduate school of the solitary life, which even Justinian had defined as the higher calling.[27] The great monastic colonies in the mountains, deserts and wildernesses of Byzantium – Mount Sinai by the Red Sea, Mount Olympos in Bithynia, Mount Athos, or the Meteora rocks in Thessaly – as often as not owed their origins to a hermit or anchorite whose fame and sanctity attracted a group of disciples. There were of course also numerous urban monasteries, in the cities and their suburbs, in Constantinople and Thessalonica. But the anchorite, the hermit, or the stylite always represented one ideal of monasticism. And this ideal received a new impetus in the last centuries of Byzantium, in the revival

26 On the spread of hesychast influence in the Balkans and Russia, see Obolensky, *Byzantine Commonwealth*, pp. 301–8, 336–43; A. N. Tachiaos, Ἐπιδράσεις τοῦ ἡσυχασμοῦ εἰς τὴν ἐκκλησιαστικὴν πολιτικὴν ἐν Ῥωσίᾳ 1328–1406 (Thessalonike, 1962).

27 Justinian, Novel 5, c. 3 (AD 535), ed. by G. Schoell and G. Kroll, *Corpus Iuris Civilis*, 5th edn (Berlin, 1928), pp. 31–2.

of the spiritual life of which Hesychasm, in its technical sense, was only one manifestation.

Byzantine hagiographical literature of this period abounds in tales of solitary anchorites, many of whom led wandering lives like the *startsy* of later Russian society. They moved from place to place without regard to frontiers or ethnic distinctions, finding friends at every turn. For such men the whole Orthodox world was their native land, irrespective of the political tensions that divided Greeks, Serbians, Bulgarians, Albanians and the rest. They were the heralds of what has been described as the 'Hesychast International'.[28] Gregory of Sinai, the master of the hesychast method, tramped around the deserts and wildernesses of Cyprus, Sinai, Crete and Athos before settling in the remote mountains of north-eastern Bulgaria.[29] His contemporary, Sabas of Vatopedi, one of the most spectacular of these 'spiritual athletes', spent twenty years wandering in the wastes of Palestine, Egypt, Cyprus, Crete and the Peloponnese before coming to rest as a simple monk on Athos.[30] Maximos Kavsokalyvites was so called because of his propensity to burn down his *kalyvion* (hut) and move on to new spiritual pastures, though he confined his wanderings to the wilder parts of Mount Athos.[31] The Patriarch Athanasios led a somewhat vagabond existence before he settled in Constantinople.[32]

28 See the remarks of F. Halkin, 'Un ermite des Balkans au XIVe siècle. La Vie grecque inédite de Saint Romylos', *B*, XXXI (1961), p. 113. Cf. Obolensky, *Byzantine Commonwealth*, p. 302.
29 For the Life of Gregory of Sinai, see n. 19.
30 Philotheos, *Life of Sabas*, ed. A. Papadopoulos-Kerameus, pp. 190–359. Cf. *BHG*³, II, p. 227.
31 There are two fourteenth-century Lives of Maximos, one by his disciple the hermit Niphon, the other by Theophanes, Abbot of Vatopedi and later Metropolitan of Peritheorion in Thrace. F. Halkin, 'Deux Vies de S. Maxime le Kausokalybe ermite au Mont Athos (XIVe siècle)', *AB*, LIV (1936), pp. 38–112. Cf. *BHG*³, II, p. 107.
32 There are two fourteenth-century Lives of Athanasios, one attributed to Theoktistos the Studite, the other by Joseph Kalothetos. The first was edited by A. Papadopoulos-Kerameus, 'Žitija dvuch Vselenskich Patriarchov XIV v., svv. Afanasija I i Isidora I', *Zapiski istoriko-filolog. fakulteta Imperatorskago S.-Petersburgskago Universiteta*, LXXVI (1905), pp. 1–51. The

But the prize for stylite endeavour and endurance must
surely go to his namesake, Athanasios, founder of the
Monastery of the Transfiguration or Meteoron in Thessaly,
who, about 1340, established the first of those aerial
communities on the tops of gigantic rocks which are now,
alas, peopled more by tourists than by monks.[33] The
spiritual father of this Athanasios, with whom he had
earlier shared a cave in one of those rocks, was indeed
known as Gregory the Stylite.[34]

The significance of such holy men for late Byzantine
society could well be further studied. There are many
hagiographies of them yet to be properly explored or even
edited.[35] They were revered as living icons or channels of
divine grace. They were consulted as oracles, for some of
them had the gift of prophecy among their divinely
acquired *charismata*. This was not just a matter of vulgar
credulity. The practised hesychast, the holy man *par
excellence*, was generally recognised to be one of the links
between time and eternity. Though he often shunned
society and the things of this world he knew, and society
knew, that men of the world could use him as one uses
a radio receiver to make contact with the ether of
transcendental reality. The common people held such men
in great esteem. But so also did many persons in high

second was edited by A. Pantokratorinos, 'Calotheti Vita Athanasii',
Thrakika, XIII (1940), pp. 56–107. Cf. *BHG*³, I, p. 71.
33 The fourteenth-century Life of Athanasios of the Meteoron was edited
by N. A. Bees, Συμβολὴ εἰς τὴν ἱστορίαν τῶν Μονῶν τῶν Μετεώρων,
Βυζαντίς, I (1909), pp. 208–60 (Greek text: pp. 237–60). For later versions
of the saint's Life, see D. M. Nicol, *Meteora. The Rock Monasteries of
Thessaly*, 2nd edn (London, 1975), pp. 73–6, 88–105. Cf. *BHG*³, I, pp. 71–2.
34 Life of Athanasios, ed. Bees, p. 248 lines 21–2.
35 The *Bibliographia Hagiographica Graeca*, 3rd edn, ed. F. Halkin (Brussels,
1957), lists twenty-six saints in the late thirteenth to fourteenth centuries.
There are others: e.g., Hosios Neilos Erichiotes in Epiros, who died about
1335 and whose Life and Testament exist in late copies in the library of
the monastery that he founded at Geromeri near Philiates. Partial
transcriptions of these documents have been printed by P. Aravantinos,
in *Pandora*, XV (Athens, 1865), pp. 470–4 and by B. Krapsites, in *Thesprotika*,
II (Athens, 1972), pp. 160–7. Cf. L. I. Vranoussis, in Θρησκευτικὴ καὶ
Ἠθικὴ Ἐγκυκλοπαιδεία, IV (Athens, 1964), cols. 496–502.

places, from the emperors downwards, seeking their
advice and company and reading their biographies. Many
of the lives of these latter-day Byzantine saints are written
in such sophisticated Greek that only the educated could
have understood them. They are not aimed at impressing
a gullible audience of common illiterate people. The
Patriarch Athanasios in fact wrote not very learned Greek.
But his successor Philotheos (Kokkinos), a prolific hagio-
grapher, wrote in a style so verbose and convoluted that
even grammarians and lexicographers must have been
bemused. (Philotheos was perhaps overcompensating for
his own unusually humble background and upbringing.)[36]
Sometimes one finds that there are alternative versions of
these lives composed for the edification of the less well
educated.[37] But in the fourteenth and fifteenth centuries
there was evidently a thriving market for such productions
among the upper-class literati.

A few examples may be cited. The scholar and historian
Nikephoros Gregoras, by no means a dunce, wrote a life
of his pious and learned uncle John, by whom he had been
brought up, and who became a bishop. He recalls how
John had first been inspired to sanctity by a chance encounter with 'a sort of holy cynic who pretended to be

36 Philotheos, who was Patriarch of Constantinople from 1353–4 and again
  from 1364–6, was born of Jewish parents in Thessalonica about 1300 and
  worked as a kitchen-hand to pay for his education before becoming a
  monk. But he had the good fortune to be taught by the celebrated
  philologist and orator Thomas Magister. See Beck, *Kirche und theologische
  Literatur*, pp. 723–7; and V. Laurent, in *DTC*, xii, 2 cols. 1498–1509
  (where his numerous hagiographies and other works are listed). An
  Akolouthia and Life of Philotheos written in the late eighteenth century
  are published by B. Dentakis in Ἐπιστημονικὴ Ἐπετηρὶς τῆς Θεολογικῆς
  Σχολῆς τοῦ Πανεπιστημίου Ἀθηνῶν, xvii (1971), pp. 513–637.
37 As, e.g., in the case of Athanasios of the Meteoron, the popular version
  of whose Life was edited by Sp. P. Lambros, in *NH*, ii (1905), pp. 51–93
  (Greek text: pp. 61–87). Some such saints merited hagiographies in Slav
  as well as in Greek: e.g., St Romylos, the fourteenth-century hermit of
  Macedonia, who was of mixed Greek and Bulgarian parentage. F. Halkin,
  'Un ermite des Balkans', pp. 111–47 (Greek text: pp. 114–45); P. Devos,
  'La version slave de la Vie de S. Romylos', *ibid.* pp. 149–87. Cf. *BHG*,
  Auctarium (Subsidia Hagiographica, 47: Brussels, 1969), nos. 2383, 2384.

mad'. This Christian Diogenes had made his way into the palace without ceremony and naked to the waist to see the Empress.[38] To feign madness was to play 'the fool for Christ's sake', a gambit recommended by St Paul (1 Cor. 4: 11, 12) and taken literally by several Byzantine monks. Maximos Kavsokalyvites in his younger days, before he became a pyromaniac, had tramped the streets of Constantinople bareheaded and in rags, acting the fool for Christ's sake to such effect that the word of his 'divine madness' reached the Emperor Andronikos II. The holy man was invited to the palace where he amazed his audience by his ability to recite the scriptures from memory.[39] Later in his life Maximos is said to have been visited in his hut on Athos by two emperors and by the Patriarch Kallistos, whose murder he predicted.[40] The great Sabas of Vatopedi, whose prowess impressed Muslims as well as Christians, added a show of dumbness to his foolishness, preserving almost continuous silence for twenty years.[41] On one occasion in Cyprus, when he felt that he was becoming too much of a celebrity or superman ($\dot{v}\pi\epsilon\rho\acute{a}\nu\theta\rho\omega\pi o\nu$), 'in the sight of all he sat himself down in an evil-smelling ditch of muck and pretended to be an idiot for a whole day'.[42] His humility was such that he

38 V. Laurent, 'La Vie de Jean, Métropolite d'Héraclée du Pont', *Archeion Pontou*, VI (1934), pp. 1–67, esp. p. 38 lines 5–10. Cf. Laurent, 'La personnalité de Jean d'Héraclée, oncle et précepteur de Nicéphore Grégoras', *Hellenika*, III (1930), pp. 297–315. Cf. *BHG³*, III, no. 2188.

39 Life of Maximos by Theophanes, ed. F. Halkin, *AB*, LIV (1936), pp. 70–1.

40 Life of Maximos, ed. Halkin, pp. 93–4. These events are recorded also in the Life of Maximos by Niphon, *ibid*. pp. 46, 48. As Halkin says (p. 46 n. 2), the alleged visit to the saint on Athos by the Emperors (John VI) Cantacuzene and John (V) Palaiologos is not supported by any other evidence. If it occurred, it must have been between the years 1347 and 1352, when the two emperors were not at war with each other. It is, however, certain that John Cantacuzene visited Athos before 1341 (Kantakouzenos, III, p. 173). The legend of the Patriarch Kallistos's death by poison is reported, and refuted, by Kantakouzenos, III, pp. 360–2.

41 Philotheos, *Life of Sabas* (see n. 30), pp. 235–6; cf. pp. 218–21, 227, 230–2, 292, 294. For his fame among 'Ishmaelites' (i.e. Muslims) as well as Christians, see *ibid*. pp. 285–6.

42 Philotheos, *Life of Sabas*, pp. 241–3.

always refused to be ordained as a priest. But at the end of his vagabond career Sabas became spiritual father of the future Patriarch Philotheos and was very nearly made patriarch himself at the insistence of the Emperor John Cantacuzene, who set great store by holiness.[43]

Cantacuzene was a man of many parts, deeply religious and deeply involved in the theology and politics of Hesychasm. But as a Byzantine he fully believed in the possibility of miracles, provided the working of them was left to those qualified – namely God or holy men who had trained themselves to be the intermediaries of God's special, supernatural graces. Such a man was Hilarion, who became Bishop of Didymoteichon, Cantacuzene's headquarters in Thrace during the second civil war. Hilarion had trained under a celebrated ascetic called Makarios, whose sanctity attracted people of all ages and classes to his cell for guidance – among them the emperor. He was one of those who contrived to lead his holy life in one of the smaller monasteries of Constantinople, deaf to the distractions of an urban environment. Hilarion was one of his four most successful pupils.[44] In his case we are fortunate in having not only the stylised account of a typical Byzantine hagiography but also the independent testimony of the Emperor John Cantacuzene, who frequently sought the saint's advice and recorded his debt in the memoirs which he wrote later in life.[45] He recalls, for

43 Philotheos, *Life of Sabas*, pp. 301, 339–47. Cantacuzene himself in fact says nothing about the proposed election of Sabas as patriarch, though Philotheos refers to it again in his Life of Isidore (see below, n. 53), pp. 116–17.
44 The *Life of Makarios* by Philotheos of Selymbria was edited by A. Papadopoulos-Kerameus, Ὁ ἐν Κωνσταντινουπόλει Ἑλληνικὸς Φιλολογικὸς Σύλλογος, XVII, Παράρτημα (Μαυρογορδάτειος Βιβλιοθήκη) [᾿Ανέκδοτα Ἑλληνικά] (Constantinople, 1886), pp. 46–59. The career of Hilarion is outlined at pp. 55–7. On Philotheos of Selymbria, see Beck, *Kirche und theologische Literatur*, pp. 776–7; Meyendorff, *Introduction*, index, s.v. Philothée; BHG³, II, no. 1000.
45 Kantakouzenos, II, pp. 169–73, 287–9, 340–4, 401–2, 426. Cantacuzene elsewhere names the three saints whom he had personally known and whose miraculous powers he had witnessed: the Patriarch Athanasios I, Hilarion of Didymoteichon, and one Gabriel, archimandrite of the

instance, how, at the time of his proclamation as emperor in 1341, he asked for Hilarion's blessing. The saint replied: 'To be Emperor of the Romans is, as you know, something ordained by God; but those who eat unripe figs will surely get swollen lips.' This cryptic remark was meant to imply that the new Emperor would encounter many dangers and difficulties – which was proved true. 'But', the Emperor goes on, 'the pronouncements of Hilarion on future events were regarded as oracles, for he had from God the gifts of prophecy and of thaumaturgy which are granted only to the pure in heart.'[46]

There are several other references to the prophetic and miraculous powers of Hilarion in the otherwise sober memoirs of John Cantacuzene. It is true that Hilarion consistently foretold that Cantacuzene was God's favourite for the throne – which again proved to be true in the end. But to suppose that this was the sole reason for the Emperor's trust in him would be to misrepresent the place of the holy man in Byzantine society. Cantacuzene reports another strange event that occurred at the time of his investiture. When he came to put on his imperial robes it was found that the inner garment was too tight to meet round his chest, however much it was stretched; the outer robe on the other hand was far too wide – though both had been carefully made to measure. This led someone to predict that the beginning of his reign would be strained and hard but the latter part peaceful and easy. But the 'someone' was not a holy man. Therefore it was possible to say, as the Emperor does say, 'whether this happened through God's will or just by chance, who knows? For the will of God in human affairs is predictable only by the pure in heart and by those whom God judges worthy of special gifts.'[47]

Monastery of the Pantokrator in Didymoteichon. See Meyendorff, *Introduction*, p. 34 n. 33 (citing an autograph marginal note in Cod. Paris. gr. 1347, fol. 93^v).

46 Kantakouzenos, II, pp. 169–71.
47 Kantakouzenos, II, pp. 167–8.

The gift of prophecy was acknowledged to be one of the rewards of long years of application to the 'inner' wisdom. Some of the scholars of the new 'enlightenment' of fourteenth-century Byzantium inveighed against false prophets, against 'ventriloquists' and fortune-telling quacks. But none of them seems to have doubted that a saint might possess a true gift of prophecy.[48]

There was then a double revival or renaissance in Byzantium – of learning and of spirituality. How far was there a conflict between the scholars and the saints, between the practitioners of the outer and of the inner wisdom?[49] The saints as well as the scholars tended to live in the ivory towers of their own pursuits. The prime purpose of monasticism was after all the salvation of one's own soul; the performance of good works for the rest of humanity was a secondary consideration. The prime purpose of scholarship as practised in late Byzantium seems

48 Gregoras, I, p. 411 lines 23–4, writes scornfully of 'false prophets and ventriloquists' ($\psi\epsilon\upsilon\delta o\mu\acute{a}\nu\tau\epsilon\iota\varsigma$ $\kappa a\grave{\iota}$ $\grave{\epsilon}\gamma\gamma a\sigma\tau\rho\acute{\iota}\mu\upsilon\theta o\iota$). Cf. pp. 722–6. So also George Pachymeres warns against astrologers and horoscope-mongers, 'who speak vain and empty words from their bellies'. P. Tannery, *Quadrivium de Georges Pachymère* (Studi e Testi, 94: Vatican City, 1940), p. 391 lines 12–20. Yet Gregoras recounts with admiration the prophetic dream of St Merkourios which foretold the death of Julian the Apostate (R. Guilland, *Essai sur Nicéphore Grégoras* (Paris, 1926), pp. 185–6); and in a letter to a friend on the subject of prediction from the stars he writes: 'But we acknowledge a prescience of the future only in those who receive a divine inspiration, like a ray of the flame of truth, or those who have recourse to some technique or method higher than that of ours or than any other science' (*Correspondance de Nicéphore Grégoras*, ed. R. Guilland [Paris, 1927], no. 33, p. 143).

49 There has been much discussion on this subject. See, e.g., L. Bréhier, 'L'enseignement classique et l'enseignement religieux à Byzance', *Revue d'histoire et de philosophie religieuses*, XXI (1941), pp. 34–69 (esp. pp. 59–63); H.-G. Beck, 'Humanismus und Palamismus', *Actes du XIIe Congrès International des Etudes Byzantines*, I (Belgrade, 1963), pp. 63–82; G. Schirò, in *ibid.* pp. 323–7; J. Meyendorff, in *ibid.* pp. 329–30; Meyendorff, 'Society and culture in the fourteenth century. Religious problems', *Actes du XIVe Congrès International des Etudes Byzantines*, I (Bucharest, 1974), pp. 51–65, esp. pp. 54–8; Runciman, *Last Byzantine Renaissance*, pp. 30ff.; Nicol, 'Byzantine Church and Hellenic learning' (see above, n. 7); and most recently G. Podskalsky, *Theologie und Philosophie in Byzanz* (see above, n. 16).

often to have been the gratification of one's own ego and
sometimes the discomfiture of one's intellectual opponents,
as in the case of the notorious academic feud between
Theodore Metochites and his social and political rival
Nikephoros Choumnos.[50] Beyond the discipline of the
master-pupil relationship there was little observable co-
operation among Byzantine scholars. Each worked alone
as an individualist. He would often express his debt to the
giants of Antiquity – to Plato, Aristotle or Ptolemy. But
he would seldom acknowledge the work of any of his
immediate predecessors, still less that of one of his contemporaries. Byzantine historians likewise behaved as
though no one since Herodotus and Thucydides had ever
put historical pen to paper. It is obvious, for example, that
Gregoras in his *History* relied heavily on the historical
work of his predecessor, George Pachymeres. But the
fact is nowhere acknowledged.[51] Certainly the scholars
congratulated each other on their expertise in their
elaborate correspondence. Flattery was a part of rhetoric.
Sometimes they borrowed books from each other. But
only rarely did they collaborate in their researches.

Yet it does not follow that all the saints and scholars
were so wrapped up in their own spiritual or intellectual
cocoons as to be oblivious of the world around them.
Some of the holy men actually preferred to live in
the world rather than in the wilderness. One such was
Makarios, the spiritual father of Hilarion. He spent

50 I. Ševčenko, *Etudes sur la polémique entre Théodore Métochite et Nicéphore
Choumnos* (Brussels, 1962); J. Verpeaux, *Nicéphore Choumnos homme d'état
et humaniste byzantin (ca. 1250/1255–1327)* (Paris, 1959), pp. 52–62.
51 On the sources of the *History* of Gregoras, see R. Guilland, *Essai sur
Nicéphore Grégoras*, pp. 244–8. Theodore Metochites repeatedly congra-
tulates himself on having rediscovered the lost sciences of astronomy and
mathematics, though he must surely have known of the *Handbook of the
Four Sciences* (*Quadrivium*) composed by George Pachymeres some years
before his time. See the Introduction to his own treatise on astronomy,
ed. K. N. Sathas, Μεσαιωνικὴ Βιβλιοθήκη, I (Venice, 1872), p. ρια΄; R.
Guilland, 'Les poésies inédites de Théodore Métochite', in Guilland,
Etudes Byzantines (Paris, 1959), pp. 181, 200; Ševčenko, *Etudes sur la
polémique*, pp. 78 n. 3, 109–11, 115 n. 2, 201–3.

most of his life in one of the city monasteries in Constantinople.[52] Another was Isidore, who was twice Patriarch of Constantinople (1347–50; 1355–63). No less a saint than the great Gregory of Sinai is said to have advised Isidore that he was not called to be an anchorite but to live in the world in a monastic community, to be a public example of the Christian way of life.[53] Similarly, many of the scholars such as Theodore Metochites led active public lives in the intervals of their researches. Finally, most of the saints and all of the scholars shared a common educational background. Isidore, for example, before he became a monk had taught grammar and literature to upper-class boys in Thessalonica. His biographer tells us, however, that he was different from many schoolmasters in rejecting the myths and fables of the Hellenes as being unpalatable for Christian ears. For his own pupils Isidore recommended three mentors who in philosophy, dialectic, physics, astronomy and rhetoric were more than the equals of the Hellenes – namely, Basil the Great, Gregory of Nazianzus and John Chrysostom.[54] The problem of how to reconcile the 'wisdom of the

52 Makarios was a monk of the Monastery of the Virgin called Kalliou in the heart of Constantinople and frequented several other monasteries in the city, among them that of the Chora; Philotheos of Selymbria, *Life of Makarios*, ed. Papadopoulos-Kerameus (see above, n. 44), pp. 49–50. For the Monastery of Kalliou, or of Kyr Antonios, see R. Janin, *La Géographie ecclésiastique de l'Empire byzantin*, I: *Le Siège de Constantinople et le Patriarcat œcuménique*, III: *Les Eglises et les Monastères* (Paris, 1953), pp. 44–6.

53 Philotheos (Kokkinos), *Life of Isidore*, ed. A. Papadopoulos-Kerameus, 'Žitija dvuch Vselenskich Patriarchov XIV v., svv. Afanasija I i Isidora I', *Zapiski istoriko-filolog. fakulteta Imperatorskago S.-Petersburgskago Universiteta*, LXXVI (1905), pp. 52–149, esp. p. 77 lines 21–6: Οὐκ ἐν ἐρήμοις οὐδ' ἐν ὄρεσι τούτοις ἐβουλόμην ἔγωγε τέως, ὦ βέλτιστε, διατρίβειν σε – διατί γάρ; –, ἀλλ' ἐν τῷ κόσμῳ μᾶλλον καὶ τοῖς ἐκεῖ ζῶσι μονάζουσι καὶ κοινωνικοῖς, ἵν' ἐκείνοις ὁμοῦ πᾶσι τύπος εἴης τῆς κατὰ Χριστὸν ἀγαθῆς πολιτείας καὶ παντοδαπῆς ἀρετῆς, καὶ σιωπῶν καὶ φθεγγόμενος. Cf. R. Guilland, 'Moines de l'Athos, patriarches de Constantinople (Nicolas II, Isaïe, Isidore)', *EEBS*, XXXII (1963), pp. 40–59.

54 Philotheos, *Life of Isidore*, pp. 63–5, esp. p. 64 lines 3–9. See also the *Testament* of Isidore (dated February 1350), in *MM*, I, no. CXXX, pp. 287–94, esp. pp. 287–8.

Hellenes' with the 'inner wisdom' of Christian revela-
tion was as old as Christianity itself. St Basil had given it
much thought and wrote a sensible address to the young
on how to derive benefit from Hellenic literature without
endangering their Christian souls.[55] St John of Damascus
in the eighth century thought that Christians could safely
flavour the message of salvation with the sweetness of
pagan learning, as the bee sips honey from the flowers.[56]
But the balance was a delicate one. The flowers held more
than honey, and the bees ran the risk of poisoning
themselves. Such at least was the apprehension of those
who guarded the Christian conscience of the Christ-named
people. Everyone knew what had happened to John Italos,
the pupil and successor of Michael Psellos as Professor of
Philosophy in Constantinople in 1082. Italos had become
so enamoured of the wisdom of the Hellenes that he had
fallen into heresy. His errors were read out in every
Orthodox church on the first Sunday of Lent as a
perpetual reminder and warning.[57] The problem was not
made easier by the sheer quantity and quality of Hellenic
learning which was available to the Byzantines. By the
eleventh century and still more by the fourteenth the
legacy of ancient scholarship encompassed not only the
works of respectable sages like Plato and Aristotle (though
they too had their dangers), but also the whole corpus of
neoplatonic literature, hermetic texts, the speculations of
the Pythagoreans and much more besides. Only an expert
could pick his way safely through these quicksands.

It could be said that the wandering mystics, the holy
men and hesychasts of this latter age, tipped the balance

---

55 *Saint Basil on the Value of Greek Literature*, ed. N. G. Wilson (London,
   1975) (Greek text: pp. 19–36). P. Lemerle, *Le premier humanisme byzantin.
   Notes et remarques sur l'enseignement et culture à Byzance des origines au Xe
   siècle* (Paris, 1971), esp. pp. 43ff.
56 John of Damascus, *Fons Scientiae* (Πηγὴ Γνώσεως), in *MPG*, XCIV, cols.
   524C–525A, 532B.
57 J. M. Hussey, *Church and Learning in the Byzantine Empire, 867–1185*
   (London, 1937), pp. 89–102; P. E. Stéphanou, *Jean Italos, philosophe et
   humaniste* (*OCA*, 134; Rome, 1949).

too far in the other direction by their total rejection of the wisdom of this world, past or present. Gregory Palamas, the doctor of hesychast theology, firmly believed that the pursuit of the 'outer' learning was irrelevant if not positively harmful to the life of the spirit. Scholarship was not a monk's business, unless it were the study of theology. The monk should be wholly detached from the things of this world.[58] In his earlier life Palamas had, like every educated Byzantine, been grounded in ancient Greek philosophy. But from the moment of his monastic vocation he turned his back on scholarly pursuits. In one of his homilies he compares the uses which a Christian may make of pagan philosophy to the uses which doctors make of snakes. 'The flesh of snakes', he writes, 'is of use to us if we kill and dissect them and make preparations from them, which can be applied with discretion as a remedy against their own bites.'[59] But even though men of the world might extract some beneficial serum from profane studies, for a man of the spirit, a monk, they could be nothing but a hindrance. 'The Lord did not expressly forbid scholarship', he says. 'But neither did he forbid marriage, or the eating of meat, or cohabitation between married persons. . . There are many things that ordinary Christians may do which are strictly forbidden to monks by reason of their special way of life.'[60]

Many of the scholars and teachers of the time, excited as they were by the rediscovery of so much of their Greek heritage, found such illiberal views to be unpalatable. It was not that they were on the way to questioning the

---

58 The first treatise of the first of the *Triads* of Gregory Palamas is wholly devoted to denying the uses of profane philosophy in the search for the knowledge of God, especially as expounded by Barlaam of Calabria: *Grégoire Palamas. Défense des saints hésychastes*, ed. Meyendorff, I, pp. 1–69. The same theme runs through the first treatise of *Triad* II, *ibid.* pp. 225–317. These two works constitute 'l'attaque la plus violente et la plus solide qu'ait connue la littérature grecque chrétienne du Moyen Age contre les dangers et les tentations de l'hellénisme païen' (Meyendorff, *Introduction*, p. 349).

59 *Défense des saints hésychastes*, ed. Meyendorff, I, 1, §11, pp. 34–7.

60 *Défense des saints hésychastes*, ed. Meyendorff, II, 1, §35, pp. 294–7.

eternal truths of their Christian religion. Byzantine scholars of the fourteenth century were well aware that, in the last resort, philosophy was only the handmaid of theology. But men like Metochites and Gregoras believed that there was a lot to be said for Christians, and even monks, being in touch with the world as much as possible. They felt that the total rejection of the wisdom of this world was a form of spiritual pride and that the rabble of ignorant monks that demonstrated in favour of the Arsenites or the hesychasts would be the better for a little further education. Sanctity was being used as an excuse for illiteracy. Metochites went so far as to say that the eremitic life of the solitary monk was a kind of escapism, contrary to Christian ordinances and to nature.[61]

This was an extreme if not an eccentric opinion for a Byzantine. On the whole the saints and scholars mixed happily enough. There was a bit of both in most educated Byzantines; though there were perhaps more scholars who aspired to sanctity than there were saints who aspired to scholarship. In either case one is dealing with an élite. The scholars were never more than a tiny minority of the population; and only a chosen few answered the call to sanctity. It is easy to exaggerate the piety and depth of spiritual feeling of the ordinary people of Byzantium. The constant complaints of patriarchs and bishops about the moral and spiritual shortcomings of their flocks cannot be all baseless rhetoric. Religion and the performance of religious duties were, as often, matters of habit, tradition, social custom and superstition. But they were always an essential ingredient of the mixture that went to make up a Romaios or Byzantine, the citizen, however worldly, of a theocratic society.

Theirs was a Church and world in which it was thought nothing strange that a man of affairs should be an erudite

61 Metochites, *Miscellanea philosophica et historica*, ed. Müller and Kiessling, no. 73, pp. 484–91 (esp. p. 486); cf. nos. 74–6, pp. 491–511. H.-G. Beck, *Theodoros Metochites. Die Krise des Byzantinischen Weltbildes im 14. Jahrhundert* (Munich, 1952), pp. 31ff.; Verpeaux, *Nicéphore Choumnos*, p. 185.

theologian, that a priest should be a married man with a family, that a holy man such as Sabas should remain unordained, or that a layman should suddenly be appointed as patriarch. Thirteen of the one hundred and twenty-two Byzantine Patriarchs of Constantinople were elevated from the laity, among them the great Patriarch Photios (though the Pope had disapproved).[62] John Glykys, who became patriarch in 1315, was a civil servant with an academic turn of mind.[63] Most self-respecting statesmen or courtiers even of the later age turned their leisure hours to the production of religious or hagiographical works. George Akropolites, historian, scholar, diplomat and Grand Logothete in the thirteenth century, found time to write two polemical tracts denouncing the fatal errors of Latin theology.[64] His son Constantine, who rose to the same high office of state, wrote no less than twenty-nine lives of saints as well as other works of a religious nature.[65] Nicholas Kabasilas, who came of a well-to-do family in Thessalonica in the fourteenth century, wrote some of the most penetrating mystical literature ever written; and yet he was a layman, at least until the close of his life.[66]

62 L. Bréhier, 'Le recrutement des Patriarches de Constantinople pendant la période byzantine', *Actes du VIe Congrès d'Etudes Byzantines*, I (Paris, 1950), pp. 221–7; Bréhier, *Les Institutions de l'Empire byzantin* (*Le monde byzantin*, II, 2nd edn, Paris, 1970), pp. 384–8. Cf. Hunger, *Reich der neuen Mitte*, pp. 276–7.
63 On the Patriarch John XIII Glykys, see S. I. Kourousis, Ὁ λόγιος οἰκουμενικὸς πατριάρχης Ἰωάννης ΙΓ' ὁ Γλυκύς (Athens, 1975).
64 *Georgii Acropolitae Opera*, ed. A. Heisenberg, II (Leipzig, 1903), pp. 30–45, 45–66.
65 D. M. Nicol, 'Constantine Akropolites. A prosopographical note', *DOP*, XIX (1965), pp. 249–56; F. Winkelmann, 'Nachrichten über das Nikaia des 13. Jahrhunderts in einer Laudatio des Konstantinos Akropolites', *Studia Balcanica*, I (Sofia, 1970), pp. 113–15; Winkelmann, 'Leningradskij fragment žitija Mitrofana', *VV*, XXXI (1971), p. 145; K. A. Manaphis, Κωνσταντίνου Ἀκροπολίτου λόγος εἰς τὴν ἀνακαίνισιν τοῦ ναοῦ τῆς Κυρίου ἡμῶν Ἀναστάσεως διαθητικός, *EEBS* XXXVII (1969–70), pp. 459–65; D. I. Polemis, 'The speech of Constantine Acropolites on John Merciful the Young', *AB*, XCI (1973), pp. 31–54.
66 On Nicholas Kabasilas, see Myrrha Lot-Borodine, *Un maître de la spiritualité byzantine au XIVe siècle. Nicolas Cabasilas* (Paris, 1958); Beck, *Kirche und theologische Literatur*, pp. 780–3; Tatakis, *Philosophie byzantine*,

Emperors too turned their hands to religious composition. John Cantacuzene, who spent the last thirty years of his long life as a monk, wrote a variety of theological works as well as lengthy tracts against the Muslims and against the Jews.[67] His son and co-emperor Matthew Cantacuzene composed a number of philosophical and theological works.[68] His grandson, the Emperor Manuel II Palaiologos, wrote treatises designed to confound both Latin and Muslim theologians, as well as an ethical discourse on marriage – about which he was something of an expert, having reared six legitimate children and an unspecified number of bastards.[69] (Manuel's son, the Emperor John VIII, who had doubtless read his father's advice, married three times, was divorced once and produced no issue whatever.)[70]

What is still more striking is that, for all the strictures of Palamas and his like, a number of the latter-day scholars of Byzantium were in fact monks. Perhaps the most outstanding was Maximos Planoudes, who died in 1305. Allusion has already been made to his philological work in the way of editing and commenting on texts. Hesiod, Sophocles, Euripides, Aristophanes, Pindar, Aratus, Thucydides, Euclid, Aesop, Plutarch, Ptolemy and Diophantos

pp. 277–81; A. A. Angelopoulos, Νικόλαος Καβάσιλας Χαμάετος. Ἡ ζωὴ καὶ τὸ ἔργον αὐτοῦ (Ἀνάλεκτα Βλατάδων, 5: Thessalonike 1970); J. Gouillard, 'L'autoportrait d'un sage du XIVe siècle', *Actes du XIVe Congrès International des Etudes Byzantines*, II (Bucharest, 1975), pp. 103–8; M. A. Poljakovskaja, 'Politiceskie idealy vizantijskoj intelligentzii serediny XIV v. (Nikolaj Kavasila)', *Anticnaja drevnost' i srednie veka*, XII (1975), pp. 104–16.

67 Nicol, *Byzantine Family of Kantakouzenos*, pp. 98–100.
68 Nicol, *Byzantine Family of Kantakouzenos*, p. 120.
69 J. W. Barker, *Manuel II Palaeologus (1391–1425). A Study in Late Byzantine Statesmanship* (New Brunswick, N.J., 1969), pp. 402–3, 474–8, 579–81. Manuel's *Moral Dialogue or Concerning Marriage* remains unpublished; see *The Letters of Manuel II Palaeologus*, ed. G. T. Dennis (*CFHB*, VIII: Washington, D.C., 1977), pp. xxii–xxiii, 172–4.
70 On John VIII, see A. Th. Papadopulos, *Versuch einer Genealogie der Palaiologen, 1259–1453* (Munich, 1938: reprinted Amsterdam, 1962), no. 90, p. 59. Cf. J. Gill, 'John VIII Palaeologus: a character study', in Gill, *Personalities of the Council of Florence and Other Essays* (Oxford, 1964), pp. 104–24.

– all in one way or another received the attention of Planoudes – not to mention his great collection of epigrams, which still goes by the name of the Planudean Anthology.[71] Even more remarkable is his work as a translator from Latin into Greek. Knowledge of Latin was a very rare accomplishment in Byzantium in his day. But Planoudes knew enough to translate not only St Augustine and Boethius (who might qualify for the 'inner' learning) but also Cicero, Cato, Ovid and Caesar.[72] In addition he wrote a treatise on mathematics entitled *Arithmetic after the Indian Method* in which he introduced the use of the zero into Greek numerals.[73] He and his most successful pupil, Manuel Moschopoulos (died 1316), studied and taught for part of their time in the Monastery of Chora, which was later to be rebuilt by Theodore Metochites. Some of the books which they acquired or copied remained in the library of that monastery. Moschopoulos too composed numerous commentaries on classical texts as well as a popular grammatical handbook, the *Erotemata grammatica*.[74]

George Pachymeres, besides writing the history of his time, composed a summary of Aristotelian philosophy and

71 See above, p. 34 and notes 10 and 11. On the life and work of Planoudes, see C. Wendel, in Pauly-Wissowa (ed.), *Real-Enzyclopädie der klassischen Altertumswissenschaft*, XX, 2 (1950), *s.v.* 'Planudes', pp. 2202–53; Tatakis, *Philosophie byzantine*, pp. 239–41; Hunger, 'Von Wissenschaft und Kunst', *JÖBG*, VIII (1959), pp. 139–42; Runciman, *Last Byzantine Renaissance*, pp. 59–60.

72 W. O. Schmitt, 'Lateinische Literatur in Byzanz. Die Übersetzungen des Maximos Planudes und die moderne Forschung', *JÖBG*, XVII (1968), pp. 127–47; A. Lumpe, 'Abendland und Byzanz, III: Literatur und Sprache. A. Literatur. Abendländisches in Byzanz', in *Reallexikon der Byzantinistik*, ed. P. Wirth, Reihe A, Bd. I. Heft 4 (Amsterdam, 1970), cols. 304–47; M. Papathomopoulos (ed.), Μαξίμου Πλανούδη μετάφρασις τῶν ᾿Οβιδίου ἐπιστολῶν (Ioannina, 1973).

73 See G. Sarton, *Introduction to the History of Science*, II (Baltimore, 1931), pp. 973–4; III, 1 (1947), pp. 119–21, 681–2. K. Vogel, 'Byzantine Science', in *Cambridge Medieval History*, IV, 2 (1967), pp. 277, 278.

74 On Manuel Moschopoulos, see Sarton, *Introduction*, III, 1, pp. 679–81; I. Ševčenko, 'The Imprisonment of Manuel Moschopulos in the year 1305 or 1306', *Speculum*, XXVII (1952), pp. 133–57; Hunger, 'Von Wissenschaft und Kunst', pp. 142–3.

also a handbook of the four sciences (*Quadrivium* or *tetraktys*) – arithmetic, music, geometry and astronomy. He was not a monk, though he was ordained as a deacon and for a while held the title of Professor of New Testament exegesis.[75] His younger contemporary, Thomas Magister, who was a monk with the name of Theodoulos, wrote commentaries on the tragedians and on Pindar as well as a lexicon of Attic Greek and several rhetorical works.[76] He and his pupil Demetrios Triklinios, perhaps the greatest of the late Byzantine editors, lived and worked in Thessalonica, a fact which is enough to indicate that the fourteenth-century world of learning was not confined to Constantinople.[77] The Patriarch Philotheos was proud to be a native of Thessalonica and describes it as 'the very home of civilised men'.[78] The holy Sabas of Vatopedi, the 'fool for Christ's sake', was also born there and must indeed have been a contemporary of Thomas Magister and Triklinios. We are told that Sabas as a boy was sent to the grammar school where, although his mind was already on higher things, he romped through the curriculum, studying the best of the ancient writers as a necessary basis for his later introduction to the 'inner' wisdom. Mythology, however, he rejected as pure nonsense.[79] One is left wondering how a scholar-monk like Thomas Magister and an incipient anchorite like

75 On George Pachymeres, see Sarton, *Introduction*, II, 2, pp. 972–3; Tatakis, *Philosophie byzantine*, pp. 239–40. For his *Quadrivium*, see n. 48.
76 On Thomas Magister, see Hunger, 'Von Wissenschaft und Kunst', pp. 143–5.
77 On Demetrios Triklinios, see Sarton, *Introduction*, III, 1, pp. 996–7; Hunger, 'Von Wissenschaft und Kunst', pp. 145–7; A. Turyn, 'Demetrius Triclinius and the Planudean Anthology', Λειμών. Προσφορὰ εἰς N. B. Τωμαδάκην (= EEBS, XXXIX–XL (1972–3)), pp. 403–50; L. D. Reynolds and N. G. Wilson, *Scribes and Scholars*, 2nd edn (Oxford, 1974), pp. 66–8, 156, 206, 210, 211. On scholarship in Thessalonica in the fourteenth century, see O. Tafrali, *Thessalonique au Quatorzième Siècle* (Paris, 1913), pp. 148–69; B. Laourdas, Ἡ κλασσικὴ φιλολογία εἰς τὴν Θεσσαλονίκην κατὰ τὸν δέκατον τέταρτον αἰῶνα (Thessalonike, 1960).
78 Πολιτευομένοις ἀνθρώποις κόσμος οἰκεῖος: Philotheos, *Life of Sabas*, ed. Papadopoulos-Kerameus (see above, n. 30), p. 193 line 9.
79 Philotheos, *Life of Sabas*, ed. Papadopoulos-Kerameus, pp. 192–3, 197.

Sabas, both members of that higher estate of the monastic life, would have got on together if and when they met in Thessalonica.

What was it that impelled one kind of monk to immerse himself in the 'outer' learning of the Hellenes and another to reject it outright? What indeed was the attitude of the Church to this unmonkish pursuit of pagan scholarship? Part of the answer to both of these questions may be illustrated in the career of one further Byzantine scholar-monk of this age – Joseph the Philosopher. Joseph, who liked to be known as the humble Rakendytes or threadbare monk, was born about 1280 on the island of Ithaka. He studied in Thessalonica, became a monk and for a time lived the vagabond hermit life, in Thessaly, Athos and elsewhere, before settling in Constantinople. More than once he was nominated for the patriarchate, but he declined the honour; and he died in Thessalonica about 1330.[80] His great project, which was never finished and has still to be edited, was the compilation of an encyclo-paedia. This was to be in the nature of a synthesis of the outer and inner wisdom. It was to include rhetoric, logic, physics, anthropology, mathematics (with music and astronomy), the four virtues and theology. It was something of a scissors-and-paste job and far from original. But the very idea of the project is interesting. Joseph admitted that it might be thought strange that a monk, whose profession was the perfection of his soul, should devote his time to the natural sciences. But the real object of all scholarship was the true wisdom of the knowledge of God. If by studying natural philosophy one comes to a greater awareness of the wondrous works of the Creator then that is not time wasted or misspent. Clearly such delving into the 'outer' learning had its hazards for the Christian, as Joseph observes in his comments on Aristotle's views

80 On Joseph the Philosopher, see M. Treu, 'Der Philosoph Joseph', *BZ*, VIII (1899), pp. 1–64; J. Dräseke, 'Zum Philosophen Joseph', *Zeitschrift für wissenschaftliche Theologie*, XLII (1899), pp. 612–20; Hunger, 'Von Wissenschaft und Kunst', pp. 150–3; Nicol, 'Byzantine Church and Hellenic learning', pp. 35–6.

about the soul. But his idea was to reconcile what could
be reconciled between the two forms of wisdom.[81]

Joseph the Philosopher was much admired by his
contemporaries. Theodore Metochites wrote an epitaph
for him.[82] But if either of these men, the one a scholar-
monk, the other a pious layman, had proposed that
scholarship had any object other than the further knowledge of God and the works of God, he would have been
condemned by Church and State as John Italos had been
condemned in the eleventh century. The fact is that
neither did. Metochites got as near to doing so as anyone
in his day. But even he, who claimed (somewhat pre-
sumptuously) to have revived the study of astronomy
single-handed, defended it on the ground that it could
elevate the spirit and lead men to a deeper understanding
of the divine purpose.[83] (Metochites was in fact, for a
Byzantine, abnormally quiet on the matter of theology,
perhaps because his own father had disgraced himself by
adopting a strong unionist position at the time of the
Council of Lyons.)[84] His pupil Gregoras recalls with pride
how his saintly uncle John had by his spiritual instruction
led him towards the good, and by initiating him into
astronomy had brought him closer to the divine. 'For the
observation of the heavens is by its nature a great and most
noble pursuit. It is the ladder that leads to the knowledge
of God, making it possible for a mortal to peep at the
mysteries of theology.'[85] A slightly later astronomer,

81 Nicol, 'Byzantine Church and Hellenic learning', p. 36 and refs.; R.
   Criuscolo, 'Note sull' "Enciclopedia" del filosofo Giuseppe', *B*, xliv
   (1974), pp. 255–79.
82 Ed. M. Treu, 'Der Philosoph Joseph', pp. 2–31.
83 See, e.g., Metochites, *Miscellanea*, no. 43, pp. 264–8; Guilland, 'Les poésies
   inédites', p. 195. In his poem 'On Mathematics, a branch of Philosophy',
   and more especially 'On Harmonics', Metochites observes that the
   harmonious movement of the spheres gives one a clearer admiration of
   the power and wisdom of the Creator.
84 Theodore's father, George Metochites, archdeacon of St Sophia, was and
   remained until his death a fervent supporter of the Union of Lyons. He
   was exiled in 1283 and died in prison in 1328. R.-J. Loenertz, 'Théodore
   Métochite et son père', *Archivum Fratrum Praedicatorum*, xxiii (1953), pp.
   184–94; Beck, *Kirche und theologische Literatur*, p. 684.
85 Laurent (ed.), 'Vie de Jean d'Héraclée', p. 60 lines 8–15.

Theodore Meliteniotes, who wrote a three-volume work on the subject, ranked astronomy next to theology as the noblest branch of that philosophy which makes us capable of imitating God. As a scientist he pointed out that the eclipse at the time of the Crucifixion went against the astronomical evidence. But as a Christian, and a hesychast as well, he concluded that the eclipse must be accepted as a miracle wrought by God.[86]

The idea of knowledge for its own sake did not appeal to these scholars. The 'outer' learning must have an educative purpose, the 'inner' learning a perfective one. But ultimately the goal of both was the same. There was no place for idle curiosity and consequently not much danger of the devil finding work for idle hands to do.[87] The Byzantines in one sense may be said to have been stunted in their intellectual development. They had all the materials to hand for a true renaissance of learning: the libraries, the texts, the scribes and the enthusiasm. But they made very little of their opportunity. This was partly because they were brought up to regard philosophy as the handmaid of religion, and partly because they liked things that way. The scholars of the fourteenth century were not really breaking new ground. Even in those subjects such as mathematics, astronomy and medicine, in which new material from Persian and Arabic sources became available to them, they made few original observations or calculations.[88] They paid proud homage to the literature

86 Theodore Meliteniotes, Ἀστρονομικὴ τρίβιβλος, Prologue, in MPG, CXLIX, cols. 988–1001, esp. col. 992 A–C. Cf. Sarton, Introduction, III, 2, pp. 1512–14; Vogel, 'Byzantine science', pp. 277–8; Hunger, 'Von Wissenschaft und Kunst', pp. 148–9; D. Pingree, 'Gregory Chioniades and Palaeologan Astronomy', DOP, XVIII (1964), pp. 133–60.

87 See the remarks of V. Laurent in P. Tannery, Quadrivium de Georges Pachymère, pp. xx–xxi. Cf. Guilland, Essai sur Nicéphore Grégoras, p. 77; Beck, Theodoros Metochites, pp. 48–9.

88 On Byzantine medicine in this period, see Guilland, Essai sur Nicéphore Grégoras, p. 74; Vogel, 'Byzantine science', pp. 291–4; Hunger, 'Von Wissenschaft und Kunst', p. 149; Sarton, Introduction, II, 2, pp. 1094–6, III, 1, pp. 859–92. Runciman, Last Byzantine Renaissance, pp. 91–2, takes a somewhat optimistic view of the late Byzantine contribution to medical research.

of Greek Antiquity. But it is often hard to believe that they read it for pleasure. Certainly they read it for style. They exploited it as a mine of prefabricated phrases and ideas for their own artificial literary language, the language of rhetoric in which they communicated and wrote, whether their subject was an address to an emperor or a life of a saint.

How far then did such men achieve a synthesis between pagan and Christian learning? How fairly could Metochites or Gregoras be described as Christian humanists or Christian Hellenists? As early as the 1250s the Emperor-in-exile, Theodore II Laskaris, in his *Encomium* of the city of Nicaea, had envisaged a fruitful co-existence between Hellenic learning and Christian theology. He writes of 'the double kingdom of (ancient) philosophy and of the theology built upon it and rising above it'. The scholars of Nicaea, he says, 'have mingled philosophy with theology in new ways, as one grafts a wild olive branch to a cultivated tree'.[89] Much the same ideas were expressed by Gregoras in the Life that he wrote of his uncle and mentor John. 'Spiritual virtue is lame', he writes, 'if it lacks [a foundation of] worldly wisdom.'[90] And John did all in his power to see that his nephew got the best of both worlds, tending him as a gardener tends a plant, 'mixing and mingling Hellenic and divine instruction so as to preserve intact the harmony between them and, by familiarising him with the wisdom of the Hellenes, directing his mind to things more divine'.[91]

But the grafting and the mingling were self-conscious,

89 *Theodori Ducae Lascaris imperatoris in laudem Nicaeae urbis oratio*, ed. L. Bachmann (Programm Rostock, 1847), pp. 5, 6; reprinted by Hunger, 'Von Wissenschaft und Kunst', p. 136. See also the Κοσμικὴ Δήλωσις of the same Emperor Theodore II Laskaris, ed. N. Festa, in *Giornale della Società Asiatica Italiana*, XI (1898), pp. 97–114, XII (1899), pp. 1–52. Extracts from this, with commentary, are in Hunger, 'Von Wissenschaft und Kunst', pp. 128–35. Cf. Hunger, *Reich der neuen Mitte*, p. 357f.

90 Ed. Laurent, *Vie de Jean d'Héraclée*, p. 46 lines 13–15: ...ἐπόθει καὶ τὸ τῆς ἐπιστήμης λαβεῖν ἐντελές· χωλεύειν γὰρ ἔλεγε τὴν πνευματικὴν ἀρετήν, εἴ τις ἐκείνης ἀφέλοι τουτί.

91 Laurent, *Vie de Jean d'Héraclée*, p. 57 line 27–p. 58 line 2.

artificial processes and they produced very little new fruit or blossom. The nature of Christian humanism is at best debatable, that of Christian Hellenism still more so. Neither tag seems wholly apt to the scholars of late Byzantium. Had they fallen into either of these categories they would have ceased to be 'Byzantines'. They would have lost that special if elusive quality which may be described as 'Byzantinism'. Their saints were trained by vigilance and by *askesis* to reach the higher calling of monasticism. Likewise their scholars were the perfected products of an intensive training in 'Byzantinism'. They were the members of an exclusive club in which the rules were determined by cultured manners and sophisticated language, by the initiation into a style.[92] They prided themselves on being civilised (πολιτευόμενοι) and on their urbanity. 'Urbanity' (ἀστειότης) may indeed be the nearest Greek equivalent to the Latin *humanitas*.[93] But it was not the product of a blend of Hellenism with Christianity; it was cultivated by a grafting of Hellenism on to Byzantinism. This, like 'Byzantine', was not a word which these people would have used of themselves. It is a term of convenience to convey the flavour of that society, unfamiliar to our palate, which could at the same time accommodate a rude holy man and a cultured aesthete – an Athanasios and a Metochites.

Just as there were two kinds of wisdom, the outer and the inner, so there were two kinds of experience, the tangible and the intangible, the temporal and the spiritual. It is typical that the Byzantines should have continued to use Platonic terms to describe the two levels of human experience – τὰ αἰσθητά and τὰ νοητά (or νοερά, ἐπιστη-μονικά) – things perceived by the senses and things perceived by the intellect.[94] But beyond and above the purely

92 See the penetrating remarks of P. Lemerle, *Le premier humanisme byzantin*, pp. 300–7, which, though concerned with the tenth century, are no less applicable to the fourteenth and fifteenth centuries.
93 Beck, *Theodoros Metochites*, p. 64. Cf. Verpeaux, *Nicéphore Choumnos;* pp. 189–90; Medvedev, *Vizantijskij Gumanism*, pp. 22ff., 88–103.
94 See, e.g., the *Quadrivium de Georges Pachymère*, ed. P. Tannery, p. 7 lines

human level of experience lay that of the spirit, supernatural and supra-intellectual, in which the whole human
being, body, mind and soul, could be illuminated,
transfigured and eventually deified. Theodore Metochites
writes of the difficulties of reconciling the active and the
contemplative life – the βίος πρακτικός and the βίος
θεωρητικός.[95] Gregory Palamas, however, writes of experiences far beyond those expressible in Platonic or
Aristotelian terms. 'Those who possess something more
than the faculties of sense and intellect, who have acquired
spiritual and supernatural grace, will not be limited to
created beings in their understanding, for they will understand also spiritually, above sense and intellect, that God
is spirit, for they become God with all their being and
know God in God.'[96] This was the inner wisdom, the true
philosophy. It is instructive that the Greek word *philo-
sophos* should have come to mean a monk and the word
phrontisterion a monastery.[97] Nikephoros the Hesychast
adapted the Aristotelian definition of philosophy to
Orthodox Christian purposes when he wrote: 'The
monastic life has received the name of science of sciences
and art of arts.'[98]

As so often, it is in the visual arts that we can best
perceive the Byzantine mentality at work. Byzantine art
is a form of art for which no other epithet will serve. It
is a genre on its own. It performs at once an aesthetic and
a noetic function. Its artists worked in a style and idiom

11f.: Δῆλον γὰρ ὅτι κλίμαξί τισι καὶ γεφύραις ἔοικε ταῦτα τὰ μαθήματα,
διαβιβάζοντα τὴν διάνοιαν ἡμῶν ἀπὸ τῶν αἰσθητῶν καὶ δοξαστῶν ἐπὶ τὰ
νοητὰ καὶ ἐπιστημονικά. Similarly, the ideas of Metochites and Gregoras
on astronomy as a science that purifies the mind are clearly indebted to
Plato.

95 Cf. Beck, *Theodoros Metochites*, pp. 26ff.; Hunger, 'Von Wissenschaft und
Kunst', p. 138; Medvedev, *Vizantijskij Gumanism*, pp. 93–5.

96 Palamas, *Défense des saints hésychastes*, ed. Meyendorff, II, p. 531 line 31–p.
533 line 2.

97 F. Dölger, 'Zur Bedeutung von *ΦΙΛΟΣΟΦΟΣ* und *ΦΙΛΟΣΟΦΙΑ* in
byzantinischer Zeit', in Dölger, *Byzanz und die europäische Staatenwelt*
(Ettal, 1953), pp. 197–208; Hunger, *Reich der neuen Mitte*, pp. 284–5.

98 Nikephoros the Hesychast (Nicephorus Monachus), in *MPG*, CXLVII, col.
947A: Διὰ τοῦτο γὰρ τέχνη τέχνων, καὶ ἐπιστήμη ἐπιστήμων ἡ μοναδικὴ
πολιτεία ὠνόμασται.

into which they were initiated and from which they
hardly ever deviated. To us it appears unreal – 'shade
more than man, more image than a shade', as W. B. Yeats
has it.[99] But there is ample evidence that to Byzantine eyes
it was, as we would say, quite naturalistic. The figure in
the icon is said to be so lifelike that it is constantly about
to speak or even to come down, as the Virgin did from
her icon in St Sophia to advise the future Patriarch
Isidore.[100] If the saints in their mosaics and icons really
seemed so human to the Byzantines then their view of
humanity, and of humanism, must have been different
from ours, and also different from that of their western
contemporaries.[101]

The monastery Church of the Chora in Constantinople
remains as one of the most exquisite jewels of Byzantine
art. This is no monument to Christian Hellenism or
Byzantine humanism. Yet it is, or it was, a work of
sanctity and scholarship combined. Restored and decorated
at fabulous expense by the scholar and statesman Theodore
Metochites, it was the focal point of a huge complex of
buildings, charitable and administrative; but its founder's
pride and joy was the library. All that remains now is the
church with its mosaics and the side chapel with its
wall-paintings – executed, as always, by anonymous artists, themselves, like the holy images they created or like
the holy men on earth, media or channels of divine
grace.[102] And among the mosaics, above the entrance

99 W. B. Yeats, *Byzantium*, line 10.
100 Philotheos, *Life of Isidore*, p. 111 lines 3–11.
101 On the 'naturalism' of Byzantine art in the eyes of its contemporaries,
see C. Mango, 'Antique statuary and the Byzantine beholder', *DOP*,
XVII (1963), pp. 55–75, esp. pp. 65ff.; Mango, *The Art of the
Byzantine Empire, 312–1453* (Englewood Cliffs, N.J., 1972), pp. xiv–xv.
For other views, see H. Maguire, 'Truth and convention in Byzantine
descriptions of works of art', *DOP*, XXVIII (1974), pp. 111–40; R.
Cormack, 'Painting after Iconoclasm', in *Iconoclasm*, ed. A. Bryer and
Judith Herrin (Centre for Byzantine Studies, University of Birmingham,
1977), pp. 157ff.
102 For the comparatively humble status of the artist in Byzantine society,
see G. Mathew, *Byzantine Aesthetics* (London, 1963), pp. 114ff.; Runciman, *Last Byzantine Renaissance*, pp. 49–52; Runciman, *Byzantine Style
and Civilization* (Harmondsworth, 1975), pp. 119, 180.

into the nave, kneels the figure of Metochites in person, presenting his church to the enthroned Christ. Metochites fell from imperial favour in 1328 and was exiled. But his monks and his friends protected his library until he was allowed to return two years later; and it was here that he died, having become a monk himself, in 1332.[103]

Once again the middle of the fourteenth century can be seen as a turning-point. The coterie of intellectuals whose luminaries included such men as Metochites or Gregoras depended very much on imperial patronage.[104] Andronikos II had readily supplied his patronage for scholars as well as saints. John Cantacuzene was the friend of both. But after his abdication in 1354 things changed. Not all of his successors were interested in scholarship and none could afford to subsidise the arts and sciences. The preoccupations of Church and society changed too. The debate over union with the Roman Church again became a burning issue; to some it seemed the only means of survival. There were still individual men of learning, many of them monks. But most of them were personally and theologically committed to one camp or the other. The ideal of the scholar-monk became harder to sustain when most of the monastic world of Byzantium was engaged in jealous and argumentative preservation of the inherited truths of Orthodox theology. The monk Joseph Bryennios, for example, who died in 1431, was proud to list the books in his library, which included works on mathematics, music and the sciences. But his own literary output was almost entirely confined to tracts supporting Hesychasm and attacking Latin doctrine.[105] The growing

---

103 The concern of Metochites for his library is expressed in his letter to the monks of the Chora (Logos 15); ed. I. Ševčenko, 'Theodore Metochites', *The Kariye Djami*, IV, §§ 23–4, pp. 80–2. Cf. Ševčenko, 'Observations sur les recueils des *Discours* et des *Poèmes* de Th. Métochite et sur la Bibliothèque de Chora à Constantinople', *Scriptorium*, V (1951), pp. 279–88.

104 See esp. Ševčenko, 'Society and intellectual life', pp. 17ff.

105 On Joseph Bryennios, see the following works by N. B. Tomadakes: 'Ο 'Ιωσὴφ Βρυέννιος καὶ ἡ Κρήτη κατὰ τὸ 1400 (Athens, 1947); Μελετήματα

influence and authority of the Orthodox Church as the guardian of the true Byzantine conscience meant that Hellenic learning was relegated to a secondary place. In the latter half of the fourteenth century the balance between sanctity and scholarship, between the inner and the outer wisdom, was decisively tipped in favour of sanctity; and in the world of the intellect, theology, in the form of polemics, took over to the exclusion of almost all other pursuits. It was, after all, along with rhetoric, the favourite pursuit of the Byzantines.

περὶ 'Ιωσὴφ Βρυεννίου, *EEBS*, xxviii (1958), pp. 1–33; *Σύλλαβος Βυζαντινῶν μελετῶν καὶ κειμένων* (Athens, 1961), pp. 489–611; *Ἁγιορειτικοὶ κώδικες τῶν ἔργων 'Ιωσὴφ Βρυεννίου*, *EEBS*, xxxii (1963), pp. 26–39; *'Ιωσὴφ Βρυεννίου δημηγορία περὶ τοῦ τῆς πόλεως ἀνακτίσματος* (1415 μ. Χ.), *EEBS*, xxxvi (1968), pp. 1–15; and R.-J. Loenertz, 'Pour la chronologie des œuvres de Joseph Bryennios', *REB*, vii (1949), pp. 12–32; Beck, *Kirche und theologische Literatur*, pp. 749–50. Bryennios lists the books which he bequeathed to the Great Church in his *Testament*, ed. A. Papadopoulos-Kerameus, *Varia Graeca Sacra* (St Petersburg, 1909), pp. 295–6.

3

Byzantium between east and west:
the two 'nations'

In 1352 Philotheos, then Bishop of Herakleia in Thrace, addressed a letter to his flock. He was writing from Constantinople. News had reached him of a devastating raid on his city, not by the Turks but by a marauding band of Genoese sailors. Many of the inhabitants had been carried off as slaves or driven out as refugees. To the survivors he wrote words of comfort and consolation. He compared their misfortunes with the fate that had befallen the cities of Kyzikos and Bithynia, 'the great Nicaea, Prousa, Nikomedeia and Chalcedon, those ancient adornments of the Church and the Christian Empire'. All these and more had passed not temporarily but permanently, as it seemed, under alien rule, under the rule of the infidel.[1]

The Byzantines were hardened to living between two fires, between the Slavs and the Persians, the Bulgars and the Arabs, the Normans and the Turks. For many years after the restoration of the Empire in 1261 they had been forced to neglect their eastern frontiers in order to protect themselves from their western enemies, notably Charles of Anjou and his papal supporters. The consequence of that neglect was the loss to the Turks of the Christian cities of Asia Minor which the Bishop of Herakleia lamented. The extent of the loss and of the catastrophe for the Church and the Christ-named people can be illustrated by

---

1 Philotheos, *Letter to the citizens of Herakleia*, ed. C. Triantafillis and A. Grapputo, *Anecdota Graeca*, I (Venice, 1874), pp. 35–46. Philotheos was to become Patriarch of Constantinople two years later. Much the same words were subsequently put into the mouth of John Cantacuzene by Nikephoros Gregoras (*Historia*, II, pp. 816–17).

statistics. About the year 1204 there were forty-eight metropolitanates and four hundred and twenty-one bishoprics in Anatolia. By the fifteenth century these numbers had been reduced to seventeen and three respectively.[2] The emperors and patriarchs put a brave face on it by revising their diocesan lists, appointing titular bishops and creating more metropolitanates in eastern Europe.[3] The loss was measurable not only in terms of property and revenues but also, as the patriarchs were well aware, in Christian souls. The rate of apostasy to Islam among the Christians in Asia Minor was a matter for deep concern; and the remaining clergy quickly discovered that the only means of survival was to come to some arrangement with the new conquerors.

What were bishops to do when the only secular administration in their district was Turkish? What were the Christian laity to do when they had no bishop and when they were under pressure to adopt the faith of Islam? The Patriarch Athanasios repeatedly urged absentee bishops to return to their sees in Asia Minor. 'Now, if ever', he writes, 'they should be there to die with their own flocks.'[4] In 1338, and again in 1340, the then Patriarch sent an appeal to the people of Nicaea. The 'most Christian city' of Nicaea had fallen to the Osmanlis only seven years before, in 1331. But even in that short space of time many Christians there had already apostatised, whether voluntarily or under duress. The Patriarch pledged that the Church of God would forgive those

2 S. Vryonis, *The Decline of Medieval Hellenism in Asia Minor and the Process of Islamization from the Eleventh through the Fifteenth Century* (Berkely–Los Angeles–London, 1971), p. 303.

3 The Emperors Andronikos II and Andronikos III both issued revised lists, the effects of which were to establish more metropolitanates than had ever existed before, fifty-six (or fifty-four) in Asia Minor and fifty-six (or fifty-four) in Europe. See H. Gelzer, 'Ungedruckte und ungenügend veröffentlichte Texte der *Notitiae episcopatuum*', *Abhandlungen der Bayerischen Akademie der Wissenschaften*, XXI, Abh. 3 (Munich, 1903), pp. 597–601, 607–9.

4 *Letters of Athanasios*, ed. Talbot, no. 30, p. 64 lines 32–3; cf. nos. 31 and 32.

who returned to it and truly renounced 'the evil of the
Muslims' into which they had lapsed. But to do this they
must, as he implied, either expect a crown of martyrdom
or become crypto-Christians 'practising the Christian way
in the secrecy of their hearts'.[5] There were both neo-
martyrs and crypto-Christians in Asia Minor for many
centuries after the Turkish conquest.[6] But the Christian
Church, and so Christian society, disintegrated very
rapidly after the fourteenth century with the collapse of
its institutions and the disillusionment of its people.

Shock at the Turkish conquest first of the countryside
and then of the walled cities of Bithynia, almost within
sight of Constantinople, was compounded by despair at
the clear inability of the Byzantine government to provide
any substantial protection. The last real attempt at a
military confrontation between Byzantine and Osmanli
armies was in 1329. The Byzantines were humiliated in
two encounters; and if after that date the emperors
themselves elected to cut their losses and come to terms
with the Turks as equals, it is no wonder that the
Christians already under Turkish rule should have felt
abandoned.[7] In 1346 the Emperor John Cantacuzene gave
his own daughter in marriage to Orchan, son of the
founder of the Osmanli people.[8] The Church, so far as is
known, made no protest, although canon law forbade
unions between Christians and infidels. The marriage set
the seal of recognition on the already established fact that

---

5 Letters of the Patriarch John XIV Kalekas to the citizens of Nicaea, in *MM*,
  I, pp. 183–4, 197–8; trans. in Vryonis, *Decline of Medieval Hellenism*, pp.
  341–2.
6 At least two neo-martyrs in Asia Minor are attested as early as the time
  of Andronikos II: one, Niketas the Young, was tortured, hanged and
  burnt by the Turks at Ankara some time between 1282 and 1308. See H.
  Delehaye, 'Le martyre de Saint Nicétas le Jeune', *Mélanges offerts à M.
  Gustave Schlumberger*, I (Paris, 1924), pp. 205–11. St Michael, a Christian
  slave who became a Muslim soldier and reverted to Christianity, was
  executed and burnt at the same period. See *Acta Sanctorum Bollandiana*,
  Nov. IV, pp. 671–6. Cf. Vryonis, *Decline of Medieval Hellenism*, p. 361.
7 Nicol, *Last Centuries*, pp. 174–6.
8 Nicol, *Last Centuries*, pp. 209–10.

Asia Minor was no longer Christian. It was indeed already, in some sense, Turkey. That this was in line with the Emperor's policy of dividing the world between Europeans and Asiatics can have brought no comfort to the Christians whose fate was thus determined.

Some of the more energetic bishops, seeing that no help would reach them from the capital, took what measures they could to protect their own sees. Niphon of Kyzikos and Theoleptos of Philadelphia both personally directed the fortification and defence of their cities against the encroaching enemy.[9] But there were limits to the measures that Byzantine priests could take in such circumstances; and the limits were imposed by their own Church. In 1306, for example, a young monk called Hilarion was summoned from Bithynia to stand trial before the Patriarch in Constantinople for having organised an army of peasants to fight the Turks.[10] Even in such desperate circumstances the Church maintained its ban on the taking up of arms by the clergy. On the other hand there were bishops who retained their rights and their revenues by open collaboration with the Turks. In 1381 Dorotheos, Metropolitan of Peritheorion, was accused of defying his patriarch and his emperor by continuing to exercise tyrannical authority over his see with the support of Turkish troops. He had also made and honoured an agreement with the Turks to hand over to them all Christian refugees who came his way; and he publicly proclaimed that he regarded the Turks as his own emperors, patriarchs and protectors. He was, quite rightly, excommunicated *in absentia*.[11]

The problems faced by bishops who tried to minister to their flocks during the first years of the Turkish

9 Pachymeres, II, p. 390. Gregoras, I, p. 221. Nikephoros Choumnos, *Epitaph for Theoleptos of Philadelphia*, ed. J. F. Boissonade, *Anecdota Graeca*, v (Paris, 1832), pp. 231–4.
10 Pachymeres, II, p. 596. Cf. V. Laurent, 'L'idée de guerre sainte et la tradition byzantine', *Revue historique du sud-est européen*, XXIII (1946), pp. 71–98.
11 *MM*, II, pp. 37–9. Cf. Vryonis, *Decline of Medieval Hellenism*, pp. 332–3.

conquest are well illustrated by the case of Matthew of
Ephesos. Ephesos was in Turkish hands as early as 1304.
Many of its inhabitants were massacred, many more
evicted to make room for Muslim colonists. Some of its
churches, including the cathedral of St John, were turned
into mosques and their treasures were confiscated. Matthew was appointed Bishop of Ephesos in 1329 after a long
period when the see was, of necessity, vacant. But not until
1339 did it become possible for him to travel from
Constantinople to his diocese.[12] Matthew was not a very
saintly character. He had schemed to win the title if not
the duties of a bishop. His letters, recently edited, are heavy
with rhetorical artifice; yet they give a sombre picture of
the plight of Christians in southern Asia Minor.[13] His
journey down to Ephesos was hazardous. There were
Turkish pirates on the seas and brigands in the mountains;
and such forces of law and order as there were along his
route put every obstacle in his way. Matthew soon learnt
the lesson which Orthodox patriarchs and bishops were
to know so well in later years: that a little timely bribery
worked wonders with the Turks. The local bey of Ephesos
accepted the gifts which the bishop had brought with him
but declined to let him use the cathedral and its properties.
Instead Matthew was given a peasant's cottage with a small
allotment. He was amused by the fact that an old Turkish
woman was turned out of the cottage to make room for
him. He found that his flock consisted mainly of prisoners
and slaves, many of them priests and monks: and the local
Turks made it abundantly clear that he was not welcome
in Ephesos by hurling stones on to the roof of his modest
residence every night.[14] Such circumstances were not
propitious for the survival of Christianity.

12 S. I. Kourousis, *Μανουὴλ-Ματθαῖος Γαβαλᾶς εἶτα Ματθαῖος Μητροπολίτης Ἐφέσου (1271/2–1355/60)*, I (Athens, 1972). Cf. Vryonis, *Decline of
   Medieval Hellenism*, pp. 343–8.
13 D. Reinsch, *Die Briefe des Matthaios von Ephesos im Codex Vindobonensis
   Theol. Gr. 174* (Berlin, 1974) [edn, with German trans., of sixty-four letters
   of Matthew of Ephesos].
14 Reinsch, *Briefe*, esp. nos. 54–7, pp. 173–83. Vryonis, *Decline of Medieval
   Hellenism*, pp. 344–7.

Was it then a fact that the Christian Church and society in Asia Minor could *not* survive without the material structure and support of a Christian Empire? That a Church without an emperor was an impossibility? The circumstances described by Matthew of Ephesos are those of a triumphant Muslim minority imposing its will on a humiliated and desperate Christian population. In southern Asia Minor the conquerors were not even Osmanli or Ottoman.[15] These were early days of the Turkish conquest. The conquerors had not yet established a stable and centralised administration based upon the law of the Koran, which provided for religious tolerance. It was the Osmanlis in Bithynia, in north-western Asia Minor, who most successfully imposed the rules of Islamic law and applied them to the government of non-Muslim people – rules which were later to be applied in the Ottoman provinces in Europe.[16] In Asia Minor the Christian Church declined. In Europe it did not. There is room for research into the reasons for this.[17]

What did the Byzantines of the fourteenth century think of the new 'nation' of infidels that had burst upon

15 The bey of Ephesos whom Matthew encountered was Khidir Beg, brother of Umur, emir of Aydin (d. 1348), one of the several Turkoman principalities in western and south-western Asia Minor at this time. P. Lemerle, *L'Emirat d'Aydin, Byzance et l'Occident. Recherches sur 'La geste d'Umur Pacha'* (Paris, 1957); Nicol, *Last Centuries*, pp. 150–6 and refs.

16 H. A. Gibbons, *The Foundation of the Ottoman Empire. A History of the Osmanlis up to the death of Bayezid I, 1300–1403* (Oxford, 1916); P. Wittek, *The Rise of the Ottoman Empire* (London, 1938); H. Inalcik, 'Ottoman methods of conquest', *Studia Islamica*, II (Paris, 1954), pp. 103–29; S. Vryonis, 'Nomadization and Islamization in Asia Minor', *DOP*, XXIX (1975), pp. 41–71; P. Charanis, 'Cultural diversity and the breakdown of Byzantine power in Asia Minor', *ibid.* pp. 1–20.

17 See, e.g., S. Vryonis, 'The condition and cultural significance of the Ottoman Conquest in the Balkans', *Rapport: IIe Congrès International des Etudes du Sud-Est Européen* (Athens, 1970), pp. 3–10 (reprinted in Vryonis, *Byzantium: Its Internal History and Relations with the Muslim World. Collected Studies* [Variorum: London, 1971], no. XI); Vyronis, 'Religious changes and patterns in the Balkans, fourteenth to sixteenth centuries', *Aspects of the Balkans* (The Hague, 1972), pp. 151–76; Vyronis, 'Religious change and continuity in the Balkans and Anatolia from the fourteenth through the sixteenth centuries', in Vyronis (ed.), *Islam and Cultural Change in the Middle Ages* (Wiesbaden, 1975), pp. 127–40.

them? Their ancestors had had ample time to reflect upon Islam, ever since the first Arab onslaughts on the Empire in the seventh century. To begin with men like John of Damascus had supposed that here was another heresy or deviation from the Christian norm. There was much of Judaism and indeed of a form of Christianity in Islam. It happened to be a monophysite and iconoclast form and therefore in error; but where error could be identified it could also be discussed.[18] Slavs and other lesser breeds of pagans whose religion had no recognisable creed were susceptible to conversion through a mixture of evangelisation and diplomacy. But the Arabs, and the Turks, came with a religion of revealed truths and credos which had many of the convictions of Christianity and which seemed to bring them material victory almost wherever they went. It was very hard for Christians to convert them; but it was possible to engage them in debate on specific points.

In March 1354 Gregory Palamas, then Metropolitan of Thessalonica, was taken prisoner by the Turks. His ship had been blown into the harbour of Gallipoli on its way to Constantinople, and he was as surprised as anyone to find that Gallipoli, recently ruined by earthquake, was full of Turkish settlers. Palamas and his companions were escorted under guard over to Bithynia, to Prousa (the first Osmanli capital), and eventually to Nicaea. He spent over a year in Turkish Asia Minor before being ransomed and allowed to return to Constantinople. In the course of his enforced travels Palamas wrote letters describing his adventures and some accounts of theological debates with his adversaries.[19] Palamas was no St Francis, striding out

18 See A.-Th. Khoury, *Les Théologiens byzantins et l'Islam. Textes et auteurs (VIIIe–XIIIe s.)* (Louvain-Paris, 1969); Khoury, *Der theologische Streit der Byzantiner mit der Islam* (Paderborn, 1969); A. Ducellier, 'Mentalité historique et réalité politique: L'Islam et les Musulmans vus par les byzantins du XIIIème siècle', *Byzantinische Forschungen*, IV (1972), pp. 31–63; Ducellier, 'L'Islam et les Musulmans vues de Byzance au XIVe siècle', *Actes du XIVe Congrès International des Etudes Byzantines*, II (Bucharest, 1975), pp. 79–85.

19 Gregory Palamas: *Letters to the Thessalonians*, ed. K. Dyobouniotes, *NH*, XVI (1922), pp. 3–21; *Letter to David Dishypatos*, ed. M. Treu, *DIEE*,

across the desert to convert the heathen by holy example. His mission was thrust upon him. But he was a more saintly Christian than Matthew of Ephesos; and he had the comparatively good fortune to find himself in Bithynia, where under the enlightened rule of Orchan, Islamic law and tolerance prevailed in a way that they did not in other parts of Anatolia. Palamas clearly regarded the Osmanli conquest as permanent. But he reported that Christians, though demoralised, were still allowed to practise their religion; and, being a saint, he saw that the circumstances presented a challenge and a new possibility for true Christianity to survive and prevail. The Turks were, of course, barbarians and unbelievers, but their tolerance of Christians was in line with that usually displayed by Muslims elsewhere. They were not partial to proselytisers but they respected holy men, as St Sabas of Vatopedi had found during his travels in Syria and Palestine. Palamas persuaded himself that the amalgamation of Turks and Greeks in Asia Minor might well in the end lead to the christianisation if not hellenisation of the former by the latter.

The theological discussions in which he became involved were spontaneous affairs. One was conducted with a group of Jews (the Chiones) who had found the Osmanlis to be more tolerant masters than the Christians.[20] But inevitably, as time went on, Byzantine writers began to compose set pieces to explain the differences between

III (1889), pp. 227–34; *Dialogue with the 'Chiones'*, ed. I. A. Sakelliou, *Sotir*, xv (1892), pp. 240–6. The capture and alleged ill treatment of Palamas are recorded with some satisfaction by his enemy Nikephoros Gregoras, *Historia*, III, pp. 226–35. See G. Georgiades-Arnakis, 'Gregory Palamas among the Turks and documents of his captivity as historical sources', *Speculum*, XXVI (1951), pp. 104–18; Meyendorff, *Introduction*, pp. 157–62; Meyendorff, 'Grecs, Turcs et Juifs en Asie Mineure au XIVe siècle', *Byzantinische Forschungen*, I (1966), pp. 211–17 (reprinted in Meyendorff, *Byzantine Hesychasm*, no. IX); Vryonis, *Decline of Medieval Hellenism*, pp. 426–7.

20 On the 'Chiones', see P. Wittek, Χίονες, B, XXI (1951), pp. 421–3; Meyendorff, *Introduction*, pp. 160–2; Meyendorff, 'Grecs, Turcs et Juifs', pp. 211–17.

Islam and Christianity. Among them were two emperors
– one, John Cantacuzene, who wrote eight treatises *Against
the Mohammedans*, the other his grandson Manuel II, who
recorded a lengthy *Dialogue* with a Persian (that is, a
Turk).[21] Cantacuzene, who gave his daughter as wife to
the son of Osman and who professed a knowledge of the
Turkish language, yet regularly refers to his quite civilised
son-in-law as 'the barbarian'.[22] It was of course a deliberate
archaism to call the Turks the 'Persians'. Byzantine style
required that the Empire's neighbours and enemies should
be translated into Herodotean terms. The Mongols were
the 'Scythians', the Bulgarians the 'Mysians' the French
the 'Celts', and so on. Likewise the struggle between the
Byzantines and the Turks could be glorified as another
chapter in the war between Greeks and Persians, between
civilisation and barbarism. The Turks were considered to
be 'barbarians' in the technical sense of not belonging to
the theocratic society of Byzantium. They were among
the 'nations' who lived beyond the pale. The Greek word
is ἔθνη. It is the term applied in the New Testament to the
Gentiles, to those living outside the flock of God's chosen
people. The modern concept of a nation would have been
inconceivable in Byzantium. But the idea of the 'nations'
was as old as Constantinople.[23]

The people of western Europe, collectively known as
the 'Latins', were also thought to be among the 'nations'.
They were in a different category from the Turks because
they were in a sense Christians, however misguided, and
because they were, at first, better known. Latins had

21 John Kantakouzenos: *Contra Sectam Mahometicam Apologiae IV*, and
   Contra Mahometem Orationes Quatuor, in *MPG*, CLIV, cols. 371–584,
   583–692. Manuel II: E. Trapp, *Manuel II Palaiologos, Dialoge mit einem
   "Perser"* (Wiener byzantinische Studien, II: Vienna, 1966). See also
   Vryonis, *Decline of Medieval Hellenism*, pp. 421–36. Joseph Bryennios
   concocted a similar debate: A. Argyriou, Ἰωσὴφ τοῦ Βρυεννίου μετά τινος
   Ἰσμαηλίτου Διάλεξις, *EEBS*, XXXV (1966/7), pp. 158–95.
22 Kantakouzenos, II, p. 588 lines 17–18. For his knowledge of Turkish, see
   ibid. III, p. 66 lines 5–8.
23 Cf. H. Hunger, 'On the imitation (*mimesis*) of Antiquity in Byzantine
   literature', pp. 17–38 (reprinted in Hunger, *Byzantinische Grundlagenforschung*, no. XV).

infiltrated into the Empire as merchants long before the Fourth Crusade. And after that disaster they had invaded and colonised large stretches of the provinces, notably Greece and the Greek islands, where they lorded it over the Greek-speaking population as a feudal ascendancy. The behaviour of the French in the Peloponnese or of the Venetians in Crete was not calculated to produce a symbiosis. The Latins were not much better than the Turks. In many ways they were worse because, being of the Christian faith, they ought to have known better. Philotheos of Herakleia, describing the attack on his city by the Genoese, blames the Latins for having forgotten that they too were once members of the theocratic society before, in their folly, they detached themselves as a 'nation' from the universal Church and Empire.[24] There was little to choose between the two 'nations'. A fugitive from Byzantine justice could consider taking himself off, 'either to the Latins or to the Turks'. Voluntary exile to one or other of the 'nations' was an acceptable form of penance and punishment.[25] Politically the alternatives were much the same. After the loss of Asia Minor the Byzantine Empire could survive only by reaching a *modus vivendi* with the Turks or by courting the favour of the Latins.

The year 1354 was a memorable one. In March the Turks settled in Gallipoli, in Europe. Palamas was taken prisoner there. In December the Emperor John Cantacuzene abdicated and became a monk. It was an admission of defeat – defeat for his policy of co-existence with the Turks. He was succeeded by his young son-in-law John V Palaiologos.[26] Almost at the same moment, in

---

24 Philotheos, *Historical Discourse on the Siege and Capture of Herakleia by the Latins*, ed. C. Triantafillis and A. Grapputo, *Anecdota Graeca*, I (see n. 1), pp. 1–33, esp. p. 11 lines 6–15.

25 *MM*, II, p. 55 (AD 1383):...ἔτι ἐλαλήθη κατ' αὐτοῦ, ὅτι μετὰ τὴν προτέραν ἀπόφασιν τὴν συνοδικὴν ἔλεγεν αὐτός, ὅτι ἐὰν μὴ συγχωρηθῇ, ἢ εἰς τοὺς Φράγγους ἢ εἰς τοὺς Τούρκους μέλλει ἀπελθεῖν.

26 See Nicol, *Last Centuries*, pp. 249–53 and refs. The exact date of John VI's formal abdication should now be amended to 9 December 1354. A. Failler, 'Nouvelle note sur la chronologie du règne de Jean VI Cantacuzène', *REB*, XXXIV (1976), pp. 119–24.

December 1354, Demetrios Kydones, prime minister and
friend of both emperors, completed his translation into
Greek of the *Summa contra Gentiles* of Thomas Aquinas.[27]
There is a thread that connects these disparate events. One
of the first acts of the new Emperor John V was to reverse
his predecessor's policy with regard to the 'two nations'.
In December 1355 he wrote a personal letter to the Pope
appealing for help against the Turks. In return he promised
to do all in his power to heal the schism, to promote the
union of the Churches and eventually to make his own
submission to the Holy See. He had to admit that he could
not force the idea of union on his people for fear that they
would rise in revolt against him.[28] The idea was indeed
far from popular. It ran counter to almost everything that
Church and society in Byzantium held most dear. What
then prompted the new Emperor to propose it?

One might more aptly ask who prompted him? It has
often been noted that his mother, Anne of Savoy, had been
a westerner and a Catholic. It has even been claimed that
she entered a Franciscan convent; but in truth she was
completely Byzantinised and died as an Orthodox nun.[29]
A far greater influence upon her son was exercised by a
small circle of Byzantine intellectuals who were then
coming round to the opinion that there might be some
good in the Latins after all. Prominent among them was

27 R.-J. Loenertz, 'Démétrius Cydonès, I. De la naissance à l'année 1373',
    OCP, XXXVI (1970), pp. 47–72, esp. p. 55.
28 The Greek and Latin texts of John V's appeal to Pope Innocent VI are
    in A. Theiner and F. Miklosich, *Monumenta spectantia ad unionem ecclesiarum
    Graecae et Romanae* (Vienna, 1872), no. VIII, pp. 29–33, 33–7. Cf. *DR*,
    V, no. 3052. O. Halecki, *Un empereur de Byzance à Rome. Vingt ans de travail
    pour l'union des églises et pour la défense de l'empire d'Orient, 1355–1375*
    (Warsaw, 1930: reprinted London, 1972), pp. 31ff.; Nicol, *Last Centuries*,
    pp. 268ff.
29 The myth of the Empress Anne's death as a tertiary of the Order of St
    Francis is enshrined in Halecki, *Un empereur*, p. 43. The fact of her death
    as an Orthodox nun with the name of Anastasia in Thessalonica about
    1365 is confirmed by the Synodikon of Orthodoxy and by a letter of
    Demetrios Kydones. J. Gouillard, 'Le Synodikon de l'Orthodoxie, édition
    et commentaire', *Travaux et Mémoires*, II (1967), pp. 100–3 lines 869–73;
    R.-J. Loenertz, *Démétrius Cydonès, Correspondance*, I (Studi e Testi, 186:
    Vatican City, 1956), p. 128, no. 94 line 17f.

Demetrios Kydones, the leading courtier and minister of state in Constantinople for most of the second half of the fourteenth century.[30] He and his friends were excited to discover that the Latins were not all boors and barbarians. Kydones took Latin lessons for professional reasons. The Dominican who taught him made him translate passages from Thomas Aquinas for his homework. He was swept off his feet by the beautiful certainties of Latin theology; and in due course he was converted to the Roman faith. Knowledge of Latin was, as has been noted, a very rare accomplishment in Byzantium. John V, in his appeal to the Pope, had proposed that Latin schools be founded in Constantinople to remedy this defect.[31] They never were. Few Byzantines visited the west. They therefore judged Latin culture by the example of the Italian merchants and sailors who frequented the docks and warehouses of the Golden Horn, or by the behaviour of the feudal lords in the Peloponnese and the Greek islands. These were not the best criteria for a proper assessment of western civilisation.

There were, however, a few educated men who tried to look a little further and to bridge the cultural gap by making translations of Latin literature into Greek. Indeed, the art of translation constituted a new literary genre in the Palaiologan age.[32] Maximos Planoudes was one of the

---

30 On Demetrios Kydones, see: R.-J. Loenertz, 'Démétrius Cydonès, I', pp. 47–72; 'II. De 1373 à 1375', *OCP*, XXXVII (1971), pp. 5–39; Loenertz, *Démétrius Cydonès, Correspondance*, 2 vols. (Studi e Testi, 186, 208: Vatican City, 1956, 1960); G. Mercati, *Notizie di Procoro e Demetrio Cidone, Manuele Caleca e Teodoro Meliteniota ed altri appunti per la storia della teologia e della letteratura bizantina del secolo XIV* (Studi e Testi, 56: Vatican City, 1931); Beck, *Kirche und theologische Literatur*, pp. 733–9; Beck, *Theodoros Metochites*, pp. 117–21; Tatakis, *Philosophie byzantine*, pp. 266–70; K. M. Setton, 'The Byzantine background to the Italian Renaissance', *Proceedings of the American Philosophical Society*, C, 1 (1956), pp. 52–8 (reprinted in Setton, *Europe and the Levant in the Middle Ages and the Renaissance. Collected Studies* [Variorum: London, 1974], no. I); Runciman, *Last Byzantine Renaissance*, pp. 74–5, 99–100; *Letters of Manuel II*, ed. Dennis, pp. xxxviii–xl and *passim*.
31 Halecki, *Un empereur*, p. 33.
32 H.-G. Beck, 'Besonderheiten der Literatur in der Palaiologenzeit', in *Art et Société à Byzance sous les Paléologues* (Venice, 1971), pp. 41–52, esp. p. 43; Lumpe, 'Abendland und Byzanz, III', cols. 304–5; Podskalsky, *Theologie und Philosophie in Byzanz*, pp. 173–80.

first and the most prolific in this field, though his motives
were perhaps more academic than emotional. Certainly
his interests were more in classical than in contemporary
Latin, and he showed no inclination to abandon his
Orthodoxy.[33] The teachers of Latin, for those few Greeks
who wished to learn it, were the Dominicans. Both
Dominicans and Franciscans had come to Constantinople
on the crest of the wave of the Fourth Crusade. The
Franciscans in particular worked hard to prepare the
ground for the Union of Lyons in 1274. But both orders
were expelled from the city after the restoration of
Orthodoxy in 1282.[34] They moved their houses across the
Golden Horn to the Genoese colony of Pera (or Galata).
The founder of the Dominican house in Pera in 1299 was
charged with the mission of 'preaching the word of the
Lord and disputing the errors of the Greeks'. He was a
contemporary of Planoudes and is said to have made the
first translation of Thomas Aquinas into Greek.[35] The

33 W. O. Schmitt, 'Lateinische Literatur in Byzanz. Die Übersetzung des
Maximos Planudes und die moderne Forschung', *JÖBG*, XVII (1968), pp.
127–47.

34 R.-J. Loenertz, 'Les établissements Dominicains de Péra-Constantinople.
Origines et fondations', *EO*, XXXIV (1935), pp. 332–49 (reprinted in
Loenertz, *Byzantina et Franco-Graeca* [Rome, 1970], pp. 209–26); Loenertz,
La Société des Frères Pérégrinants. Etudes sur l'Orient Dominicain, I (Institutum
historicum FF. Praedicatorum Romae: Dissertationes historicae, fasc. 7
[Rome, 1937]); Loenertz, 'Les missions dominicains en Orient au XIVe
siècle', *Archivum Fratrum Praedicatorum*, II (1932), pp. 2–83. The expulsion
of the 'Friars' ($\phi\rho\acute{\epsilon}\rho\iota o\iota$) from Constantinople in 1305 is related at some
length by Pachymeres, II, pp. 536–9, and apparently alluded to by the
Patriarch Athanasios, *Letters*, ed. Talbot, no. 23, p. 52 and commentary
p. 330. Cf. Loenertz, 'Les établissements', p. 335 (212). See also R. L.
Wolff, 'The Latin Empire of Constantinople and the Franciscans',
Traditio, II (1944), pp. 213–37 (reprinted in Wolff, *Studies in the Latin
Empire of Constantinople. Collected Studies* [Variorum: London, 1976], no.
VII). Elizabeth A. R. Brown, 'The Cistercians in the Latin Empire of
Constantinople and Greece 1204–1276', *Traditio*, XIV (1958), pp. 63–120;
Brenda M. Bolton, 'A mission to the Orthodox? The Cistercians in
Romania', *Studies in Church History*, XIII (*The Orthodox Churches and the
West*), ed. D. Baker (Oxford, 1976), pp. 169–81; D. J. Geanakoplos,
'Bonaventura, the two Mendicant Orders, and the Greeks at the Council
of Lyons (1274)' in *ibid*. pp. 183–211.

35 Loenertz, 'Les missions dominicaines', Document I, p. 66. His name was
Guillaume Bernard de Gaillac. Loenertz, 'Les établissements', p. 336 (213);
Loenertz, *La Société*, pp. 78–9.

Dominicans prided themselves on their proficiency in Greek, and they lived in closer contact with the Byzantines than any other section of the Latin community. The emperors employed them as ambassadors to the west and counted some of them among their personal acquaintances.[36] It was from one of them that Demetrios Kydones learnt his Latin. He was a close friend of Philip Incontri, who spent twenty-five years in the Dominican house at Pera and who in 1356 was made Inquisitor in the Orient.[37] Most of the works which Kydones selected for translation were such as one would expect to find in a Dominican library – among them Thomas Aquinas and Ricoldo da Monte Croce, whose *Improbatio Alcorani* was also exploited by John Cantacuzene in his own treatises *Against the Mohammedans.* Kydones's brother Prochoros, who co-operated in the translation of Aquinas, also translated parts of the *Commentary on the Sentences of Peter Lombard* by Herveus Natalis, who was General of the Dominicans from 1318 to 1323.[38]

36 B. Altaner, 'Die Kentniss des Griechischen in den Missionsordnen während des 13. und 14. Jahrhunderts', *Zeitschrift für Kirchengeschichte*, LIII (1934), pp. 436–93. The following were among those sent as imperial ambassadors to the popes: Frater Andreas, sent in 1326 (cf. Laiou, *Constantinople and the Latins*, p. 324); Francesco da Camarino and Richard of England, in 1333 (*DR*, IV, no. 2792). John of Pera, whom John Cantacuzene sent to congratulate Pope Innocent VI on his election in 1353, is described by the Emperor as 'one of my friends in Galata, of the Order of Preachers' (Kantakouzenos, III, p. 62); Nicol, *Byzantine Family of Kantakouzenos*, p. 67 n. 85. See R.-J. Loenertz, 'Ioannes de Fontibus Ord. Praedicatorum Epistula ad Abbatem et Conventum monasterii nescio cuius Constantinopolitani', *Archivum Fratrum Praedicatorum*, XXX (1960), pp. 163–95, esp. pp. 164–9.
37 R.-J. Loenertz, 'Fr Philippe de Bindo Incontri, O. P. du couvent de Péra, Inquisiteur en Orient', *Archivum Fratrum Praedicatorum*, XVIII (1948), pp. 265–80; T. Kaepelli, 'Deux nouveaux ouvrages de Fr Philippe Incontri de Péra, O. P.', *Archivum Fratrum Praedicatorum*, XXIII (1953), pp. 163–83.
38 On Ricoldo da Monte Croce, see E. Trapp, *Manuel II. Palaiologos, Dialoge mit einem "Perser"*, pp. 35*–44*; A. Dondaine, 'Ricoldiana. Notes sur les œuvres de Ricoldo da Montecroce', *Archivum Fratrum Praedicatorum*, XXXVII (1967), pp. 119–79; J.-M. Mérigoux, Un précurseur du dialogue islamo-chrétien: Frère Ricoldo (1243–1320)', *Revue Thomiste*, LXXIII (1973), pp. 609–21. On translations made by Prochoros Kydones, see Mercati, *Notizie di Procoro e Demetrio Cidone*, pp. 28–40. Cf. Lumpe, 'Abendland und Byzanz, III', cols. 319–23.

The Dominicans, for all their obsession with the 'errors of the Greeks', did much to break down the barriers between Byzantines and Latins, at least at a personal level. Philip Incontri wrote a pamphlet explaining how far the Greeks had lapsed from obedience to the Roman Church, in which he congratulated himself on his efforts as a mediator. 'At first', he says, 'when I used to talk to them, their bishops, monks, priests and people fled from us as though we were excommunicates or heretics, and there was a great fuss even to get permission to look inside their churches and monasteries. If one of our men happened to be thirsty we could hardly find anyone to give him some water; and when he had drunk they would break or throw away the cup. Rarely could we find anyone who would talk to us about anything. However, when I began to deal with them more familiarly, visiting their monasteries, meeting them informally, debating with them and answering their points, I have so tamed them that within ten years they no longer avoid us; indeed they eat and drink together with us and we with them.'[39] The Dominicans' most notable convert was Demetrios Kydones. His was an intellectual conversion, a change of mind rather than of heart. He remained a Hellene by culture and a Byzantine by instinct. To explain his action he wrote three *Apologies* – one addressed to his Orthodox friends, the second a defence of his own sincerity, and the third his spiritual testament. They are among the most interesting documents of all late Byzantine literature.[40]

As a statesman and man of affairs (Kydones served three emperors as prime minister) he was understandably

39 Philip Incontri, *De oboedientia Ecclesiae Romanae debita*, in Kaepelli, 'Deux nouveaux ouvrages', p. 179.
40 Demetrios Kydones, *Apologie della propria fede*, 1: *Ai Greci Ortodossi*; 2: *Difesa della propria sincerità*; 3: *Il Testamento religioso*, ed. Mercati, in *Notizie di Procoro e Demetrio Cidone*, pp. 359–403, 403–25, 425–35. German trans., 'Die "Apologia pro vita sua" des Demetrios Kydones', by H.-G. Beck, in *Ostkirchliche Studien*, I (1952), pp. 208–25, 264–82. Two other apologetic works of Kydones, one on the authority of the Latin Fathers, the other on St Thomas Aquinas, remain unpublished. See *Letters of Manuel II*, ed. Dennis, p. xxxviii and n. 53.

depressed by the inexorable advance of the Turks. He encouraged his emperor to look for help from the popes and princes of the west. When in 1369 the Emperor John V fulfilled his promise and went to Rome to make his personal submission to the Pope, Kydones went with him; he had made the diplomatic arrangements for the visit. As a scholar Kydones was excited by discovering the philosophical and literary quality of Latin theology. He was annoyed by the complacency of his own people. He condemned them for their wilful ignorance of the writings of such as Jerome, Ambrose and Augustine. 'How absurd it is', he writes, 'that people calling themselves Christians should put their trust only in what is written in Greek and refuse to listen to anything in Latin, as if the truth were a monopoly of one language.'[41] Kydones uses the word *ethnos* in a different sense. For him the two 'nations' are the Greeks and the Latins; and the gap between them is mainly a linguistic and cultural gap, widened by ignorance and prejudice.[42] He could no longer tolerate the superiority complex of the Byzantines and their division of the world into 'Hellenes and barbarians', Byzantines and Gentiles. 'Previously', he says, 'there was no one to persuade our people that there is any intelligence in the Latins, or that they are able to raise their minds to consideration of anything more exalted than shipping, trade and war.'[43]

Given his political and cultural interest in the west it was easier for Kydones to swallow the pills that stuck in the throats of most Byzantines. The universal primacy of

---

41 Kydones, *Apologie*, ed. Mercati, p. 382 lines 35–40; p. 429 lines 9–12: ληρεῖν γὰρ ᾤμην καὶ τετυφῶσθαι εἴ τις χριστιανὸς φάσκων εἶναι τοὺς μὲν τὴν Ἑλλάδα προϊεμένους ἀξιοπίστους ἡγοῖτο, τῶν δ' Ἰταλιστὶ διαλεγομένων οὐδ' ἀκούειν ἀνέχοιτο, ὥσπερ μιᾷ μόνον φωνῇ τοῦ ἀληθεύειν ἀποκεκληρωμένου, ταῖς δ' ἄλλαις ἐπιτακτέον εἶναι σιγᾶν. Cf. p. 382 lines 13ff.

42 For Kydones's use of the term 'nations', see *Apologie*, ed. Mercati, p. 386 lines 51–2: 'the division between the nations has lasted almost five hundred years' (τοσαῦτα γὰρ ἡ τῶν ἐθνῶν διάστασις ἔχει). Cf. *Ibid.* pp. 367 line 43, 428 lines 85, 105.

43 *Apologie*, ed. Mercati, p. 365 lines 77–86.

the See of Rome, for example, could be defended as a
safeguard against anarchy in the Church.[44] The Orthodox
objection to the *Filioque* in the Creed could be dismissed
as contentious hair-splitting, calculated to obscure the
basic harmony and to perpetuate dissension between the
two 'nations' of Christians.[45] All this would have been
music to the ears of the Latins. But Kydones addressed his
Apologies to the Greeks; and to the Greeks they were
mostly foolishness. There is no doubt that the discovery
of the works of Aquinas caused some stir among Byzantine
theologians.[46] Prochoros Kydones, like his brother, admired them greatly. But he seems never to have taken the
plunge and joined the Church that produced such geniuses.
Prochoros was and probably remained an Orthodox
monk, though he was an active anti-Palamite and freely
used Thomistic arguments to refute the hesychasts.[47] The
techniques of scholasticism were new to the Byzantines
and some found them intriguing. The teacher of Kydones,
Neilos Kabasilas, congratulated his pupil on his translations
and then sent him an essay composed in Thomistic form
refuting the Latin doctrine on the Procession of the Holy
Spirit.[48]

44 *Apologie*, ed. Mercati, pp. 377–9, 430–1.
45 *Apologie*, ed. Mercati, p. 429 lines 28–30: 'on the Procession of the Holy
   Spirit I have found much agreement between the two (nations), if only
   people did not want to squabble and to reduce the majesty of the truth
   to verbal hair-splitting' (πολλὴν τῆς τοῦ ἁγίου Πνεύματος ἐκπορεύσεως
   εὕρισκον ἀμφοῖν συμφωνίαν, εἴ τις ἐρίζειν οὐκ ἐβούλετο μηδὲ τῇ τῶν λέξεων
   μικρολογίᾳ τὸ τῆς ἀληθείας μέγεθος ἐπιτρέπειν).
46 M. Rackl, 'Die griechische Übersetzung der Summa theologiae des hl.
   Thomas von Aquin', *BZ*, xxiv (1923/24), pp. 48–60; S. G. Papadopoulos,
   Ἑλληνικαὶ μεταφράσεις θωμιστικῶν ἔργων. Φιλοθωμισταὶ καὶ ἀντιθωμισταὶ ἐν Βυζαντίῳ (Athens, 1967); Papadopoulos, 'St Thomas in Byzanz.
   Thomas-Rezeption und Thomas-Kritik in Byzanz zwischen 1345 und
   1453', *Theologie und Philosophie*, xlix (1974), pp. 274–304; A. D.
   Karpozilos, 'Thomas Aquinas and the Byzantine East (De essentia et
   operatione)', *Ekklesiastikos Pharos*, lii (1970), pp. 129–47; Meyendorff,
   Byzantine Theology, pp. 105–7.
47 On Prochoros Kydones, see Beck, *Kirche und theologische Literatur*, pp.
   737–9; Mercati, *Notizie*, *passim*. His unrepentant anti-Palamism led to
   his being excommunicated shortly before his death in 1368 or 1369.
48 On Neilos Kabasilas, who succeeded Gregory Palamas as Metropolitan of
   Thessalonica and died in 1368, see Beck, *Kirche und theologische Literatur*,

To our minds Demetrios Kydones is perhaps a more sympathetic figure than many of his Orthodox contemporaries. There were others like him who, for various reasons, followed his lead. Some were intellectual refugees from the doctrine of Hesychasm. John Kyparissiotes, a pupil of Gregoras, fled first to Cyprus and then to Italy, where in 1376 he was granted a pension by Pope Gregory XI and immersed himself in scholastic theology. His anti-Palamite effusions had the distinction of being refuted by the ex-Emperor John Cantacuzene in person. His systematic exposition of Orthodox theology, employing the scholastic method, earned him the title of *Sapiens* among his Italian admirers.[49] Another anti-Palamite, Manuel Kalekas, a pupil of Demetrios Kydones, was carried away by his master's translation of St Thomas. He too learnt Latin from the Dominicans at Pera and made his own contributions to the translation industry with renderings into Greek of Boethius and St Anselm of Canterbury. He travelled in Italy and in the Italian-occupied islands of Crete and Lesbos, where he died in 1410 as a member of the Dominican Order.[50] Still more remarkable were the careers of the brothers Maximos and Andrew Chrysoberges, both of whom became Dominicans under the influence of Kydones and his Thomistic circle. Andrew taught philosophy and theology at Padua, served as an interpreter at the Council of Constance in 1414, and was to play an active part in the Council of Florence twenty-five years later with the title of Latin Archbishop of Nicosia. The greatest of such converts was one of the heroes of that Council, Cardinal Bessarion.[51]

pp. 727–8. Kydones relates that his teacher was 'madly in love with the works of Thomas': *Apologie*, ed. Mercati, p. 391 line 28. See also G. Schirò, 'Il paradosso di Nilo Cabasila', *SBN*, IX (1957), pp. 362–88.

49 On John Kyparissiotes, see Beck, *Kirche und theologische Literatur*, pp. 739–40; D. J. Geanakoplos, *Interaction of the "Sibling" Byzantine and Western Cultures in the Middle Ages and Italian Renaissance (330–1600)* (New Haven–London, 1976), pp. 101–4, 140–5.

50 On Manuel Kalekas, see Beck, *Kirche und theologische Literatur*, pp. 740–1; R.-J. Loenertz, *Correspondance de Manuel Calécas* (Studi e Testi, 152: Vatican City, 1950).

51 On the brothers Chrysoberges, see Beck, *Kirche und theologische Literatur*,

Kydones thus made his influence felt throughout the last two generations of Byzantine scholars and theologians. But it was never more than a limited influence. Far more typical of the mood of the society in which he lived are the polemics of comparatively obscure anti-Latinists and anti-Thomists which were never translated. Kydones had the zeal and the blindness of a convert. The anti-Latin polemicists had the confidence and the arrogance of those who hold fast to their own traditions. A basic element in the Byzantine Orthodox tradition was the view that beyond a certain point theology was above reason. A recently published anti-Thomistic tract of the later fourteenth century by one Kallistos Angelikoudes well illustrates the fundamental Byzantine mistrust of an intellectual approach to theology.[52] Theology for Angelikoudes is 'the expression in words of the event and consequences of the union of man with God through divine grace'.[53] He is scandalised by St Thomas's constant emphasis on the role of the intellect in the knowledge of God. To him it is a matter of vision, of personal experience, vouchsafed through the uncreated energies of God, through the divine light. He utterly rejects the Aristotelian, rationalistic conception of God and man.[54] This rejection of the rationalisation of the faith was, and still is, a powerful factor in misunderstanding between the Greek and Latin Churches. Orthodox theology is often called 'apophatic', a theology of 'unknowing'.[55] The Greek privative *alpha* (English 'un-') qualifies much of its

pp. 742–3; Setton, 'Byzantine background', p. 60. R.-J. Loenertz, 'La Société de Frères Pérégrinants de 1374 à 1475. Etudes sur l'Orient Dominicain, II', *Archivum Fratrum Pradedicatorum*, XLV (1975), pp. 122–8. For Bessarion, see below, Ch. 4, pp. 111f.

52 S. G. Papadopoulos, Συνάντησις ὀρθοδόξου καὶ σχολαστικῆς θεολογίας (ἐν τῷ προσώπῳ Καλλίστου Ἀγγελικούδη καὶ Θωμᾶ Ἀκινάτου (Ἀνάλεκτα Βλατάδων, 4: Thessalonike, 1970).

53 Papadopoulos, Συνάντησις..., p. 137.

54 Papadopoulos, Συνάντησις..., pp. 133–9, 174f.

55 One of the works of Prochoros Kydones is entitled: Περὶ καταφατικοῦ καὶ ἀποφατικοῦ τρόπου ἐπὶ τῆς θεολογίας. Cf. Beck, *Kirche und theologische Literatur*, p. 738.

terminology. God is said to be unknowable, ineffable, incomprehensible, indefinable, uncircumscribable. The truths of the inner wisdom cannot be reached by syllogising. The production of proofs by syllogism, says Gregoras, is a method of argument zealously cultivated by the Italians and others of mediocre intelligence, but worse than useless in the search for the divine truths.[56] The Byzantines might have approved of W. H. Auden's observation,[57]

> That Eve and Adam till the Fall
> Were totally illogical,
> But, as they tasted of the fruit,
> The syllogistic sin took root.

The doctrine of Hesychasm was in the main stream of such apophatic theology. Not all Byzantines, as we have seen, accepted its implications. Kydones was, as one would expect, an anti-hesychast and anti-Palamite. He was embarrassed by the fact that the formal acceptance of hesychast doctrine in 1351 had driven yet another wedge between the Greek and Latin Churches. His friend Paul of Smyrna, the papal legate to Constantinople, as early as 1355 reported to the Pope that the Byzantines appeared to have introduced another new heresy into the Church.[58] Hesychasm, or what was scathingly called 'Palamism', was soon denounced in the west as still further proof of the stubborn and melancholy aberrations of the Greeks.

Thus, although some good came of individual contacts between the Dominicans and the erroneous Greeks, at a more general level there was little improvement in understanding. The conversion of the Emperor John V,

56 Gregoras, I, pp. 507–9, 512–20.
57 W. H. Auden, *New Year Letter* (London, 1941), lines 498–501.
58 The papal legate Paul, like Barlaam of Calabria an Italo-Greek, was present at a theological debate between Palamas and Gregoras in the palace in 1355 (Gregoras, III, pp. 262–5). See Meyendorff, *Introduction*, pp. 164–6. His letter to the Pope, Urban V, is in *MPG*, CLIV, cols. 835–8. There may be some question of its authenticity; see Meyendorff, *Introduction*, p. 166 n. 54.

like that of Kydones and others, was a purely personal matter. The Emperor's submission took place at an impressive ceremony in St Peter's in 1369, and he was allowed to take back with him to Constantinople a portable altar, on condition that it would never be used by other than a Latin priest.[59] This was a very personal privilege. Neither the Emperor nor the Pope claimed that any union of the Churches had been achieved. The best that the Pope could say was that the Emperor, like his predecessor Constantine the Great, had set an example for others to follow. A few people did. But what is remarkable is that the Byzantine Church and people regarded their emperor's action with such detachment, as a matter for his own conscience. They understood, because Kydones kept telling them, that the Emperor's purpose in courting the western powers was to secure sympathy and support against the infidel. Most people believed that he was wrong; and he was to be proved wrong in this respect within his own lifetime. But so long as he did not imitate Michael VIII by trying to force his example on his subjects, they were prepared to put up with his eccentricities.

John V seems to have worn his religion unusually lightly for a Byzantine. He was not a theologian and was not much interested in the niceties of dogma. For much of his reign he was overshadowed by patriarchs trained in the hard school of Athonite Hesychasm. His conversion may have been sincere at the time. But he was soon led to abandon the hope that it would produce tangible rewards. Barely a year after his return from Italy he was obliged to make a new agreement with the Turks, in which his status was for the first time defined as that of a vassal of the Ottoman Sultan. In 1373 the Emperor of the Romans was to be found with the Sultan's army in Asia Minor, fighting for a master to whom he had now to pay tribute.[60] The Pope deplored this 'impious alliance'

59 Halecki, *Un empereur*, pp. 199–212; Nicol, *Last Centuries*, pp. 281–3.
60 G. Ostrogorsky, 'Byzance, état tributaire de l'Empire turc', *ZRVI*, v (1958), pp. 49–51; Nicol, *Last Centurties*, pp. 287–8.

of a newly converted Catholic prince with the infidel.[61] The Pope lived far away from the scene of action. Nor could he be expected to understand that the Byzantine Church would rather see its emperor humiliated by the infidel than be indebted to the Latins for its material survival. Towards the end of John V's reign, about 1380, the Church expressed its confidence in him, not as a person but as the holder of the supreme office, by agreeing to the terms of a document that clarified and defined the constitutional rights of the emperor in ecclesiastical affairs. The Byzantines had left it rather late in the day to commit their constitution to writing. But this concordat reemphasised their certainty that there could be no Church without an emperor.[62]

It also emphasised the Church's certainty that it would survive, whatever the vacillations of its emperors. The continuing vitality of the Byzantine Church in the late fourteenth century is witnessed not only by its spate of anti-Latin polemics, but more significantly by the enhanced stature and authority of the Patriarchate of Constantinople. As the Empire sank ever deeper into its material decline, the Church came to exert and to claim a moral as well as a spiritual leadership as the only permanent institution in a dissolving world. The Patriarchs of Constantinople in the last seventy years of the Empire commanded an authority which was more universally respected in the Orthodox world than that of the emperors, not only among the Greeks but also in Serbia, Bulgaria, Roumania, Cyprus, Trebizond, Georgia and Russia. Patriarchs are found advising and admonishing the temporal as well as the spiritual leaders of their Slav neighbours, with all the assurance of popes.[63] The Emperor John V

---

61 Letter of Pope Gregory XI, cited by Halecki, *Un empereur*, p. 301 n. 3: '...inter Grecos et Turchos quaedam impia colligatio adversus fideles Christi...'.

62 V. Laurent, 'Les droits de l'empereur en matière ecclésiastique. L'accord de 1380–1382', *REB*, xiii (1955), pp. 5–20. Cf. Runciman, *Byzantine Theocracy*, pp. 158–9.

63 See D. M. Nicol, 'The papal scandal', *Studies in Church History*, xiii (*The Orthodox Churches and the West*), ed. D. Baker (Oxford, 1976), pp. 165–7.

proved to be incapable of organising any collective resistance to the Turks, whether with the Latins or with the Slavs. It was left to the Patriarch to encourage the idea, proposed by the Serbians, of a kind of Byzantine–Slav coalition. It was not their fault that the proposal was never adopted.[64]

The reawakening of Byzantine spirituality had its effects far beyond the shrinking boundaries of the Byzantine Empire in Europe. It lit up the whole Orthodox world. The 'international' appeal of Hesychasm is in marked contrast to the ingrown and esoteric nature of the intellectual revival. Much has been made of individual conversions of Byzantines to the Roman Church at this time. But, given the vitality of Orthodoxy, it is not surprising that there were also conversions in the other direction. Some occurred through intermarriage, which neither popes nor patriarchs were able to prevent, for all the objections of their canonists. But the patriarchal registers of the late fourteenth century record several cases of the personal conversion to Orthodoxy of Genoese, Venetians and Catalans.[65] Such converts were obliged to submit a declaration to the patriarchal synod in Constantinople. There was a set form of words. After reciting the Creed in its Orthodox form they had to make the following profession: 'I reject the addition to the Creed made by the Latins, to the effect that the Holy Spirit proceeds also from the Son; for I believe that it proceeds from the Father alone. And I renounce all their customs and way of life in so far as these are foreign to the ways of the apostolic and catholic church . . . and I adhere to and believe the same

64 On this proposal, see Halecki, *Un empereur*, pp. 179–80, 241–2; Ostro-gorsky, *History of the Byzantine State*, pp. 540–1; Obolensky, *Byzantine Commonwealth*, pp. 256–7.

65 E.g., in *MM*, II, pp. 8, 9, 48, 84, 159, 160, 200, 266, 296, 343, 344, 449, 454, 488; all of these conversions occurred between the years 1382 and 1401. On the canonical impediments to mixed marriages between Orthodox and Catholics, see D. M. Nicol, 'Mixed marriages in Byzantium in the thirteenth century', *Studies in Church History*, I, ed. C. W. Dugmore and C. Duggan (London–Edinburgh, 1964), pp. 160–72 (reprinted in Nicol, *Byzantium...Collected Studies* [London, 1972], no. IV).

as the Holy Church of Constantinople, devoting myself wholeheartedly to my most holy lord the Oecumenical Patriarch and his holy synod. . . .[66] Some of these conversions, notably among the Genoese, were undoubtedly contracted with an eye to business. Genoese traders in the Anatolian city of Philadelphia, for example, which miraculously held out against a sea of Turks until 1390, found that being Orthodox brought them more trade.[67] The Italian merchants wore their religion even more lightly than John V. But at least this shows that the Orthodox Church was far from dead, even in such unpromising circumstances.

By that time, by 1390, it was perhaps difficult any longer to sustain the theory that Church and society were one. In most of the rest of Asia Minor the Church as an institution had practically disappeared, the monasteries were deserted and the dwindling society of Christians struggled on as a grudgingly tolerated sect of second-class citizens. Many of them gave up the struggle and embraced Islam. As early as 1303 the Patriarch Athanasios was deploring the 'countless numbers' of apostasies.[68] Kydones reports the frightening news that 'every day floods of Christians are drawn off into unbelief'.[69] The Orthodox assurance that the Church exists, and exists in its fullness, wherever two or three are gathered together was always there to give heart to the steadfast. But the evidence suggests that the Turkish conquest of Anatolia was fol-

66 *MM*, II, p. 449.
67 E.g., *MM*, I, pp. 227–8. Cf. Hélène Ahrweiler, 'L'histoire et la géographie de la région de Smyrne entre les deux occupations turques (1081–1317), particulièrement au XIIIe siècxle', *Travaux et Mémoires*, I (1965), pp. 27–8; P. Schreiner, 'Zur Geschichte Philadelpheias im 14. Jahrhundert (1293–1390)', *OCP*, XXXV (1969), pp. 375–431.
68 *Letters of Athanasios*, ed. Talbot, no. 110, pp. 272–3 lines 14–18: 'not only have certain people, in an excess of wickedness, repudiated piety of their own accord, but also countless numbers (even more than the grains of sand) of unwilling people have been driven to this by irresistible necessity...'.
69 Demetrios Kydones, *Apologie*, ed. Mercati, p. 374 lines 46–7: καὶ ὁ μηδ' ἄν τις ἄνευ τοῦ φρίττειν ἀκούσειεν, ὅτι καὶ καθ' ἡμέραν τὸ πλεῖστον ἐπὶ τὴν ἀσέβειαν ὥσπερ ῥεῦμα ἀποχετεύεται.

lowed by a remarkable process of religious syncretism, initiated not least by the Bektashi and Mawlawi orders of dervishes and similarly fervent missionaries of Islam.[70] Whole Christian villages were converted, sometimes as a result of miracles performed by a dervish; and the early establishment of dervish colleges provided numerous centres for Muslim propaganda.[71] Furthermore, the followers of Osman did not regard themselves as Turks but as the Osmanli people into whose ranks persons of all races and creeds were welcome, provided they renounced their former beliefs and accepted Islam. Even if they remained Christians they knew that they were assured of their legal status as *dhimmis*, or members of a protected religious minority, in Islamic society.[72] But the Osmanlis in Asia Minor did everything to make conversion attractive. The German traveller Schiltberger has a chapter on 'How a Christian becomes an Infidel'. 'If the convert is poor', he writes, 'they make a large collection and give it to him, and their great lords show particular honour to him, and make him rich; this they do, that Christians may be more willing to be converted to their faith.'[73]

The patriarchs and bishops of Byzantium naturally lamented this development. And yet, if given the choice between surrendering to the Turks or submitting to the Latins, most of them would have opted for the former. Those who had to live under French or Italian rule in Greece and the islands could testify that the Turks were not alone in treating the Greeks as second-class citizens and the Orthodox faith as a troublesome deviation. The Latins

---

70 Vryonis, *Decline of Medieval Hellenism*, pp. 351ff.
71 Vryonis, *Decline of Medieval Hellenism*, pp. 365–96; Vryonis, 'Nomad-ization and Islamization', pp. 64–71.
72 Vryonis, 'Nomadization and Islamization', pp. 60, 62.
73 Johann Schiltberger, *Reisebuch*, ed. J. B. Telfer (Hakluyt Society: London, 1879), pp. 74–5. Vryonis, *Decline of Medieval Hellenism*, pp. 357–8. Cf. the account of mixed marriages between Turks and Greeks in fourteenth-century Asia Minor given by Ludolph of Suchem (Sudheim), *De itinere terre sancte*, ed. G. A. Neumann, *Archives de l'Orient Latin*, II (1884), *Documents*, pp. 375–6 (cited by Vryonis, *Decline of Medieval Hellenism*, p. 228 n. 510).

too had their concept of the 'nations' – the *nationes christianorum orientalium*, of wayward and dissident sects. The Greeks were often uncritically lumped together in western minds with the other heretical Christians of the Orient, the Armenians, Jacobites, Copts, Nestorians and the rest.[74] Opinions were divided as to whether the Greeks were in fact heretics as well as schismatics; but the Byzantines themselves were uncomfortably aware that some Latins rated them no higher than 'pale-faced Arabs'.[75] Humbertus de Romanis, Dominican General at the Council of Lyons in 1274, was unusually tolerant and understanding; but even he concluded that the Greeks of his day were to be regarded not only as schismatics but also as manifest heretics ('non tantum schismatici sunt censendi, sed etiam haeretici manifesti').[76] A less enlightened Dominican, William Adam, suggested that, were it not for the fact that Greek was one of the languages inscribed on the Cross, it should be stamped out. Failing that, all Greek books, ancient or modern, which did not accord with Roman doctrine, should be burnt, and every second Byzantine child should be forcibly educated in Latin.[77] A more humane and more romantic solution to the problem of the 'oriental nations' was proposed by Pierre Dubois in 1306. His idea was that their salvation might be effected through the marriage of their rulers,

74 Anna-Dorothee v. den Brincken, *Die "Nationes Christianorum Orientalium" im Verständnis der lateinischen Historiographie von der Mitte des 12. bis in die zweite Hälfte des 14. Jahrhunderts* (Cologne–Vienna, 1973), esp. pp. 15–76. The popes of the fourteenth century tended to regard the Greek Church merely as a corporation or 'sect'. Pope Clement VI declared that the Patriarch of Constantinople had 'made himself another Church' (*aliam sibi confinxit ecclesiam*). See W. de Vries, 'Die Päpste von Avignon und der christliche Osten', *OCP*, xxx (1964), pp. 85–128, esp. pp. 99–103.
75 Pachymeres, I, p. 367 lines 8–9: λευκοὺς Ἀγαρηνοὺς εἶναι Γραικοὺς παρ' ἐκείνοις.
76 Humbertus de Romanis, *Opus Tripartitum*, in J. D. Mansi, *Sacrorum Conciliorum nova et amplissima collectio*, xxiv (Venice, 1780), col. 126.
77 'Brocardus' (William Adam), *Directorium ad passagium faciendum*, viii, in *Recueil des historiens des Croisades, Documents Arméniennes*, ii (Paris, 1906), pp. 468–71. See v. Brincken, *Die "Nationes Christianorum Orientalium"*, pp. 64–5.

Muslim as well as Christian, to carefully selected and trained convent girls from western Europe.[78]

The popes, for all their good intentions, could hardly help making things difficult for the Byzantines. It was impossible for them to preach a crusade for the rescue of schismatics or heretics. To them the solution seemed simple. It required the Greeks only to admit the error of their ways and return to the fold of Rome. The process was described as a *reductio*, a bringing back. There was no need to go to the trouble of convening a council, as the Greeks always proposed, to debate theological issues which had already been defined by the authority of previous popes. The point was clearly put to the Emperor Michael VIII by Pope Clement IV in 1267. 'The Emperor', he wrote, 'may ask for the convocation of a council . . . But we have not intention of summoning such a gathering for discussion or definition of the faith, not because we are afraid of losing face or of being outwitted by the Greeks, but because it is not proper nor permissible to call into question the purity of the true faith, confirmed as it is by the authority of so much holy writ, by the judgment of so many saints and by the firm definition of so many Roman pontiffs.'[79] The terms of union as spelt out by Clement IV to Michael VIII in 1267 served as the model for all succeeding popes in their dealings with the Byzantines. They were repeated, often verbatim, in nearly all papal communications with Constantinople up to the fifteenth century. Not until the emperor and his Church and people had accepted and professed every single item

78 Pierre Dubois, *De Recuperatione Terrae Sanctae*, ed. Ch.-V. Langlois, in *Collection de Textes pour servir à l'Etude et à l'Enseignement de l'Histoire* (Paris, 1891), pp. 51ff. (English trans., *The Recovery of the Holy Land*, by W. I. Brandt [Columbia University Records of Civilization, 51: New York, 1956], p. 172); v. Brincken, *Die "Nationes Christianorum Orientalium"*, pp. 62–4; D. J. Geanakoplos, 'Byzantium and the Crusades, 1261–1354', in Setton (ed.), *A History of the Crusades*, III, p. 52.

79 Letter of Clement IV dated 4 March 1267, in A. L. Tăutu, *Acta Urbani IV, Clementis IV, Gregorii X (1261–1276)* (*Pontificia Commissio ad redigendum CIC orientalis*, Fontes, ser. III, vol. v, 1: Vatican City, 1953), no. 23, pp. 61–9.

of those terms could the union of the Greek Church under Rome be achieved. And not until then could the Greeks qualify for a crusade to rescue them from the Turks.[80]

Here was the heart of the matter. The Byzantines found it very difficult to do business with people who refused to discuss things except on their own prearranged terms. Especially in their declining years they felt put upon by an organisation stronger and more materialistic than their own. Even in their darkest hours few of them would willingly contemplate 'reduction' to Rome as the answer to their problems. The word itself struck a jarring note. It emphasised the ideological gulf that separated Latins from Greeks. It symbolised the legalistic, authoritarian attitude of the western Church which the Orthodox found to be so alien. They could not see why it was they who were expected to make all the concessions in the way of accepting what went against their traditions and convictions; and they were never in sympathy with the Latin passion for defining every article of the faith.

The doctrine of Purgatory is a case in point. At the time of the Council of Lyons it was patiently explained to the Byzantines by a learned Franciscan in Constantinople, and they duly coined a Greek word for Purgatory so that it could go into the profession of faith that the Pope required of their delegates to the Council.[81] But one hundred and sixty-five years later, at the Council of Florence, the Latins were dismayed to find that there was still no Orthodox definition of Purgatory; and the Greek bishops at Florence, when asked to clarify their position on the subject, had to admit that their opinions were divided.[82] To say honestly that they did not know what exactly happened to souls

80 D. M. Nicol, 'Byzantine requests for an oecumenical council in the fourteenth century', *Annuarium Historiae Conciliorum*, I (Amsterdam, 1969), pp. 69–95, esp. pp. 71–2 (reprinted in Nicol, *Byzantium...Collected Studies*, no. VIII).

81 Greek and Latin texts of the profession of faith are in Tǎutu, *Acta Urbani IV*, pp. 116–23, esp. p. 119 (πουργατωρίου, ἤτοι καθαρτηρίου...). Cf. Nicol, 'The papal scandal', pp. 156–7.

82 Gill, *Council of Florence*, pp. 117–25, 272.

after death would have been embarrassing. So once again
they were pressed into formulating a definition of what
they preferred to leave undefined.

The most intractable symptom of misunderstanding
between the two Christian 'nations' was without doubt
the problem of the Procession of the Holy Spirit – the
addition of the *Filioque* clause to the Creed. From the ninth
century to the present day this has been a fruitful source
of quarrels between Orthodox and Catholic theologians;
and in the theological exchanges in the last centuries of
Byzantium it occupied more time than any other single
subject. The Orthodox as a rule preferred not to go too
far in exact definitions of articles of their faith; and yet
for years they argued passionately for their own definition
of the Holy Trinity. They did so partly because they
believed that the Roman addition to the Creed made a
muddle of Trinitarian theology, and partly because the
nature of the Trinity was one of the basic tenets of the faith
which had been defined once and for all by the Fathers
of the Universal Church under the inspiration of the Holy
Spirit itself. No one bishop of that Church, however
exalted his see, had a right to add anything to the form
and wording of that Creed, certainly not without first
consulting his colleagues in the hierarchy, which would
require the holding of another general council. Some
Byzantine churchmen were in fact prepared to concede
that a compromise might be reached on the theology of
the matter by juggling around with prepositions. The
Holy Spirit could be said to proceed *through* the Son *from*
the Father. Greek patristic texts could be found to support
this view, and indeed this view was expounded at tedious
length at the Council of Florence.[83]

Demetrios Kydones and other intellectual converts
found the matter to be tiresome and hoped that it could
be played down. But to the Orthodox it was of vital

83 On the debates about the *Filioque* at the Council of Ferrara-Florence, see
Gill, *Council of Florence*, pp. 194–223; Geanakoplos, *Byzantine East and
Latin West*, pp. 99–106; Runciman, *Great Church*, pp. 106–9.

concern. If, as everyone was agreed, something had been added to the Creed in its Roman form, then the question arose 'on whose authority had the addition been made?' People were not very clear how the *Filioque* clause had slipped in. Some said that it was through German or Arian influence. But there could be no doubt that it had been sanctioned by the papacy. This, to the western Church, seemed quite in order, since the Pope was the Supreme Pontiff of the Church Universal. But the Byzantines saw the addition as a scandal, a stumbling-block. The *Filioque* was therefore symptomatic of the whole range of differences between the Greek and the Latin Churches. It represented a Latin attempt to define more closely the indefinable, thereby upsetting the relationship between the persons of the Trinity which had already been defined as nearly as it ever could be. The acceptance or rejection of the *Filioque* depended upon a definition that could more easily be made, the definition of where in the Church authority lay. The Roman insistence on preserving it seemed to the Byzantines to be perverse and high-handed. If, as the Latins admitted at the Council of Florence, the *Filioque* was really a slight and unimportant matter, why could the Roman Church not simply accept or at least approve the Greek point of view? The matter was succinctly put at that Council by Mark Eugenikos, Bishop of Ephesos. 'The addition of a word', he said, 'seems to you (Latins) to be a small matter and of no great consequence. So then to remove it would cost you little or nothing; indeed it would be of the greatest profit, for it would bind together all Christians. But what was done was in truth a big matter and of the greatest consequence, so that we are not at fault in making a great consequence of it. It was added in the exercise of mercy; in the exercise of mercy remove it again so that you may receive to your bosoms brethren torn apart who value fraternal love so highly.'[84]

84 Trans. by Gill, *Council of Florence*, p. 163. The Greek text is in J. Gill, *Quae supersunt actorum graecorum Concilii Florentini* (Rome, 1953), p. 216. Cf. the

The *Filioque* dispute demonstrated a fundamental difference in mentality, the difference between what the Greeks would have called the distressing materialism of the Latins and what the Latins would have called the maddening obscurantism of the Greeks. For this reason if for no other, relationships between the two Christian 'nations' in the last centuries of Byzantium were never very promising; nor did they engender that kind of response from the Catholic west that might have saved Constantinople or driven the infidel from Christian Europe. Some intelligent Byzantines, like Kydones, tried to persuade the Latins that a show of practical help in the form of an army and navy would do more good for east–west relations than any number of papal legates armed with professions of faith, and might even encourage many Greeks to take more kindly to the Roman point of view.[85] But to the papacy this was a reversal of proper priorities. The popes insisted that union must come before rescue, that unless the Greeks repented of their schism they were not worthy objects of a crusade for their salvation. The order of priorities on either side is well expressed by Edward Gibbon: 'The Greeks insisted on three successive measures, a succour, a council, and a final reunion, while the Latins eluded the second, and only promised the first as a consequential and voluntary reward of the third.'[86]

In the final years of Byzantium crusades from the west did come marching down the Danube, one to Nikopolis in 1396, the other to Varna in 1444. But neither got

Oration of Mark Eugenikos to Pope Eugenius IV at Ferrara, *ibid.* pp. 28–34, esp. p. 41: "Ἤκουσα τοῦ τῶν παρ' ὑμῖν φιλοσόφων οἰκονομίας χάριν καὶ διορθώσεώς τινων οὐκ ἁγίως περὶ τὴν πίστιν ἐχόντων τὴν προσθήκην ταύτην ἐξ ἀρχῆς ἐπινοηθῆναι· οὔκουν οἰκονομίας χάριν ἀφαιρηθήτω πάλιν, ἵνα προσλάβησθε ἀδελφούς....

85 See the speech of Demetrios Kydones, *De admittendo Latinorum subsidio*, in *MPG*, CLIV, cols. 961–1008. Barlaam of Calabria, on his mission to Pope Benedict XII in 1339, had suggested that if the Pope would help to secure military aid for the Greeks against the Turks before insisting on their reunion he would win their gratitude and favour. Barlaam, *Oratio pro Unione habita*, in *MPG*, CLI, cols. 1331–42, § 19.

86 Gibbon, *Decline and Fall of the Roman Empire*, ed. Bury, VII, p. 97.

anywhere near Constantinople, and the Byzantines may well have felt that both were directed more to the protection of Catholic Hungary than to the rescue of their own Orthodox City. Their emperor and their hierarchy had been browbeaten into making every possible concession to the Latins at the Council of Florence. Many of them found it grimly comforting that after all it had made no difference. They might as well have saved their breath and their dignity. For at the end, conquest by the Ottoman Turks was less galling than survival at the cost of submission to the arrogant Latins. It was this feeling that inspired the famous outburst by one Byzantine statesman just before the fall of the city and the end of his world – 'Better the Sultan's turban in our midst than the Latin mitre'.[87]

87 The remark is attributed to the Grand Duke Loukas Notaras by the fifteenth-century historian Doukas. Ducas, *Istoria Turco-Bizantina*, ed. Grecu, p. 329 lines 11–12: Κρειττότερόν ἐστιν εἰδέναι ἐν μέσῃ τῇ πόλει φακιόλιον βασιλεῦον Τούρκων ἢ καλύπτραν Λατινικήν. Cf. Halina Evert-Kappesowa, 'Le Tiare ou le Turban?', *BS*, XIV (1953), pp. 245–57.

4

The end of the world

When the last Byzantine emperor fell fighting at the walls of his city on Tuesday 29 May 1453 a whole world came to an end. The end had been long expected. But suddenly it was a fact that the Empire of the Romans was over and that there was a Church without an emperor. Byzantium produced no St Augustine to present a teleological explanation of the collapse of the world. But various explanations were proposed.

For centuries the Byzantines had believed that the Empire would endure until the Second Coming of Christ. Its endurance, however, depended upon resolute adherence to the practice and principles of Orthodox Christianity. As the Patriarch Athanasios put it about 1300: 'inasmuch as the Empire sincerely keeps the holy commandments of Christ together with the Orthodox faith, prosperity will last as long as the Empire, "until the end of the world", as it has been proclaimed. If, on the other hand, the Empire rejects both faith and works, it will in direct proportion be deprived of his succour.'[1] The Patriarch Athanasios had a blindingly simple view of the reasons for the downfall of the Christians and the triumph of the Turks. The wages of sin is death. 'The people of God', he writes, 'have been delivered into the hands of Ishmael on account of their adultery, incest and perverted passion for sodomy and pederasty, and because of their intolerable blasphemy and sorcery and injustice.'[2] 'It is not the strength of the enemy, not their expertise in warfare that multiply our mis-

1 *Letters of Athanasios*, ed. Talbot, no. 110, p. 272 lines 43–7.
2 *Letters of Athanasios*, ed. Talbot, no. 36, p. 76 lines 8–11.

fortunes, no, it is our own passionate and unrepentant devotion to sin.'³ As one would expect, this was by far the commonest explanation of the Byzantine decline and fall, especially among churchmen. It followed that the Turkish conquests were God's punishment of the wicked Christians. If only they would repent and mend their ways they would find the moral courage to defy their enemies and the Empire would be saved.⁴ Some went so far as to say that the Turks deserved to win because they were morally superior to the Christians. Alexios Makrembolites, the only Byzantine sociologist of the fourteenth century, declared that, 'in spite of their abominable faith, many Turks are like true Christians in their deeds and lack only the name of Christ'. The Turks, after all, were ignorant barbarians. The Byzantines, being civilised, could not be forgiven for exploiting the poor and perpetrating injustice.⁵ Even some Turks, it seems, attributed their triumphs to their being the appointed agents of God's chastisement of the sinful Greeks.⁶

The tirades of the Patriarch Athanasios were echoed a century later by the monk Joseph Bryennios. About 1400, in a work entitled 'The Causes of our Sufferings', Bryennios deplores the prevalent lack of Christian faith and morals and enumerates the sins of the Byzantine clergy and people. Many priests and monks had no sense of vocation. Simony, fornication and blasphemy were rife among them. Christians could not even remember the books of the Bible or how to cross themselves. They delighted in profaning the holy mysteries and indulged in all manner

3 *Letters of Athanasios*, ed. Talbot, no. 67, p. 160 lines 29–32. Cf. no. 13, p. 30 lines 5–7: ἰσχύουσι καθ' ἡμῶν οἱ μισοῦντες ἡμᾶς, δι' ἄλλο οὐδὲν ἢ δι' ἀθέτησιν τῶν τοῦ Θεοῦ νόμων καὶ καταφρόνησιν, καὶ πλέον οὐδέν.
4 On sin as the cause of Christian defeat and Muslim victory, see Vryonis, *Decline of Medieval Hellenism*, pp. 417–21; I. Ševčenko, 'The decline of Byzantium seen through the eyes of its intellectuals', *DOP*, xv (1961), pp. 178–81. Cf. Mazal, *Die Prooimien der byzantinischen Patriarchenurkunden*, pp. 169–70.
5 I. Ševčenko, 'Alexios Makrembolites and his "Dialogue between the Rich and the Poor"', pp. 196–7.
6 Vryonis, *Decline of Medieval Hellenism*, p. 418.

of sexual irregularities, from child prostitution to sodomy and transvestism.[7] It is true that Bryennios was describing conditions in Crete, which was then under Venetian rule. But, like all good prophets of doom, he meant his remarks to have a wider significance. And again, like all good prophets, he was a highly successful preacher whose sermons drew large congregations eager to hear the catalogue of their iniquities. On the other hand, the clergy were clearly not all shining examples of the virtues that they preached; and there seems to have been a growing undercurrent of anti-clericalism. It is most vividly represented in a piece of samizdat literature (probably of the fifteenth century) called the Liturgy of the Beardless Man, or 'of the Profane and Beardless Son of a Goat'. This is an obscene parody of the celebration of the Liturgy, in which the priest marries his daughter to a eunuch.[8] Such profanity is rare in Byzantine literature. Perhaps it expressed a popular feeling that the Church, for all the revival of spirituality in the fourteenth century, had let society down. Gregory Palamas relates that when he arrived in Lampsakos as a prisoner of the Turks, men, women and children crowded round him. Some wanted to be confessed, some to have their faith fortified. 'But most wanted to know why God had forsaken them.'[9]

Among the sins of society denounced by Bryennios was the growing practice of magic, sorcery and astrology. Superstition was deeply inbred in the Byzantine mind. The pseudo-sciences of Antiquity, alchemy, astrology and the magic of numbers, were, like the works of Plato and

---

7 Joseph Bryennios, ed. L. Oeconomos, 'L'état intellectuel et moral des Byzantins vers le milieu du XIVe siècle d'après une page de Joseph Bryennios', *Mélanges Charles Diehl*, I (Paris, 1930), pp. 225–33. On Bryennios, see Beck, *Kirche und theologische Literatur*, pp. 749–50, and Ch. 2 n. 105.

8 Ἀκολουθία τοῦ ἀνοσίου τραγογενῆ Σπανοῦ, ed. E. Legrand, *Bibliothèque grecque vulgaire*, II (Paris, 1880), pp. 28–47. *Spanos. Eine byzantinische Satire in der Form einer Parodie*, ed. H. Eideneier (Supplementa Byzantina, 5: Berlin–New York, 1977).

9 Palamas, *Letter to the Thessalonians*, ed. Dyobouniotes, *NH*, XVI (1922), p. 11:...τῶν δὲ πλειόνων, τὴν αἰτίαν ἀπαιτούντων τῆς περὶ τὸ ἡμέτερον γένος παρὰ Θεοῦ ἐγκαταλείψεως.

Aristotle, a part of the Byzantine inheritance. Reputable professors of philosophy in Constantinople computed ways of foretelling the sex of an embryo by juggling around with the numbers of letters in its parents' names.[10] This kind of magic could be dignified as neo-Pythagoreanism. But below the professorial level popular superstitions of all kinds flourished. Simple people without the consolations of philosophy naturally turned more to oracle-mongers, soothsayers and magicians at a time when their Christianity no longer seemed to provide all the answers – when God had forsaken them to the tender mercies of the Turks or the Latins. Pre-Christian rituals and festivals died hard in the countryside. The ancient feasts of the Brumalia and Rosalia are attested in Greece as late as the thirteenth and fourteenth centuries – attested and denounced by the Church.[11] The bishops deplored the taking of auguries from the flight of birds and the reciting of spells to make the crops grow. The Kalends were still celebrated; people wore amulets in March, placed wreaths on their houses in May, leapt over bonfires and profaned holy days with satanic songs, dancing and drunkenness.[12]

Such survivals might be expected in remote peasant communities. But the bishops in the fourteenth century noticed with alarm that superstition was rife not only in the provinces but in the very heart of Constantinople. In 1338 the Patriarch, John Kalekas, ordered his clergy to search every corner of the city for the agents of the devil who were polluting society with their sorcery and magic. 'Such abominations are', he said, 'obviously the cause of the past and continuing destruction and enslavement of the nation of Christians... How can they escape the wrath of

---

10 K. Vogel, 'Byzantine science', pp. 298–9.
11 Demetrios Chomatianos, ed. J. B. Pitra, *Analecta Sacra*, VI (1891), no. CXX (*De Rosaliis*), cols. 509–12, esp. col. 510: τὰ παίγνια ταῦτα τοῖς θεοῖς καὶ ἱεροῖς κανόσιν ἀπηγορευμένα τυγχάνουσιν, ὡς ἐκ τῆς ἑλληνικῆς πλάνης καὶ μέθης ὁρμώμενα ὁποῖα δὴ τὰ λεγόμενα Βότα, καὶ Βρουμάλια, καὶ αὐτὰ δὴ τὰ Ῥουσάλια καὶ ἕτερα τούτοις παραπλήσια. The Patriarch Athanasios attacks the 'festivals of the Hellenes and Jews': *Letters of Athanasios*, ed. Talbot, no. 47, p. 102 lines 40–1; cf. Commentary *ibid.* p. 357.
12 Joseph Bryennios, in Oeconomos (ed.), 'L'état intellectuel', pp. 227–8.

God when such evils are afoot in the very midst of the
capital, the seat of the Church of God and the most holy
Empire, the fount of Christianity?' He called on the city's
magistrates to co-operate in tracking down and punish-
ing these 'perpetrators of demonic sorceries, magic and
incantations'.[13] The patriarchal registers of the period
record numerous cases of men and women being convicted
of what is described as the ultimate and greatest evil,
namely witchcraft and magic, and of their baneful influence on simple and impressionable people.[14] Those who
truly repented were brought before the Patriarch's tribunal
for 'therapy'. The 'therapy' here, as with those who
abjured the evils of the Roman Church, consisted of a full
confession of faith and a long round of penances and
mortifications.[15] It is to the credit of the Byzantines that
they almost never condoned the burning either of witches
or of heretics. Where therapy failed, the ultimate penalty
for a sorcerer was exile – either to the Latins or to the
Turks.[16]

The line between science and superstition was a very
narrow one. There is evidence, for example, that the
ancient Greek compilation of magic and medicine known
as the Koiranis (or Koiranides) was in circulation in
Constantinople as late as the 1370s. One copy was tran-

13 *MM*, I, pp. 188–9. Cf. pp. 184–7.
14 E.g., *MM*, I, pp. 180–1, 181–2, 184–7, 188–90, 301–6, 317–18, 342–4,
    541–50, 560, 594–5; II, pp. 84–5. For witchcraft and magic as the 'ultimate
    and greatest evil', see *MM*, I, pp. 302, 542.
15 About 1350 a woman called Amarantine, accused with many others of
    magic, of 'uttering prophetic nonsense from her belly [ventriloquism],
    denouncing Orthodoxy and Christian truth and deceiving and corrupting
    innocent Christians', made a full confession before the Patriarch's synod
    and sought 'therapy'. After her repentance she entered a convent and
    received a small pension from the Emperor. *MM*, I, pp. 302–5, 317.
16 Three men convicted of diabolical practices in 1371 were sentenced to be
    exiled from Constantinople and 'from all the land of the faithful in which
    Christians live' (*MM*, I, p. 546). The only attested case of the public
    burning of a heretic in Byzantium appears to be that of the Bogomil leader
    Basil and his associates, who were burnt at the stake on the orders of
    Alexios I. Anna Comnena, *Alexiad*, xv, x: ed. A. Reifferscheid, II (Leipzig,
    1884), pp. 301–5; ed. B. Leib, III (Paris, 1945), pp. 226–9.

scribed by a former official of St Sophia, Demetrios
Chloros. When hauled before the Patriarch to reveal the
source of his iniquities he declared in court that he had put
it all together from medical textbooks. Some of the
leading doctors who were then called to give evidence
expressed their horror at such abuse of their sacred art,
as if Hippocrates and Galen had been magicians.[17] But the
Byzantine art of medicine, when it broke away from the
anchor of its Hippocratic moorings, was not far removed
from magic. The line between astrology and astronomy
was equally tenuous. The astronomer Gregoras, who
could correctly foretell eclipses, was still inclined to
interpret them as portents of disaster.[18] The pious Emperor
Andronikos II was not above opening the Bible at random
to see what his future might hold; and when dying he
summoned Gregoras to ask him whether the stars could
do any better for him than his doctors.[19] The collapse of
one of the arches and vaults of St Sophia in 1346 was
widely believed to be a manifestation of divine wrath.
Gregoras and Makrembolites wrote whole essays on the
subject. They were aware that the structure of the building
had been weakened by earthquake. But the earthquake
itself could only be explained as a portent – a sign from
God that the end was nigh.[20]

17 *MM*, I, pp. 543–6. On this case, see F. Cumont, 'Démétrios Chloros et
les Cyranides', *Bulletin de la société nationale des Antiquaires de France* (1919),
pp. 175–80. The Koiranides or Kyranides was a compilation of magical
and medicinal remedies originally made in the third or fourth century.
The Patriarch Athanasios knew of its circulation in Constantinople: *Letters
of Athanasios*, ed. Talbot, no. 69, p. 168 lines 80–1; and Commentary
ibid. pp. 386–7.

18 The eclipse of the moon on 1 September 1327, fully described by
Gregoras, was interpreted by him as an evil omen (Gregoras, I, p. 385).
Various portents foretelling the death of Andronikos II in 1332 included
eclipses of the sun and of the moon (Gregoras, I, pp. 460–1). An invasion
of Thrace by the Tatars in 1337 was thought to have been foretold by
solar and lunar eclipses on 15 February and 3 March 1337 (Gregoras, I,
p. 536). Eclipses of the sun and moon in 1342 were taken to be presages
of disaster (Gregoras, II, p. 624).

19 Gregoras, I, pp. 358, 559.

20 S. I. Kourousis, Αἱ ἀντιλήψεις περὶ τῶν ἐσχάτων τοῦ κόσμου καὶ ἡ κατὰ
τὸ ἔτος 1346 πτῶσις τοῦ τρούλλου τῆς Ἁγίας Σοφίας, *EEBS*, XXXVII

There were two schools of thought about the approaching end of the world. Some, as we have seen, held that the 'nation of Christians' was being destroyed because of its sinfulness, of which pagan superstition was a vile symptom. This theory is well expressed in a patriarchal document of 1350: 'It is through the divine anger at such wickedness that we are visited by these plagues, famines, earthquakes, tidal waves, floods and conflagrations, and that we have to witness the murder of Christians by each other in civil war, the Black Death, and the great and terrible enslavement and diaspora of the Christian nation by their impious, godless and barbarian enemies.'[21] The Patriarch's remedy is for Christians to return to and cling to the pure and Orthodox faith of their fathers. The partisans of the other school of thought, whose numbers grew as the news became daily more hopeless, held that there *was* no remedy – that the portents and visitations of divine wrath were a sure sign that the end of the world was at hand. Everything seemed to point to the imminence of Armageddon. Repentance was surely called for, but only as a preparation for the Second Coming.[22]

There was some consensus of opinion about the date of this event, even though the method of calculating it rested partly upon pagan supersitition, upon the Pythagorean theory of the magic number seven. The final consummation was reckoned to come at the end of seven aeons or periods of 1000 years, corresponding to the seven days of

(1969/70), pp. 211–50 (includes the Greek text of Alexios Makrembolites's essay *On the collapse of St Sophia as a result of many continuous earthquakes* (pp. 235–40); and of the *Monodia* ascribed to Gregoras (pp. 247–50)). See also Gregoras, II, pp. 749–50, for the opinion that the collapse of the building was a divine warning and might have happened even without the earthquake (p. 749 lines 7–9:...καὶ μοι δοκεῖ διὰ τοῦτ' ἄνευ σεισμοῦ καὶ περικλονήσεως γῆς γεγενῆσθαι τὸ πάθος τουτί).

21 *MM*, I, pp. 303–4. 'The unexpected scourge of the plague' (ἡ ἀπροσδόκητος ῥομφαία τοῦ θανατικοῦ) must refer to the Black Death, which struck Constantinople in 1347.

22 For this view, see esp. Joseph Bryennios, Ἰωσὴφ Βρυεννίου...τὰ εὑρεθέντα, ed. E. Boulgaris, II (Leipzig, 1768), pp. 109, 191, 370f. Cf. C. Mango, 'Byzantinism and Romantic Hellenism', *Journal of the Warburg and Courtauld Institutes*, XXVIII (1965), pp. 33–4.

creation. This piece of mathematical conjuring was grafted on to the revealed truth that 'iooo years in the sight of God are as one day'. The days of creation were six, Adam having been created on the sixth day. Christ, the second Adam, must therefore have come to earth in the sixth period of iooo years or 'cosmic week' – somewhere about 5500 years after the creation. The Byzantine calendar fixed this date, the *annus mundi*, at 5509/8. On this computation the 7000th year, and so the end of the world and the Second Coming, would occur in 1492. But when that year came round Constantinople had already been in Turkish hands for nearly forty years. The fact that the world did not end when the Christian lights went out in the Queen of Cities needed some explanation. True, the Last Judgment was scheduled to take place not in Constantinople but in Jerusalem, on a Sunday at the seventh hour of the night. But doom-watchers have ever been adept at rearranging their statistics.[23]

In the years just after the Turkish conquest in 1453 some Byzantines, the Patriarch among them, did in fact derive comfort from the thought that there were not many more years to go before the Second Coming.[24] But eschatology does not as a rule appeal to intellectuals. One would not expect a Demetrios Kydones or a Theodore Metochites

23 See G. Podskalsky, *Byzantinische Reichseschatologie* (Münchener Universitätschriften, Philos. Fak., 9: Munich, 1972); Podskalsky, 'Marginalien zur byzantinischen Reichseschatologie', *BZ*, LXVII (1974), pp. 351–8; C. Diehl, 'Sur quelques croyances byzantines sur la fin de Constantinople', *BZ*, XXX (1930), pp. 192–6; A. A. Vasiliev, 'Medieval ideas of the end of the world: West and East', *B*, XVI (1944), pp. 462–502; P. J. Alexander, 'Historiens byzantins et croyances eschatologiques', *Actes du XIIe Congrès International des Etudes Byzantines*, II (Belgrade, 1964), pp. 1–8; Kourousis, *Αἱ ἀντιλήψεις...*, *EEBS*, XXXVII (1969–70), pp. 214–22; M. A. Poljakovskaja, 'Eschatologičeskaja predstvalenija Alekseja Makremvolita', *Antičnaja drevnost' i srednie veka*, XI (Sverdlovsk, 1975), pp. 87–98. See also L. Rydén, 'The Andreas Salos Apocalypse. Greek text, translation and commentary', *DOP*, XXVIII (1974), pp. 197–261.

24 The Patriarch Gennadios (George Scholarios) almost eagerly awaited the coming of Antichrist and the end of the world after 1453. See C. J. G. Turner, 'Pages from the late Byzantine philosophy of history', *BZ*, LVII (1964), pp. 346–73, esp. pp. 370–2; I. Ševčenko, 'Decline of Byzantium', pp. 167–86, esp. p. 184.

to set much store by such calculations. Kydones periodic-
ally escaped from the deepening gloom of Byzantium
to the bright lights of Italy which he so much admired.
Other Byzantine intellectuals settled there permanently
and found a living teaching Greek to growing numbers
of enthusiastic students. Others retreated into a fatalistic
acceptance of the inevitable, finding their comfort not so
much in Christian doctrine as in the sages of Antiquity,
notably Plutarch. Theodore Metochites was disenchanted
with his people not so much because of their immorality
as because they seemed to him to be 'dregs' and 'refuse'
who refused to turn their God-given minds to higher
things. He surveyed what he called 'the wreckage of the
Roman Empire' from a lofty academic height. But he had
an antiquarian's view of the reasons for the wreckage. He
sensed that he was living 'late in time', and his reading
of ancient history persuaded him to admit that he was
witnessing nothing more nor less than the end of an
Empire.[25] It was a very un-Byzantine admission, to
declare that the God-protected Empire of the Romans was
going the way of other empires which had declined and
fallen. It was still more un-Byzantine to explain this
process not in eschatological terms but as a kind of
imperial natural selection, and to ascribe it to the workings
not of providence but of fortune, of *Tyche*, that fickle
goddess of the Hellenistic age. Popular belief about the
imminent end of the world held that the 'nations', the
Latins as well as the Turks, would meet their doom in the
general conflagration. It was revolutionary to suggest that
the 'nations' would triumph and survive after the God-
guarded City had fallen; or that the ruin of the Byzantine
Empire was merely the end of a natural process of decline,
a historical reversal of fortunes such as had overtaken the
empires of the Medes and Persians and Assyrians.[26]

25 Ševčenko, 'Decline of Byzantium', pp. 173–4, 182–4.
26 On the role of Tyche in the philosophy of Metochites and his contemporaries, see H. Hunger, 'Der 'Ηθικὸς des Theodoros Metochites', *Hellenika*, Parartima IX (Thessalonike, 1958), pp. 152, 157; Beck, *Theodoros
Metochites*, pp. 96ff.; Hunger, *Reich der neuen Mitte*, pp. 116–17; Ševčenko,
'Theodore Metochites', pp. 46–7.

Belief in divine providence, however, and in the special protection of the City of Constantinople by the Virgin, survived side by side with the more fatalistic and historical theories. By the last decade of the fourteenth century Constantinople was indeed almost all that was left of the Empire. There were still outposts of Byzantine culture and society at Trebizond on the Black Sea and at Mistra in the Peloponnese. But Thessalonica, the second city of the Empire, had its first taste of Turkish conquest in 1387. In 1394 the Ottoman Sultan Bajezid began the first blockade of Constantinople. It was to last for about eight years. The City was isolated from the rest of the world. The Sultan's message to the Emperor was clear; 'Shut the gates of your City and govern what lies behind them; for everything beyond the gates belongs to me.'[27] In 1396 his armies routed the western crusade sent down the Danube to Nikopolis. It seemed as if the end had really come. But then, suddenly, those who still hoped for a miracle had their reward. In July 1402 the great Bajezid and his invincible army were defeated at a battle near Ankara by Timur the Mongol. The Ottoman Empire in Asia Minor was shattered. The blockade of Constantinople was over. Here if ever was a miracle. To many Byzantines it was evident that God and His Mother had once again winked at the wickedness of their people and intervened to save them, as they had saved their ancestors from Arabs, Slavs, Bulgars and Russians in the past.[28]

The Emperor, Manuel II, composed a hymn of thanksgiving in the form of a Psalm – thanksgiving to God for the deliverance of his people from the Saracen Thunderbolt, Bajezid Yildirim.[29] When the news of the

27 Doukas, *Istoria*, ed. Grecu, p. 77 lines 26–8. G. Ostrogorsky, 'Byzance, état tributaire', pp. 52–3.
28 Nicol, *Last Centuries*, pp. 298–9, 315–33.
29 Manuel II's Hymn of Thanksgiving is printed in *MPG*, CLVI, col. 581 A–C; and in E. Legrand (ed.), *Lettres de l'empereur Manuel Paléologue* (Paris, 1893), p. 104; trans. in Barker, *Manuel II Palaeologus*, pp. 514–15. Manuel also composed an imaginary address to the defeated Sultan Bajezid: *MPG*, CLVI, cols. 580C–581A; Legrand, *Lettres*, pp. 103–4; trans. in Barker, *Manuel II Palaeologus*, pp. 513–14. Cf. also the Thanksgiving to the Virgin composed on the anniversary of the Battle of Ankara, ed. P. Gautier,

Thunderbolt's defeat reached Constantinople in 1402 the
Emperor Manuel was in fact far away. At the height of
the Turkish blockade he had been persuaded that the best
way to rouse the conscience of the western world was to
go there himself; and in 1399 he had slipped away from
Constantinople on a journey that was to take him to the
courts of Italy, France and England. For more than three
of those critical years he was absent from Constantinople.[30]
Manuel II was an impressive and attractive figure, urbane
and scholarly, a soldier, a writer and a devoutly Orthodox
Christian. He came perhaps as near as any Byzantine ever
came to the position of a Christian humanist. It was tragic
for himself as well as for his Empire that he was called upon
to reign when he did. For in other circumstances Manuel's
varied talents would not have been so wasted and
frustrated.

His father, John V, had gone to Italy in 1369, cap in hand
and with no idea but to win the favour and support of
the Pope. He won little favour and less support, and his
visit was not much noticed in the west. Thirty years later
things had changed. Classical Greek learning had become
fashionable in Italy and Byzantine scholars were welcomed
as the purveyors of that learning. In 1396 the Emperor's
friend, Manuel Chrysoloras, a pupil of Kydones, had been
appointed to teach Greek at Florence.[31] Manuel II was a
striking advertisement for those qualities which the *cogno-
scenti* of Italy hoped to find in a Greek. He was a classical
scholar in the best sense, with a strong feeling for the style
and thought of the ancient Hellenes. But he was a
theologian as well, able to argue the merits of his faith with

'Actions de Grâces de Démétrius Chrysoloras à la Théotokos pour
l'anniversaire de la bataille d'Ankara (28 juillet 1403)', *REB*, xix (1961),
pp. 340–57.
30 Nicol, *Last Centuries*, pp. 321–30.
31 On Manuel Chrysoloras, see G. Cammelli, *I Dotti bizantini e le origini
dell'umanesimo*, 1: *Manuele Crisolora* (Florence, 1941); Setton, 'Byzantine
background', pp. 56–8; J. Thomson, 'Manuel Chrysoloras and the early
Italian Renaissance', *Greek, Roman and Byzantine Studies*, vii (1966), pp.
63–82.

Muslims and to defend the finer points of Orthodox dogma in debate with the Catholic doctors at the University of Paris. Unlike his father, Manuel offered no compromise. His strength of character was rooted in his Byzantine Christianity. At one time the humiliated vassal of the Ottoman Sultan in Anatolia, at another the honoured guest of Charles VI in Paris and of Henry IV in London, Manuel's personality and dignity won the admiration of Turks and Christians alike.[32] He did not change in changing circumstances. Nor did he offer as an incentive to the popes and princes of the west the conversion of himself or his people to the Roman Church. He asked only for the unconditional help of fellow Christians in the defence of a worthy cause of which he was a worthy representative. The tragedy was that the cause was already lost.[33]

Manuel II died in 1425. He was succeeded by his son John VIII Palaiologos. The historian Sphrantzes records a conversation that he overheard in the palace between Manuel and John. On the subject of relations with the Latins the old Emperor advised his son strongly against offering the union of the Churches as a bait. It would only make the Turks more suspicious and undermine the loyalty of the Greeks.[34] John VIII chose to ignore his father's sage advice, and reverted to the view that the only way to save the remnants of his Empire from the Turks was to win the favour of the Pope. The result was the

32 The Sultan Bajezid is said to have likened Manuel II to the Prophet and to have declared that even those ignorant of his imperial status would know from his appearance that he was an emperor. Pseudo-Phrantzes (Makarios Melissenos), in Georgios Sphrantzes, *Memorii 1401–1477*, ed. V. Grecu (Bucharest, 1966), p. 256 lines 11–12. The monk of St Denys who saw Manuel in Paris remarked that his dignified bearing marked him out as a worthy emperor: *Chronique du Religieux de Saint-Denys, contenant le règne de Charles VI, de 1380 à 1422*, ed. M. G. Bellaguet, II (Paris, 1840), p. 756. For the English reaction, see D. M. Nicol, 'A Byzantine emperor in England. Manuel II's visit to London in 1400–1401', *University of Birmingham Historical Journal*, XII, 2 (1971), pp. 204–25, esp. pp. 214–15 (reprinted in Nicol, *Byzantium...Collected Studies*, no. X).
33 On Manuel II's career in general, see Barker, *Manuel II Palaeologus*.
34 Ps.-Phrantzes, in Sphrantzes, *Memorii*, ed. Grecu, p. 320.

union of the Churches proclaimed, after weary months of
argument, at the Council of Florence in 1439. On 6 July
of that year Pope Eugenius IV, who had convened and
presided over that Council, called upon the heavens to
rejoice that the wall dividing eastern and western Christendom for 437 years had at last been demolished.[35] In the
excitement and relief of the moment there were some
Byzantines who believed this to be true. A few of them
never wavered from that belief. The Byzantine delegation
to Florence was the most impressive ever to travel from
east to west. It was led by the Emperor John VIII and the
Patriarch, and it included some 700 Orthodox bishops and
dignitaries of Church and state. This was no limited act
of submission to Rome as undertaken by John V in 1369.
It was, or it purported to be, an oecumenical act, a
declaration of the whole theocratic society of Byzantium.
But this of course it could not be and never was.

The only one of the Greek bishops who refused to sign
the act of union at Florence was Mark Eugenikos, Bishop
of Ephesos. He was the only Byzantine delegate later to
be canonised as a Confessor by the Orthodox Church.
Mark of Ephesos was a bigot, but he was made so by his
experiences at Florence. Much attention has been drawn
to his anti-Latin fulminations but very little to his ascetic
and spiritual writings. He was a hesychast monk in the
other-worldly tradition of apophatic Byzantine theology.
As such he was distressed and finally embittered by the
complacent materialism of the subtle Latin theologians at
Florence. And he was shocked by the moral compromises
which his Orthodox colleagues seemed prepared to make
for the hope of material rewards. Like the monks of
Constantinople, who were behind him to a man, Mark
felt that the surest way to forfeit the protection of God
and His Mother and bring the City to destruction was to
betray the Orthodoxy of its people. The Emperor John
VIII, who had tried to betray as little as possible of his

---

35 Gill, *Council of Florence*, pp. 270–304, esp. pp. 289–96. The Latin text of
   the Decree of Union (*Laetentur Caeli*) is reproduced *ibid.* pp. 412–15.

Orthodoxy at Florence in the hope of winning military and financial support for his dying cause, may well have suspected that Mark Eugenikos was a more honest man than himself.[36]

It was noted at the time that the Catholic spokesmen at the Council of Florence thought with one mind and spoke with one voice, whereas the Byzantines held various opinions and fought shy of rigid definitions. They seemed to have no prepared position which they unanimously defended. This was undoubtedly true. The Byzantine delegation reflected the variety of views and sentiments of a society whose nerve was failing. There were a few who, in the tradition of Demetrios Kydones, were already half in love with Italian humanism or Latin theology and who saw the future in terms of a symbiosis of two cultures. There were many who, as the months of debate and argument dragged on, grew increasingly restless and nostalgic and would sign almost anything to secure their escape. There were in particular three men who, in their widely differing ways, represented the last flowering of that Byzantine revival of sanctitiy and scholarship which had its roots in the fourteenth century. They were Bessarion of Nicaea, George Scholarios and George Gemistos Plethon.

Bessarion attended the Council as titular Bishop of Nicaea. He was a Platonist with little taste for western scholasticism. But the debates at Florence persuaded him that Greek and Latin theology were not incompatible. Like Demetrios Kydones, he believed that the west had much to offer in the way of culture and learning. He too accepted the Roman creed and doctrine. He settled in

36 On Mark Eugenikos, see J. Gill, 'The year of the death of Mark Eugenicus', *BZ*, LII (1959), pp. 23–31; Gill, *Council of Florence, passim*; A. Schmemann, Ὁ Ἅγιος Μάρκος ὁ Εὐγενικός, Γρηγόριος ὁ Παλαμᾶς, XXIV (1951), pp. 34–43, 230–41; Tatakis, *Philosophie byzantine*, pp. 295–7; L. Petit, in *DTC*, IX, 2, cols. 1968–86; Beck, *Kirche und theologische Literatur*, pp. 755–8; C. N. Tsirpanlis, *Mark Eugenicus and the Council of Florence. A Historical Re-evaluation of his Personality* (Thessalonike, 1974); Podskalsky, *Theologie und Philosophie in Byzanz*, pp. 219–20.

Italy and was made a cardinal. His Orthodox colleagues condemned him as a traitor. But he never lost his love of his Hellenic heritage. The library of Greek manuscripts which Bessarion took with him to Italy was one of the media through which that heritage was broadcast to the west. Bessarion was, as Lorenzo Valla described him, *Latinorum graecissimus, Graecorum latinissimus.*[37]

His contemporary, George Scholarios, took another road. He was a hesychast by inclination. But he too admired some aspects of western culture, in particular the works of Thomas Aquinas and the techniques of scholastic theology. His commentaries on Aristotle take note of the contributions of western and Arabic as well as of Byzantine scholars. It may then seem surprising that, having attended the Council of Florence and subscribed to the union there proclaimed, Scholarios should have had doubts when he got back to Constantinople. But his doubts were the honest if (at the time) muddled doubts of one who was first and foremost a Byzantine. He found it harder than Bessarion to sever his Byzantine roots and settle in a foreign land where his Hellenism would be well received. He felt that he had a duty to his native city and to his native culture. He was rewarded with an almost impossible challenge. For it was he who, as the monk Gennadios, was appointed the first Patriarch of Constantinople under the Ottoman dispensation after 1453; it was he who had the delicate task of working out a lasting concordat between triumphant Muslims and humiliated Christians – a task

37 On Bessarion, see: L. Mohler, *Kardinal Bessarion als Theologe, Humanist und Staatsmann*, 3 vols. (Paderborn, 1923–7, 1942); A. A. Kyrou, *Βησσαρίων ὁ ῞Ελλην*, 2 vols. (Athens, 1947); Beck, *Kirche und theologische Literatur*, pp. 767–9; L. Bréhier, in *DHGE*, viii, cols. 1181–99; Tatakis, *Philosophie byzantine*, pp. 294ff., 297–300, 303–30; Setton, 'Byzantine background', pp. 73–4; Gill, *Council of Florence, passim*; Gill, 'The sincerity of Bessarion the Unionist', *Journal of Theological Studies*, xxvi (1975), pp. 377–92; Gill, 'Was Bessarion a Conciliarist or a Unionist before the Council of Florence?', *Collectanea Byzantina* (*OCA*, 204: Rome, 1977), pp. 201–19; Z. V. Udalcova, 'Žizn' i dejatelnost' Vissariona Nikejskogo', *VV*, xxxvii (1976), pp. 74–97; Podskalsky, *Theologie und Philosophie in Byzanz*, pp. 226ff.

in which his understanding of the mentality of the Byzantines and a feeling for their own tradition must have been more helpful than a knowledge of Plato and Aristotle.[38] Gennadios was not wholly successful; and in his declining years he relieved his despair at the enslavement and decadence of his flock by ever more confident predictions that there was not long to go, that the end of the world was indeed scheduled for the year 1492.[39]

George Gemistos Plethon was surely the least representative of all the Byzantines at Florence. Like Bessarion he was interested in bridging the intellectual and cultural gap between Greeks and Latins. But in him the wind of Hellenism blew so strong that it extinguished his Christian faith. The proceedings at the Council of Florence confirmed his opinion that the only hope for the world was to dispense with Christianity altogether and to evolve a completely new philosophy of life and politics.[40] It was at Mistra in Greece, far away from the beleaguered capital,

---

38 The works of George Scholarios (Gennadios) are edited by L. Petit, X. A. Siderides and M. Jugie, Oeuvres complètes de Gennade Scholarios, 8 vols. (Paris, 1928–36). See also: M. Jugie, in *DTC*, XIV, cols. 1521–70; Beck, *Kirche und theologische Literatur*, pp. 760–3; Gill, *Council of Florence, passim*; Turner, 'Pages', esp. pp. 365–73; Turner, 'George-Gennadius Scholarios and the Union of Florence', *Journal of Theological Studies*, XVIII (1967), pp. 83–103; Turner, 'The career of George-Gennadius Scholarius', *B*, XXXIX (1969), pp. 420–55; Runciman, *Great Church*, pp. 104–7, 125–7, 168–70, 182–6, 193–4, 280–1; G. Podskalsky, 'Die Rezeption der thomistischen Theologie bei Gennadios II. Scholarios (ca. 1403–1472)', *Theologie und Philosophie*, XLIX (1974), pp. 350–73; Podskalsky, *Theologie und Philosophie in Byzanz*, pp. 222–6.
39 See esp. Turner, 'Pages', pp. 370–1.
40 From the extensive literature on George Gemistos Plethon, see esp.: F. Masai, *Pléthon et le platonisme de Mistra* (Paris, 1956); M. Anastos, 'Pletho's calendar and liturgy', *DOP*, IV (1948), pp. 183–305; A. Diller, 'Plutarch and Pletho', *Scriptorium*, VIII (1954), pp. 123–7; A. Keller, 'Two Byzantine scholars and their reception in Italy', *Journal of the Warburg and Courtauld Institutes*, XX (1957), pp. 363–70; Tatakis, *Philosophie byzantine*, pp. 281–306; Runciman, *Last Byzantine Renaissance*, pp. 77–8; A. E. Vakalópoulos, *Origins of the Greek Nation, 1204–1461* (New Brunswick, N.J., 1970), pp. 126–35, 171–2, 179–80, 184–5; T. S. Nikolaou, Αἱ περὶ πολιτείας καὶ δικαίου ἰδέαι τοῦ Γ. Πλήθωνος Γεμιστοῦ (Thessalonike, 1974); Medvedev, *Vizantijskij Gumanism, passim*; Podskalsky, *Theologie und Philosophie in Byzanz*, pp. 82–6, 220–1.

that Plethon developed his ideas for the regeneration of what he was pleased to call the Hellenic people. This was to be achieved not by breathing new life into the dying body of the Roman Empire but by a reform of society along lines suggested by Plato's *Republic*. Early in the fifteenth century Plethon addressed to the Emperor Manuel II and his son Theodore a series of memoranda on the ways in which Hellenism could be recreated on the Hellenic soil of the Peloponnese.[41] They amounted to an elaborate and comprehensive programme for the reform of the administration, the defence, the economy and the structure of society. They contain some of the most original ideas ever expressed by a Byzantine scholar. But far more strikingly – and more dangerously – original were Plethon's ideas on religion, which he committed to writing late in his life in a treatise called *On the Laws*. Here he concocted a new 'Hellenic' religion worthy of credence by his regenerated Hellenes. The myths of Christianity were to be supplanted by an artificial theology and ethical system based on Plato and neoplatonism. God reverted to being Zeus and the rest of the ancient Greek pantheon were suitably accommodated as the new presiding deities. The treatise was never published; and when the text came into the hands of Plethon's friend, the Patriarch Gennadios, he considered it his duty as a Christian to destroy it, lest

41 Plethon's memoranda on the Peloponnese are in Sp. Lambros, Παλαιο-
λόγεια καὶ Πελοποννησιακά, III (Athens, 1926), pp. 246–65; IV (Athens,
1930), pp. 113–35; also in *MPG*, CLX, cols. 821–40, 841–66. Extracts are
trans. by Barker, *Social and Political Thought in Byzantium*, pp. 198–212.
Cf. D. A. Zakythenos, *Le Despotat grec de Morée (1262–1460)* (rev. edn:
London, 1975), I, pp. 175–80; II, 322–9, 349–56 and *passim*. I. P.
Medvedev, *Mistra. Očerki istorii i kultury pozdnevizantijskogo goroda*
(Mistra. Essays on the history and culture of a late Byzantine town)
(Leningrad, 1973), *passim*. Bessarion also produced a programme of
reforms for the Empire, beginning with the Peloponnese, which he sent
to the Despot and future Emperor Constantine Palaiologos from Italy in
1444. Sp. Lambros, Ὑπόμνημα τοῦ καρδιναλίου Βησσαρίωνος εἰς Κωνσταντῖνον τὸν Παλαιολόγον, *NH*, III (1906), pp. 15–27; also in Lambros,
Παλαιολόγεια καὶ Πελοποννησιακά, IV, pp. 32–45. Cf. A. Pertusi, 'In
margine alla questione dell'umanesimo bizantino: il pensiero politico del
cardinale Bessarione e i suoi rapporti con il pensiero di Giorgio Gemisto
Pletone', *Rivista di studi bizantini e neoellenici*, N.S., V (1968), pp. 95–104.

it should lead to the spread of atheism and blasphemy. Thus was lost the only really fresh and independent development of the classical heritage that came out of the Byzantine 'renaissance' of the last centuries of the Empire.[42]

Plethon died in 1452, one year before the end. Like his friend Bessarion, though for different reasons, he had become something of a hero in Italy. It is significant that both men were buried there and not in Byzantine soil. For both were acclaimed with greater honour by the Latins than by their own people.[43] The true Renaissance in Italy was eager to use the talents of such learned men in ways that were not open to the dying culture of Byzantium. One can understand why many of the Byzantine exiles who went to Italy in the fifteenth century found the passage from Orthodoxy to Roman Catholicism to be, after all, painless. In the west they had a marketable commodity in the form of their Hellenism.[44] To Italian humanists the end of the *Byzantine* world was of little consequence. Their interest in Hellenism or *Graecitas* was directed to the past, not to the present. The reaction of Aeneas Sylvius, the future Pope Pius II, to the fall of Constantinople was not so much to weep for Byzantium or for Orthodox Christianity as to lament 'the second death of Homer and Plato'.[45] The Greeks of the diaspora

42 The surviving parts of Plethon's treatise *On the Laws* (Νόμων συγγραφή) are edited by C. Alexandre as *Pléthon, Traité des Lois* (Paris, 1858: reprinted Amsterdam, 1966). Extracts are trans. into English in Barker, *Social and Political Thought in Byzantium*, pp. 212–19, and into Russian in Medvedev, *Vizantijskij Gumanism*, pp. 171–241. Cf. Masai, *Pléthon et le platonisme*, pp. 393–404.

43 Plethon was at first buried at Mistra, but in 1465 his remains were taken to Rimini by Sigismond Malatesta. On his tomb and its inscription in the cathedral at Rimini, see Masai, *Pléthon et la platonisme de Mistra*, pp. 362–5. Bessarion, who died as a Cardinal in 1472, was buried in the Basilica of the Holy Apostles in Rome. Kyrou, *Βησσαρίων...*, II, p. 250.

44 See D. J. Geanakoplos, *Greek Scholars in Venice. Studies in the Dissemination of Greek Learning from Byzantium to Western Europe* (Cambridge, Mass., 1962) (reprinted as *Byzantium and the Renaissance* [Hamden, Conn., 1972]); Geanakoplos, *Interaction of the " Sibling" Cultures.*

45 Letter of Aeneas Sylvius to Pope Nicholas V, dated 12 July 1453, ed. R. Wolkan, *Der Briefwechsel des Eneas Silvius Piccolomini*, III, I, in *Fontes Rerum*

in Italy after 1453 found that it paid to present themselves as the descendants of Pericles and Plato rather than as rootless and pitiable Byzantines. They were admired for their expertise in the Classics, not for their Christianity. It is significant that the first text of one of the Greek Church Fathers to be printed (about 1470) was the Latin translation of St Basil's address to young Christians on how to benefit from the Greek Classics.[46] The exiles from the wreck of Byzantium naturally encouraged the belief that they were Hellenes first and foremost.

But in the world that they had left behind what survived the wreck was the Byzantine Church and Orthodox spirituality, keeping Hellenism, as the Church had always advised, subordinate to the inner wisdom and the eternal truths of Christianity. Plethon has been hailed as a Hellene before his time, 'the most ardent devotee of Hellenic civilization', 'the first true spokesman of Neo-Hellenism'.[47] But in truth he was none of these things. He was never a Hellene in any ethnic sense and he had out-thought his Byzantinism.[48] The same may be said to

Austriacarum, LXVIII (Vienna, 1918), pp. 189–202; reproduced in A. Pertusi, *La Caduta di Costantinopoli*, II: *L'eco nel mondo* (Verona, 1976), p. 46 lines 30–5: 'Quid de libris dicam, qui illic erant innumerabiles, nondum Latinis cogniti? Heu, quot nunc magnorum nomina virorum peribunt? Secunda mors ista Homero est, secundus Platoni obitus. Ubi nunc philosophorum aut poetarum ingenia requiremus? Extinctus est fons musarum.' Cf. his letter to Cardinal Nicholas of Cues in August 1453, ed. Wolkan, *Der Briefwechsel*, III, 1, pp. 206–15; Pertusi, *La Caduta*, II, p. 54 lines 79–82: 'Nunc ergo et Homero et Pindaro et Menandro et omnibus illustrioribus poetis secunda mors erit. Nunc Graecorum philosophorum ultimus patebit interitus.' Aeneas Sylvius had a rather romantic view of the level of education and culture in Constantinople. His celebrated remark that 'nemo Latinorum satis videri doctus poterat, nisi Constantinopoli per tempus studuisset' (in Pertusi, *La Caduta*, II, p. 52 lines 53–5) contrasts with the observations of George Scholarios about 1450, who sadly remarks that only three or four people in the city were concerned with learning, and that of a very superficial nature, and that the Byzantines would soon be little better culturally than the barbarians. Gennadios Scholarios, *Letter to his Pupils*, ed. Petit, Siderides, Jugie, *Oeuvres complètes*, IV, pp. 406–7.

46 Geanakoplos, *Interaction of the "Sibling" Cultures*, pp. 270–2.

47 Cf., e.g., Vacalopoulos, *Origins of the Greek Nation*, p. 126.

48 See esp. H.-G. Beck, 'Reichsidee und nationale Politik im spätbyzantin-ischen Staat', *BZ*, LIII (1960), pp. 86–94 (reprinted in Beck, *Ideen und*

a lesser extent of Bessarion and of Kydones. But George Gemistos Plethon was the only Byzantine who fundamentally questioned his inherited ideology, the concept of a theocratic society. He was typical of no one but himself. He is the odd man out.

Mark Eugenikos, Bessarion and George Scholarios, on the other hand, never allowed themselves to think beyond the frontiers of their Byzantinism. Spiritual and intellectual giants they may have been, but neither their sanctity nor their scholarship led them to question the divine order of things. They did not stray far from the middle road of Byzantine intellectualism. The road is well mapped by the career of a much lesser figure who knew them all – John Chortasmenos, whose life spanned the last decades of the fourteenth century and the first decades of the fifteenth century.[49] Neither a saint nor much of a scholar but determined to acquire the characteristics of both, Chortasmenos spent his early years as a notary in the patriarchal chancellery in Constantinople. He was there during the long blockade of the city by the Turks between 1394 and 1402.[50] But his many writings tell little of the stirring events of his time. His letters, meticulously composed according to the rules of ancient epistolography, were, like his poems and rhetorical works, meant to be admired for their style more than for their content.[51] They were to be read, discussed and criticised in the literary salon of the emperor. The circle of initiates was smaller and perhaps even more pedantic than it had been in the days of

---

Realitäten in Byzanz. Collected Studies [Variorum: London, 1972], no. VI). Cf. Medvedev, *Vizantijskij Gumanism*, pp. 126ff. Significantly enough, it was (*pace* Beck, 'Reichsidee', p. 87) the Patriarch Gennadios and not Plethon whom Constantine Sathas designated as 'the last Byzantine and the first Hellene'. C. Sathas, *Documents inédits relatifs à l'histoire de la Grèce au moyen âge*, IV (Paris, 1833), p. VII.

49 H. Hunger, *Johannes Chortasmenos (ca. 1370–ca. 1436/37). Briefe, Gedichte und kleine Schriften* (Wiener byzantinische Studien, VII: Vienna, 1969). Cf. Hunger, 'Johannes Chortasmenos, ein byzantinischer Intellektueller der späten Palaiologenzeit', *Wiener Studien*, LXX (1957), pp. 153–63 (reprinted in Hunger, *Byzantinische Grundlagenforschung*, no. XXIV).

50 Hunger, *Johannes Chortasmenos*, p. 16.

51 Hunger, *Johannes Chortasmenos*, p. 35.

Andronikos II. But it still existed at the court of Manuel II, and not to belong to it was to have missed the boat as an intellectual.

Chortasmenos claimed to be poor and in need of funds and patronage. He supplemented his salary by giving private tuition to boys of wealthy families. Yet he contrived to build up a rich library and spent long hours copying manuscripts in his own hand. His interests were wide. Copies of the ancient orators Aristides and Libanios, of Euripides, Aristotle, Plutarch, Euclid and Ptolemy sat alongside manuscripts of later and contemporary writers such as Psellos, Akropolites, Demetrios Kydones and Theodore Metochites.[52] The cult of mathematics and astronomy as the noblest of the sciences, revived by Pachymeres and Metochites, still had its devotees in the fifteenth century, and Chortasmenos was keen to be among them.[53] On the whole he was a rather tiresome, self-centred bachelor and given to complaining about his imaginary ailments.[54] Spiritually he was no great athlete. He tried his hand at hagiography as a matter of course; and he knew the social as well as the moral value of true religion. Two of his letters, one to Manuel Chrysoloras who was then on the road to Rome, reveal his position as a champion of Orthodox doctrine; and in his later years Chortasmenos became a monk with the name of Ignatios. As a result he ended his days as Metropolitan of Selymbria in Thrace, although the chances are that he continued to live in Constantinople.[55]

The works of Chortasmenos do not give the impression

52 Hunger, *Johannes Chortasmenos*, pp. 26–7. On the high cost of books in Byzantium, see Reynolds and Wilson, *Scribes and Scholars*, p. 57; N. G. Wilson, 'Books and readers in Byzantium', in *Books and Bookmen* (Dumbarton Oaks: Washington, D.C., 1975), pp. 1–15, esp. pp. 3–4.
53 Hunger, *Johannes Chortasmenos*, pp. 41–2.
54 See H. Hunger, 'Allzu Menschliches aus dem Privatleben eines Byzantiners. Tagebuchnotizen des Hypochonders Johannes Chortasmenos', *Polychronion. Festschrift Franz Dölger* (Munich, 1966), pp. 244–52.
55 Letters to Manuel Chrysoloras and to Joseph Bryennios, ed. Hunger, nos. 29 and 11, in Hunger, *Johannes Chortasmenos*. For his monastic life, see *ibid.* pp. 17–18.

that the end of the world is nigh. Style and order still
prevail among the right people, at least in the capital. The
club is smaller and membership has become even more
expensive, but the rules are the same. One of his more
original and revealing works is a collection of fourteen
precepts on the successful conduct of life in the society
of his time.[56] Nine of the precepts are 'secular' and five
'spiritual' in content. The preface makes the clear and still
valid distinction between the two estates, the monastic (or
'evangelic') and the worldly (or 'cosmic'). Those who opt
for the former will find that the regulations are plainly laid
down. Those who choose the world will find that things
are not so simple and that they are often torn between
what is pleasing to God and what is pleasing to their fellow
men.[57] The precepts, distilled from the author's personal
experience, are meant to show how it is possible to succeed
in the world without compromising too much of one's
godliness. In particular it is vital never to question the
eternal verities of religion, for to be heard doing so might
lead to all manner of unfortunate consequences and the
end of one's career. Similarly, one must bear in mind that
the only abiding realities are those revealed in Holy
Scripture and that every thought expressed by man alone,
however respectably 'Hellenic' its origins, is nothing but
an opinion, assumption or supposition.[58]

Given these self-evident truths, the road to success and
contentment in the small and jealous world of the
Byzantine establishment had to be steered through
potholes and pitfalls of a more sordid nature. The golden
rule was not to stick one's neck out. It was important to
be respectful, even to the point of servility, to those in
power. On the other hand one should not approach them
too frequently for fear of earning their contempt.[59] It was

56 The *Moral Precepts* ('Ηθικὰ παραγγέλματα) are edited by Hunger, in
   Johannes Chortasmenos, no. VII, pp. 238–42. Cf. pp. 33–4, 135–6. See also
   Ševčenko, 'Society and intellectual life', pp. 22–3.
57 Hunger, *Johannes Chortasmenos*, p. 238.
58 Hunger, *Johannes Chortasmenos*, no. 4, p. 239; no. 12, p. 241.
59 Hunger, *Johannes Chortasmenos*, nos. 2 and 5, p. 239.

a good thing to be seen to have an air of poverty, for it is better to be pitiable than enviable.[60] This precept applied to speech as well as to practice. One should never show off one's eloquence at meetings even if one has something worth saying. The man who keeps his silence on such occasions is likely to be admired as a repository of hidden wisdom.[61] It was likewise a mistake to keep company too much with one's fellow intellectuals or to initiate discussion with them. Again, better to keep one's peace, to listen rather than to speak, and to praise what others said even if it went against the truth; for no one ever gave tongue in such circles for the sake of advancing his knowledge, only for the sake of displaying it.[62]

These are not the precepts of a fearless and original seeker after truth or of one likely to present fundamental and disturbing challenges to the existing order. But they are eloquent of the mentality which respected that order in society which had been divinely ordained. John Chortasmenos, with all his conservatism, pedantry and cautious compromising, was at one time or another the teacher of such comparatively remarkable men as Mark Eugenikos, Bessarion and George Scholarios. He therefore has much to answer for.[63]

George Gemistos Plethon does not so easily fit into the Byzantine pattern. There is no certainty about the course of his education. Some of it was doubtless acquired in Constantinople, though the names of his teachers are not recorded. But he is known to have spent some time as a young man at the Turkish court at Adrianople, where he is said to have been initiated into Zoroastrianism by a mysterious Jewish scholar. Much of his learning was acquired from his own reading, of Psellos, Plutarch and

60 Hunger, *Johannes Chortasmenos*, no. 6, p. 240.
61 Hunger, *Johannes Chortasmenos*, no. 14, pp. 241–2.
62 Hunger, *Johannes Chortasmenos*, no. 10, p. 240.
63 For Chortasmenos as the teacher of Mark Eugenikos, see Hunger, *Johannes Chortasmenos*, pp. 13, 17; as the teacher of Bessarion and Scholarios, see *ibid.* pp. 13, 14, 18, 23.

above all Plato.[64] There was nothing unusual in this. The oddity about Plethon is that he went on to build new structures on the foundation of his acquired learning. He was not content to compile, to select and to imitate; and in the end he made himself guilty of the capital sin of innovation, novelty, heresy.

Could there have been more like him? Could Byzantium at the end of the world have produced the purveyors of new ideas? It seems improbable. One noticeable symptom of the failure of nerve in the Empire's last century is the total absence of historiography. Ever since the revival of classical scholarship in the tenth century almost every generation of Byzantine society had brought forth more or less literate historians, painfully modelling their works on the great prototypes of Greek Antiquity. But the writing of contemporary history comes to an abrupt end about the year 1360, at the point where Gregoras and Cantacuzene laid down their pens.[65] It seems that no one living at the time felt strong enough to record the sad events of the one hundred years before 1453. There are eyewitness accounts of isolated incidents, such as the siege of Constantinople by the Turks in 1422 or the final capture and sack of Thessalonica in 1430.[66] But the last Byzantine historians to write narrative histories in the traditional style all lived in the fifteenth century, after Constantinople had fallen to the Turks. All of them, Sphrantzes, Doukas, Kritoboulos and Chalkokondyles, were looking back on an age that had irretrievably ended. They had themselves

64 On Plethon's education and early life, see Masai, *Pléthon et le platonisme*, pp. 52ff.; Tatakis, *Philosophie byzantine*, pp. 282–3.

65 The last event recorded in the *History* of Gregoras, and that out of context, is the death of Gregory Palamas, which occurred on 14 November 1359: Gregoras, III, pp. 549–52. Cf. J. L. van Dieten (ed.), *Nikephoros Gregoras, Rhomäische Geschichte*, I (Stuttgart, 1973), pp. 34, 36–41. The last event in the *History* of Kantakouzenos is the reinstatement of the Patriarch Philotheos, which took place on 8 October 1364: Kantakouzenos, III, p. 363.

66 John Kananos (Cananus), *De Constantinopoli oppugnata (1422)*, ed. I. Bekker; John Anagnostes, *De Thessalonicensi excidio narratio*, ed. I. Bekker: both in Phrantzes (*CSHB*, 1838), pp. 457–79, 481–528.

survived, and so they were not surprised that the world had not ended with the passing of that age; and for this evident fact each had his own explanation to offer.[67]

Sphrantzes begins his work (which is in the form of memoirs) with the statement that it would have been well for him if he had not been born or if he had died as a child; but this turns out to be no more than a pious platitude.[68] He had been a prominent statesman and diplomat of the last two emperors, had been captured by the Turks and escaped first to the Peloponnese and then to Corfu, where he died after 1478.[69] His experiences had not made him a sceptic; but with hindsight he was inclined to attribute the end of the Empire more to bad foreign policy than to the workings of providence. He singles out the Council of Florence and the union of the Churches as the prime and main cause of the fall of Constantinople to the infidel, not so much because of the betrayal of Orthodoxy as because the act of union was mistaken and dangerous policy. The Turks had been driven to action by this ill-judged entente between their Greek and Latin Christian enemies.[70]

Doukas, on the other hand, who spent much of his life in the service of the Genoese lords of the island of Lesbos, regarded the union of the Churches as the only means by which Byzantium might have been saved, and the anti-unionists as the agents of disaster. The concept of divine

67 See esp. C. J. G. Turner, 'Pages', pp. 352–65.
68 G. Sphrantzes, *Memorii*, ed. Grecu, p. 2 line 5.
69 On the career and works of Sphrantzes, see: R.-J. Loenertz, 'Autour du Chronicon Maius attribué à Georges Phrantzès', *Miscellanea Giovanni Mercati*, III (Studi e Testi, 123: Vatican City, 1946), pp. 273–311 (reprinted in Loenertz, *Byzantina et Franco-Graeca*, pp. 3–44); V. Grecu, 'Georgios Sphrantzes. Leben und Werk. Makarios Melissenos und sein Werk', *BS*, XXVI (1965), pp. 62–73; A. Pertusi, *La Caduta di Costantinopoli*, I: *Le Testimonianze dei Contemporanei* (Verona, 1976), pp. 214–15.
70 Sphrantzes, *Memorii*, ed. Grecu, p. 318 lines 34–7: "Ὅτι καὶ αὐτὴ ἡ τῆς συνόδου ὑπόθεσις ἦν αἰτία πρώτη καὶ μεγάλη, ἵνα γένηται ἡ κατὰ τῆς Κωνσταντινουπόλεως τῶν ἀσεβῶν ἔφοδος, καὶ ἀπὸ ταύτης πάλιν ἡ πολιορκία καὶ αἰχμαλωσία καὶ τοιαύτη καὶ τοσαύτη συμφορὰ ἡμῶν. Cf. Turner, 'Pages', pp. 352–6.

punishment for sin runs through the pages of Doukas.[71] But he also vividly recalls the despair of the Byzantines at the eleventh hour. All that they could say was: 'Now the end of the City is at hand. Now the bell tolls for the destruction of our race. Now is the day of the Antichrist. What will become of us and what will we do? Oh Lord, let our lives be taken from us before the eyes of Thy servants witness the fall of the City and Thine enemies say, Lord, where are the Saints who protect it?'[72]

Kritoboulos and Chalkokondyles were both living in the present rather than in the past. They tried to demonstrate that the transition from a Christian to a Muslim Empire, though unfortunate, was inevitable. Both seem a little tired of 'Christian' or millenarian explanations of the transition. Like Metochites they believed more in the workings of fortune or fate than of providence or divine retribution. They tried to make the best of the changed situation by seeing the best in their conquerors. Kritoboulos dedicated his *History* to 'the supreme *autokrator*, Emperor of Emperors, Muhammad . . . by the will of God invincible lord of land and sea'; and he declares his intention of recording the deeds of that Sultan who surpassed all others 'in virtue, courage, strategy, fortune and military experience'.[73] For him the transition had been completed by the Turkish conquest of Constantinople. The Empire, however, continued, though in a different form, and the new Emperor, appointed by God,

71 On Doukas, see: W. Miller, 'The historians Doukas and Phrantzes', *Journal of Hellenic Studies*, XLVI (1926), pp. 63–71; V. Grecu, 'Pour une meilleure connaissance de l'historien Doukas', *Mémorial Louis Petit* (Paris, 1948), pp. 128–41; Turner, 'Pages', pp. 356–8; S. K. Krasavina, 'Mirovozzrenie i socialno-političeskie vzgljady vizantijskogo istorika Duki', *VV*, XXXIV (1973), pp. 97–111; Pertusi, *La Caduta*, II, pp. 160–1, 342–3.
72 Doukas: Ducas, *Istoria*, ed. Grecu, p. 297 lines 6–11.
73 Kritoboulos: *Critobul din Imbros. Din Domnia lui Mahomed al II-lea anii 1451–1467*, ed. V. Grecu (Bucharest, 1963), p. 25 lines 3ff. (English trans., *Kritovoulos, History of Mehmed the Conqueror*, by C. T. Riggs [Princeton, N.J., 1954]). Cf. Turner, 'Pages', pp. 361–3; Pertusi, *La Caduta*, II, pp. 228–9; Z. V. Udalcova, 'K voprosu o socialno-političeskich vzgljadach vizantijskogo istorika XV v. Kritovula', *VV*, XII (1957), pp. 172–97.

was the Sultan-Basileus, the Conqueror. Chalkokondyles, the last Byzantine historian, who died about 1490, takes as the theme of his *History* not the fall of Byzantium but the origins and rise to power of the Ottoman people.[74] For him too the transition was complete and, for the time being, irreversible. Fate had ordained that it should be so. With his Herodotean view of history he could echo the rather academic myth that the sack of Constantinople had been the revenge of the barbarians for the sack of Troy.[75] But the wheel of fortune could turn again; and Chalko-kondyles looked forward to a day when a Greek emperor and his heirs would once again rule over a sizeable dominion and gather together the remnants of his people.[76]

Kritoboulos hoped that his version of events would be widely read and accepted throughout Europe. He would have been disappointed to know that only one manuscript of it has survived and that even that lay dormant until 1870.[77] Graphically though he and his fellow historians of the fifteenth century describe the fall of the City in 1453, they do not really compensate for the lack of a con-temporary Byzantine historian narrating the events lead-ing up to that disaster. This lack, as has been suggested, betrays a certain numbness of spirit or failure of nerve. The Turkish conquest of Serbia, the fatal battle of Kossovo in 1389, inspired a whole series of heroic ballads and legends.[78] The Serbians went down in a blaze of glory.

---

74 On Chalkokondyles, see W. Miller, 'The last Athenian historian: Laonikos Chalkokondyles', *Journal of Hellenic Studies*, XLII (1922), pp. 36–49; Turner, 'Pages', pp. 358–61; Pertusi, *La Caduta*, II, pp. 194–5; A. Wifstrand, *Laonikos Chalkokondyles, der letzte Athenen. Ein Vortrag* (Scripta Minora Soc. Hum. Litt. Lundensis, 1971/2, 2: Lund, 1972).

75 *Laonici Chalcocandylae Historiarum Demonstrationes*, ed. E. Darkó (Budapest, 1922–7), II, p. 166 line 24–p. 167 line 4 (reproduced in Pertusi, *La Caduta*, II, p. 226 lines 420–6).

76 *Chalcocandylae*, ed. Darkó, I, p. 2. Cf. Vacalopoulos, *Origins of the Greek Nation*, pp. 232–3.

77 See *Kritoboulos*, ed. Grecu, pp. 9–10.

78 See H. W. V. Temperley, *History of Serbia* (London, 1917), pp. 99–105; C. J. Jireček, *Geschichte der Serben*, II (Gotha, 1918), pp. 119–21; M. Braun, *Kosovo, Die Schlacht auf dem Amselfeld in geschichtlicher und epischer Überlieferung* (Leipzig, 1937).

But no single battle decided the fate of Byzantium. The Byzantine Empire went down by a long process of attrition, which is not the stuff of heroics. After 1453 the fall of the City was commemorated not in ballads extolling the deeds of its heroes but in poetic Laments and Dirges which very quickly came to constitute a new genre of demotic Greek literature.[79] Some of their anonymous authors address appeals to the west, especially to Venice, to right the wrong done to Constantinople.[80] Some look ahead to the day when the last emperor will return and the Liturgy in St Sophia, so rudely interrupted when the Turks burst into the cathedral, will be resumed. St Sophia rather than the imperial palace or the hippodrome has become the symbol of continuity and of hope.[81] The Great Church had been desecrated and turned into a mosque. That in itself was a matter for Christian jeremiads. But when the dust of conquest had settled, when the Sultan Mehmed and the Patriarch Gennadios had worked out a *modus vivendi* for the Christian 'nation' under Muslim rule, it was found that the invisible Church, of which the Holy Wisdom was the symbol, had weathered the storm. The Empire of this world had gone but the Church remained. It had been proved after all that a Church without an emperor was a possibility.

The Church survived, humiliated but tolerated and

---

79 See H.-G. Beck, *Geschichte der byzantinischen Volksliteratur*, pp. 163–6; Pertusi, *La Caduta*, II, pp. 293ff.; G. Podskalsky, 'Der Fall Konstantinopels in der Sicht der Reichseschatologie und der Klagelieder', *Archiv für Kulturgeschichte*, LVII (1975), pp. 71–86.

80 In the *Threnos* for Constantinople edited by W. Wagner (*Medieval Greek Texts* [London, 1870], pp. 141–70), the author appeals first to Venice (p. 149 lines 296ff.), then to the Genoese (p. 150 lines 311ff.), then to France (p. 151 line 1f.), then to the English (p. 151 lines 345ff.) and other western nations.

81 The legend of the interrupted Liturgy and the disappearance of the priest into the wall of the sanctuary can be read in N. G. Politis, *Μελέται περὶ τοῦ βίου καὶ τῆς γλώσσης τοῦ Ἑλληνικοῦ λαοῦ. Παραδόσεις* (Athens, 1904), I, p. 23, no. 35; II, p. 678. Cf. G. Megas, 'La Prise de Constantinople dans la poésie et la tradition populaires grecques', *1453–1953. Le Cinq-Centième Anniversaire de la prise de Constantinople* (*L'Hellénisme Contemporain*: Athens, 1953), pp. 125–33, esp. p. 133; Runciman, *Fall of Constantinople*, p. 147.

protected under law. The laments and dirges were composed for the fall of a City, not of a Church. The old
Byzantine Constantinople, the Queen of Cities, may by
1453 have become seedy, depopulated and impoverished.
The new Constantinople, the Istanbul of the Turks, as it
was rebuilt and rehabilitated by the Conqueror, was to
become a splendid and thriving capital of a mighty
Empire, a monument to the worldly power and materialistic wealth of the Sultans. But the Byzantine spirit had
gone out of it, never to return. In the days before its fall
omens natural and supernatural had clearly portended the
event. On 24 May there had been a full moon and an
eclipse. The holiest icon of the Virgin had slipped from
its moorings when being carried round the walls. Thunder
and torrential hail flooded the steets, followed by a blanket
of fog. It was said that the God of the Christians was
deserting the city under cover of the cloud.[82] Turks and
Christians alike saw a mysterious light shining in the sky.
When it went out, the Sultan and his men exclaimed with
joy that God had now abandoned his city.[83] What they
were soon to discover, if they did not already know, was
that the Christians, the Christ-named people, would cling
to their God more loyally than ever when their world was
lost.

After 1453 the feeling grew stronger than ever that the
preservation of Christian society depended upon the
jealous preservation of Orthodoxy in the Church. The
Sultan fully endorsed this sentiment, since it was not in
his interest that the Greeks should find sympathy from
western Christians. Orthodoxy in its most inflexible,
anti-Latin form consequently became the inherited and
instinctive faith of the Greek people under Turkish rule.
They convinced themselves that, after all, the Sultan's
turban in their midst was preferable to the Latin mitre. The
conviction was not new. As early as the twelfth century

82 Kritoboulos, ed. Grecu, p. 119 line 14–p. 121 line 12.
83 Sphrantzes, *Memorii*, ed. Grecu, p. 40 lines 8–27. For accounts of other
    portents, see Runciman, *Fall of Constantinople*, pp. 121–2 and refs.

a patriarch had expressed his preference in these terms:
'Let the Muslim be my master in outward things rather
than the Latin dominate me in matters of the spirit. For
if I am subject to the Muslim, at least he will not force
me to share his faith. But if I have to be under Frankish
rule and united with the Roman Church, I may have to
separate myself from my God.'[84] To become a Latin or
a Frank was to endanger one's immortal soul. From the
Council of Lyons to the Council of Florence and beyond,
Church leaders had repeatedly warned the Byzantines
against the perils of 'Latinisation'. The monk Joseph
Bryennios had declared that no one should be deceived by
illusory hopes that an army from Italy might come to
their rescue. 'Even if they did come', he warned, 'it would
be not to save but to destroy our city, our race and our
name.'[85] The year before the end, in 1452, the monk
Gennadios, the future Patriarch, harangued the people on
the betrayal of their faith at Florence. By then he had seen
the error of his own ways. He posted a manifesto on the
door of his cell bearing witness before God that he would
sooner die than forswear the Orthodoxy that was his
heritage. The Union of Florence had been an evil thing.[86]

The battle of wits between Greeks and Latins at Ferrara
and Florence can be seen as the last and the greatest
confrontation between the heirs of two different traditions
and conflicting ideologies, the Byzantine and the Roman.
Walter Ullmann has recently summed it up in these

---

84 Patriarch Michael III of Anchialos, *Dialogue* with the Emperor Manuel
   I Komnenos (1170–1), ed. Ch. Loparev, 'Ob uniatstve imperatora
   Manuila Komnina', *VV*, xiv (1907), pp. 334–57 (Greek text: pp. 344–57);
   ed. K. Dyobouniotes, Διάλογος τοῦ πατριάρχου Κωνσταντινουπόλεως
   Μιχαὴλ Γʹ. τοῦ Ἀγχιάλου πρὸς τὸν αὐτοκράτορα τοῦ Βυζαντίου Μανουὴλ
   Αʹ. Κομνηνόν, *EEBS*, xv (1939), pp. 38–51. Cf. S. Runciman, *The Eastern
   Schism* (Oxford, 1955), p. 122; A. Bryer, in *Byzantium. An Introduction*,
   ed. P. Whitting (Oxford, 1971), p. 103.
85 Joseph Bryennios, Ἰωσὴφ..., ed. Boulgaris, i, p. 474.
86 Gennadios Scholarios, *Oeuvres complètes*, ed. Petit, Siderides, Jugie, iii, pp.
   165–6; Lambros, Παλαιολόγεια καὶ Πελοποννησιακά, ii, pp. 120–21. A
   slightly different version of the manifesto is recorded by Doukas, ed.
   Grecu, p. 317 lines 3–9.

words: 'Two cosmologies confronted each other. They were both universalist, though each setting out from different premises which paradoxically enough claimed Roman parentage. These premises make understandable that a genuine and enduring reconciliation of the Greek Church with the Latin Church was beyond human ingenuity.'[87] Certainly the myth of the universal, oecumenical Empire died hard in Byzantium. The Patriarch Philotheos gave a memorable account of it in 1352, part of which has already been quoted. Having explained the causes of the schism in the Christian Church and world in true Byzantine style, Philotheos concludes: 'And the situation now is such that those of the New Rome, that is to say all of us who belong to the universal Church and are subjects of the Roman Empire and therefore continue to call ourselves Romaioi, differ so greatly from those of the Old Rome and all the various principalities of that now divided nation that very few of them recognise the fact that they too were once Romans and of the same nation and Empire and that the cause of their present detachment from the Church as from the Empire is their own shortsightedness and folly.'[88] The Patriarch Antonios IV spelt out another version of the same myth to the Grand Duke of Moscow in 1393.[89]

Perhaps these men were, in Ullmann's words, clinging desperately to 'a Greek-Byzantine ideology, embedded . . . in a by now ossified historicity'.[90] But there were some Byzantines, like Kydones and Bessarion, who were able without too much pain to make the transition from one Roman-rooted cosmology to another. And it is noteworthy that the most eloquent champions of the universalist pretensions of Byzantium in its final years were not the emperors but the patriarchs. The leaders of the Church

87 W. Ullmann, 'A Greek Démarche on the Eve of the Council of Florence', *Journal of Ecclesiastical History*, XXVI (1975), pp. 337–52, esp. p. 341.
88 Philotheos, *Historical Discourse*, ed. Triantafillis and Grapputo, *Anecdota Graeca*, pp. 10–11.
89 See Ch. I, pp. 4–5 and n. 6.
90 Ullmann, 'A Greek Démarche', p. 346.

clung to the ossified ideology until the bitter end. They lost nothing by their persistence. The Orthodox Patriarchate and Church of Constantinople gained in authority and responsibility as a result of the Turkish conquest. The patriarch himself was now officially answerable to the state for all Christians under his jurisdiction; and the territory of that jurisdiction was for the first time for centuries united under single rule, infidel though that rule might be. No rescue operation from western Europe could ever have saved the whole Empire; and since the price of rescue, payable in advance, was always submission to Rome, it would have led to division rather than unity in the Church and society.

It was not because of its political ideology that the Orthodox Church survived under the infidel; and it is hard to believe that many Byzantines consciously felt that what divided them from the Latins was a different interpretation of cosmology. There was something deeper and less definable that most of them, even in their darkest hours, were afraid of losing if they accepted the Latin mitre rather than the Sultan's turban. Sir Steven Runciman, as so often, finds the appropriate words: 'The real bar to union was that Eastern and Western Christendom felt differently about religion; and it is difficult to debate about feelings.'[91] The Byzantines hardly needed to be warned against the danger to their souls of 'Latinisation'. The soul of a Byzantine was clearly understood to be more precious in the sight of God than the soul of a Latin or a Turk. But soul and body went together and the pollution of Latinisation was thought of in physical as well as in spiritual terms. One recalls the ritual cleansing of Orthodox churches which had been sullied by Latin priests, or the contaminated corpse of the Latinophile Emperor Michael VIII. Byzantinism was a psychosomatic condition, revealed at its highest spiritual level in the sanctity of an anchorite or the mystical-corporeal vision of a hesychast, revealed more commonly in the daily mysteries or sacra-

91 Runciman, *Great Church*, p. 85.

ments of the Church, revealed above all and in lasting
form for all to see and wonder at in Byzantine art.

Some modern scholars, especially Greeks, hold that the
anti-Latinism of the Byzantines was inspired by their
exclusive sense of being Hellenes and that it was this
binding force of Hellenism which in due course inspired
the War of Greek Independence and the foundation of the
modern Greek or Hellenic nation. This theory is flattering
to the Greek sense of ethnic continuity. But on other
grounds it is hard to substantiate. What the Byzantines of
the last centuries were afraid of losing was not a sense of
national identity, not their Hellenism, but their Byzantinism; and of this Orthodoxy in its pure and unadulterated
form was the noblest part. This much more than their
Hellenism marked them off from the gross and materialistic Latins and Turks. The Orthodox Church has often
been praised for having kept the torch of Hellenism alight
among the Greek-speaking people during the long years
of Turkish occupation in Europe. What the Church more
truly preserved was Byzantinism – a sense of spiritual
identity that was nourished by an irrational belief in the
interdependence of time and eternity, a sense of belonging
to a theocratic society.

EMPERORS

MICHAEL VIII Palaiologos 1259–82 (crowned Emperor at Nicaea Jan. 1259; at Constantinople 15 Aug. 1261; died 11 Dec. 1282)
Co-emperors:
  ANDRONIKOS II (from 8 Nov. 1272)
  MICHAEL IX (from 1281)

ANDRONIKOS II Palaiologos 1282–1328 (abdicated 24 May 1328; died 13 Feb. 1332)
Co-emperors:
  MICHAEL IX (crowned 21 May 1294; died 12 Oct. 1320)
  ANDRONIKOS III (crowned 2 Feb. 1325)

ANDRONIKOS III Palaiologos 1328–41 (died 14 June 1341)

JOHN V Palaiologos 1341–53 (crowned 19 Nov. 1341; dispossessed April 1353)

JOHN VI Kantakouzenos (Cantacuzene) 1347–54 (proclaimed as rival Emperor 26 Oct. 1341; crowned at Adrianople 21 May 1346; as senior Emperor with John V at Constantinople 21 May 1347; abdicated 9 Dec. 1354; died as monk 15 June 1383)
Co-emperor:
  MATTHEW Kantakouzenos (proclaimed April 1353; crowned Feb. 1354; dispossessed Dec. 1357; died 1383)

JOHN V Palaiologos 1354–76 (reinstated 9 Dec. 1354; dispossessed 12 Aug. 1376)

ANDRONIKOS IV Palaiologos 1376–9 (crowned 18 Oct. 1377; dispossessed 1 July 1379; died 28 June 1385)

JOHN V Palaiologos 1379–91 (reinstated 1 July 1379; died 16 Feb. 1391)

JOHN VII Palaiologos 1390 (usurper, 14 April–25 Aug. 1390)

MANUEL II Palaiologos 1391–1425 (proclaimed Co-emperor with John V 25 Sept. 1373; Emperor in Thessalonica 1382–7; crowned at Constantinople 11 Feb. 1392; died 21 July 1425)

Co-emperors:
  JOHN VII (10 Dec. 1399–June 1403; died Sept. 1408)
  JOHN VIII (crowned 19 Jan. 1421)

JOHN VIII Palaiologos 1425–48 (died 31 Oct. 1448)

CONSTANTINE XI Palaiologos Dragaš 1449–53 (crowned at Mistra 6 Jan. 1449; Emperor at Constantinople from 12 March 1449; died 29 May 1453)

PATRIARCHS OF CONSTANTINOPLE

Arsenios Autoreianos. 1254 – resigned Feb. 1260
Nikephoros II. March 1260 – died Feb. 1261
Arsenios Autoreianos (again). May/June 1261 – deposed May 1264
Germanos III. 25 May 1265 – deposed 14 Sept. 1266
Joseph I. 28 Dec. 1266 – resigned 9 Jan. 1275
John XI Bekkos. 26 May 1275 – deposed 26 Dec. 1282
Joseph I (again). 31 Dec. 1282 – died 23 March 1283
Gregory II of Cyprus. 28 March 1283 – resigned June 1289
Athanasios I. 14 Oct. 1289 – resigned 16 Oct. 1293
John XII Kosmas. 1 Jan. 1294 – resigned 21 June 1303
Athanasios I (again). 23 June 1303 – resigned Sept. 1309
Niphon I. 9 May 1310 – resigned 11 April 1314
John XIII Glykys. 12 May 1315 – resigned 11 May 1319
Gerasimos I. 21 March 1320 – died 20 April 1321
Esaias. 11 Nov. 1323 – died 13 May 1332
John XIV Kalekas. Feb. 1334 – deposed 2 Feb. 1347
Isidore I Boucheras. 17 May 1347 – died March 1350
Kallistos I. 10 June 1350 – resigned Aug. 1353
Philotheos Kokkinos. Aug. 1353 – resigned Nov. 1354
Kallistos I (again). Jan. 1355 – died Aug. 1363
Philotheos Kokkinos (again). 8 Oct. 1364 – 1376
Makarios. June/July 1377 – deposed July (?) 1379
Neilos. end 1379 – died 1 Feb. 1388
Antonios IV. 12 Jan. 1389 – deposed July 1390
Makarios (again). 30 July 1390 – died Feb. (?) 1391
Antonios IV (again). March 1391 – died May 1397
Kallistos II Xanthopoulos. 17 May 1397 – died Aug. 1397
Matthew I. Oct 1397 – died Aug. 1410
Euthymios II. 26 Oct. 1410 – died 29 March 1416
Joseph II. 21 May 1416 – died 10 June 1439
Metrophanes II. 4 May 1440 – died 1 Aug. 1443
Gregory III Mammas. Aug. 1443 – Aug. 1451 (left Constantinople for Rome)
Gennadios II Scholarios. 6 Jan. 1454 – 6 Jan. 1456

BIBLIOGRAPHY

Collections of sources

Acta Sanctorum Bollandiana (Antwerp–Paris–Rome–Brussels, 1643–)

Barker, E. *Social and Political Thought in Byzantium from Justinian I to the Last Palaeologus* (Oxford, 1957)

Bibliotheca Hagiographica Graeca, ed. F. Halkin (Subsidia Hagiographica, 8^a), 3 vols. (3rd edn: Brussels, 1957)

Boissonade, J. F. *Anecdota Graeca*, 5 vols. (Paris, 1829–33)

Boissonade, J. F. *Anecdota Nova* (Paris, 1844)

Chronica Byzantina Breviora, ed. P. Schreiner, *Die byzantinischen Kleinchroniken* (*CFHB* Series Vindobonensis, xii/1, xii/2: Vienna, 1975, 1977)

Corpus Fontium Historiae Byzantinae (Berlin–Rome–Washington–Vienna, 1967–) [*CFHB*]

Corpus Scriptorum Historiae Byzantinae (Bonn, 1828–97) [*CSHB*]

Darrouzès, J. *Les regestes des Actes du patriarcat de Constantinople*, I: *Les actes des patriarches*, fasc. V: *Les regestes de 1310 à 1376* (Paris, 1977).

Dölger, F. *Regesten der Kaiserurkunden des oströmischen Reiches* (*Corpus der griechischen Urkunden des Mittelalters und der neueren Zeit*, Reihe A, Abt. I), part III: 1204–82; part IV: 1282–1341; part V: 1341–1453 (Munich–Berlin, 1931–65)

Gill, J., ed. *Quae supersunt actorum graecorum Concilii Florentini* (Rome, 1953)

Lambros, Sp. P. *Παλαιολόγεια καὶ Πελοποννησιακά*, 4 vols. (Athens, 1912–30)

Laurent, V. *Les regestes des Actes du patriarcat de Constantinople*, I: *Les actes des patriarches*, fasc. IV: *Les regestes de 1208 à 1309* (Paris, 1971)

Laurent, V. and Darrouzès, J. *Dossier grec de l'Union de Lyon (1273–1277)* (Archives de L'Orient Chrétien, 16: Paris, 1976)

Mansi, J. D. *Sacrorum conciliorum nova et amplissima collectio*, 31 vols. (Florence–Venice, 1759–98)

Migne, J. P. *Patrologiae cursus completus. Series graeco-latina*, 161 vols. (Paris, 1857–66)

Miklosich, F. and Müller, J. *Acta et Diplomata graeca medii aevi sacra et profana*, 6 vols. (Vienna, 1860–90)

Papadopoulos-Kerameus, A. Ἀνάλεκτα Ἱεροσολυμιτικῆς Σταχυολογίας, 5 vols. (St Petersburg, 1891–8)

Papadopoulos-Kerameus, A. Ἱεροσολυμιτικὴ Βιβλιοθήκη, 4 vols. (St Petersburg, 1891–9)

Papadopoulos-Kerameus, A. *Varia Graeca Sacra* (St Petersburg, 1909)

Pertusi, A. *La Caduta di Costantinopoli*, I: *Le Testimonianze dei Contemporanei*; II: *L'eco nel mondo*, 2 vols. (Verona, 1976)

Rhalles, G. A. and Potles, M. Σύνταγμα τῶν θείων καὶ ἱερῶν κανόνων, 6 vols. (Athens, 1852–9)

Sathas, K. N. Μεσαιωνικὴ Βιβλιοθήκη. *Bibliotheca graeca medii aevi*, 7 vols. (Venice–Paris, 1872–94)

Sathas, K. N. Μνημεῖα Ἑλληνικῆς Ἱστορίας. *Documents inédits relatifs à l'histoire de la Grèce au moyen âge*, 9 vols. (Paris, 1880–90)

Theiner, A. and Miklosich, F. *Monumenta spectantia ad unionem ecclesiarum Graecae et Romanae* (Vienna, 1872)

Triantafillis, C. and Grapputo, A. *Anecdota Graeca e codicibus manu scriptis Bibliothecae S. Marci*, I (Venice, 1874)

Zepos, J. and Zepos, P. *Jus Graecoromanum*, 8 vols. (Athens, 1931)

Individual sources

Akropolites, George, *Historia. Georgii Acropolitae Opera*, I, ed. A. Heisenberg (Leipzig, 1903)

Anagnostes, John. *De Thessalonicensi excidio narratio*, ed. I. Bekker, in (S)Phrantzes (*CSHB*, 1838), pp. 481–528

Athanasios I, Patriarch, *Vita*. A. Papadopoulos-Kerameus, 'Žitija dvuch Vselenskich Patriarchov XIV v., svv. Afanasija I i Isidora I', *Zapiski istoriko-filolog. fakulteta Imperatorskago S.-Petersburgskago Universiteta*, LXXVI (1905), pp. 1–51; A. Pantokratorinos, 'Calotheti Vita Athanasii', *Thrakika*, XIII (1940), pp. 56–107

Athanasios I, Patriarch, *Letters. The Correspondence of Athanasius I Patriarch of Constantinople. Letters to the Emperor Andronicus II, Members of the Imperial Family, and Officials*, ed. Alice-Mary Maffry Talbot (Dumbarton Oaks Texts, III [= *CFHB*, VII]: Washington, D.C., 1975)

Athanasios of the Meteoron, *Vita*. Ed. N. A. Bees, Συμβολὴ εἰς τὴν ἱστορίαν τῶν Μονῶν τῶν Μετεώρων, Βυζαντίς, I (1909), pp. 237–60

Barlaam of Calabria. *Oratio pro Unione habita*, in *MPG*, CLI, cols. 1331–42

Bessarion, Cardinal. Ὑπόμνημα τοῦ καρδιναλίου Βησσαρίωνος εἰς Κωνσταντῖνον τὸν Παλαιολόγον, *NH*, III (1906), pp. 15–27; Lambros, Παλαιολόγεια καὶ Πελοποννησιακά, IV, pp. 32–45

Bryennios, Joseph, *Opera*. Ἰωσὴφ Βρυεννίου...τὰ εὑρεθέντα, ed. E. Boulgaris and Th. Mandakases, 3 vols. (Leipzig, 1768–94)

Bryennios, Joseph, *Letters*. M. Treu, 'Mazaris und Holobolos', *BZ*, I (1892), pp. 95–7; A. Papadopoulos-Kerameus, *Varia Graeca Sacra* (St

Petersburg, 1909), pp. 292–5; N. B. Tomadakes, Ὁ Ἰωσὴφ Βρυέννιος καὶ ἡ Κρήτη κατὰ τὸ 1400 (Athens, 1947), pp. 124–38; R.-J. Loenertz, 'Pour la chronologie des œuvres de Joseph Bryennios', *REB*, VII (1949), pp. 12–32

Bryennios, Joseph, *Testament*. Ed. A. Papadopoulos-Kerameus, *Varia Graeca Sacra* (St Petersburg, 1909), pp. 295–6

Bryennios, Joseph. Τίνες αἰτίαι τῶν καθ' ἡμᾶς λυπηρῶν, ed. L. Oeconomos, 'L'état intellectuel et moral des Byzantins vers le milieu du XIVe siècle d'après une page de Joseph Bryennios', *Mélanges Charles Diehl*, I (Paris, 1932), pp. 225–33

Cananus (*see* Kananos)

Cantacuzenus (*see* Kantakouzenos)

Chalkokondyles, Laonikos. *Laonici Chalcocandylae Historiarum Demonstrationes*, ed. E. Darkó, 2 vols. (Budapest, 1922–7)

Chomatianos, Demetrios. Ed. J. B. Pitra, *Analecta Sacra et Classica Spicilegio Solesmensi Parata*, VI (Rome, 1891)

Chortasmenos, John. H. Hunger, *Johannes Chortasmenos (ca. 1370 – ca. 1436/37). Briefe, Gedichte und kleine Schriften* (Wiener byzantinische Studien, VII: Vienna, 1969)

Choumnos, Nikephoros, *Letters* and other works. Ed. J. F. Boissonade, *Anecdota Graeca*, I–III, V (Paris, 1829–33)

Chrysoloras, Demetrios. P. Gautier, 'Actions de Grâces de Démétrius Chrysoloras à la Théotokos pour l'anniversaire de la bataille d'Ankara (28 Juillet 1403)', *REB*, XIX (1961) (*Mélanges R. Janin*), pp. 348–57

Doukas, *History*. Ducas, *Istoria Turco-Bizantina (1341–1462)*, ed. V. Grecu (Bucharest, 1958); English trans. by H. J. Magoulias, *Doukas. Decline and Fall of Byzantium to the Ottoman Turks* (Detroit, 1975)

Eugenikos, Mark. *Marci Eugenici Metropolitae Ephesi Opera Anti-Unionistica*, ed. L. Petit, *Patrologia Orientalis*, XVII, ii (Paris, 1923), pp. 307–491; reprinted in *Concilium Florentinum Documenta et Scriptores*, ser. A (Rome, 1977)

Gennadios, George Scholarios. *Oeuvres complètes de Gennade Scholarios*, ed. L. Petit, X. A. Siderides and M. Jugie, 8 vols. (Paris, 1928–36)

Gregoras, Nikephoros, *History. Byzantina Historia*, ed. L. Schopen, 3 vols. (*CSHB*, 1829, 1830, 1855); German trans. in progress, ed. J. L. van Dieten, *Nikephoros Gregoras, Rhomäische Geschichte*, I (Stuttgart, 1973)

Gregoras, Nikephoros, *Letters*. Ed. M. Bezdeki, 'Nicephori Gregorae epistulae XC', *Ephemeris Dacoromana*, II (1924), pp. 239–377; ed. R. Guilland, *Correspondance de Nicéphore Grégoras* (Paris, 1927)

Gregoras, Nikephoros, *Life of John of Herakleia*. V. Laurent, 'La vie de Jean, Métropolite d'Héraclée du Pont', *Archeion Pontou*, VI (1934), pp. 29–66

Isidore I, Patriarch, *Testament*. *MM*, I, pp. 287–94

Kabasilas, Nicholas, *Letters*. Ed. P. Enepekides, 'Der Briefwechsel des

Mystikers Nikolaos Kabasilas', *BZ*, xlvi (1953), pp. 18–46; I. Ševčenko, 'Nicolaus Cabasilas' Correspondence and the treatment of late Byzantine literary texts', *BZ*, xlvii (1954), pp. 49–59; R.-J. Loenertz, 'Chronologie de Nicolas Cabasilas', *OCP*, xxi (1955), pp. 205–31

Kabasilas, Nicholas, *Commentary on the Divine Liturgy*. *MPG*, cl, cols. 367–491; English trans. by J. Hussey and P. McNulty (London, 1960)

Kabasilas, Nicholas, *On the Life in Christ*. *MPG*, cl, cols. 491–726; French trans. by S. Broussaleux (Amay, 1932; Chevetogne, 1960); English trans. by C. J. de Catanzaro (New York, 1974)

Kabasilas, Nicholas, *Discourse*. I. Ševčenko, 'Nicolas Cabasilas' "Anti-zealot" Discourse: a reinterpretation', *DOP*, xi (1957), pp. 79–171

Kalekas, Manuel, *Letters*. R.-J. Loenertz, *Correspondance de Manuel Calécas* (Studi e Testi, 152: Vatican City, 1950)

Kallistos I, Patriarch, *Life of Gregory of Sinai*. Ed. I. Pomjalovskij, *Žitie iže vo svjatych otsa našego Grigorija Sinaita* (St Petersburg, 1894)

Kananos (Cananus), John. *De Constantinopoli oppugnata (1422)*, ed. I. Bekker, in (S)Phrantzes (*CSHB*, 1838), pp. 457–79

Kantakouzenos (Cantacuzenus), John. *Historiae*, ed. L. Schopen, 3 vols. (*CSHB*, 1828–32)

Kodinos (*see* Pseudo-Kodinos)

Kourousis, S. I. Αἱ ἀντιλήψεις περὶ τῶν ἐσχάτων τοῦ κόσμου καὶ ἡ κατὰ τὸ ἔτος 1346 πτῶσις τοῦ τρούλλου τῆς Ἁγίας Σοφίας, *EEBS*, xxxvii (1969–70), pp. 211–50

Kritoboulos of Imbros. *De rebus per annos 1451–1467 a Mechemete II gestis*, ed. V. Grecu, *Critobul din Imbros. Din Domnia lui Mahomed al II-lea anii 1451–1467* (Bucharest, 1963); English trans., *Kritovoulos, History of Mehmed the Conqueror*, by C. T. Riggs (Princeton, N.J., 1954)

Kydones, Demetrios, *Letters*. Ed. R.-J. Loenertz, *Démétrius Cydonès, Correspondance*, 2 vols. (Studi e Testi, 186, 208: Vatican City, 1956, 1960); ed. G. Cammelli (Paris, 1930)

Kydones, Demetrios, *Apologies*. Ed. G. Mercati, *Apologie della propria fede*, in *Notizie di Procoro e Demetrio Cidone, Manuele Caleca e Teodoro Meliteniota* etc. (Studi e Testi, 56: Vatican City, 1931), pp. 359–435

Kydones, Demetrios, *Speeches*. *Occisorum Thessalonicae Monodia*, in *MPG*, cix, cols. 639–52; *De admittendo Latinorum subsidio*, in *MPG*, cliv, cols. 961–1008; *De non reddenda Callipoli*, in *MPG*, cliv, cols. 1009–36; to John Cantacuzene and John Palaiologos, ed. G. Cammelli, *BNJ*, iii (1922), pp. 67–76; iv (1923), pp. 77–83, 282–95; ed. Loenertz, *Correspondance*, i, pp. 1–23

Makrembolites, Alexios, *Historical Discourse on the Genoese*. Ed. A Papadopoulos-Kerameus, Ἀνάλεκτα Ἱεροσολυμιτικῆς Σταχυολογίας, i (1891), pp. 144–59

Makrembolites, Alexios, *Dialogue between the Rich and the Poor*. Ed. I.
    Ševčenko, 'Alexios Makrembolites and his "Dialogue between the Rich
    and the Poor" ', *ZRVI*, VI (1960), pp. 203–28.
Makrembolites, Alexios, *On the Collapse of St Sophia* [Εἰς τὴν 'Αγίαν
    Σοφίαν πεσοῦσαν ὑπὸ πολλῶν κατὰ συνέχειαν γενομένων σεισμῶν]. Ed.
    S. I. Kourousis, *EEBS*, XXXVII (1969–70), pp. 235–40
Manuel II, Emperor, *Address to Sultan Bajezid*. Ed. E. Legrand, *Lettres de
    l'empereur Manuel*, pp. 103–4 (*MPG*, CLVI, cols. 280C–281A)
Manuel II, Emperor, *Hymn of Thanksgiving*. Ed. E. Legrand, *Lettres de
    l'empereur Manuel*, p. 104 (*MPG*, CLVI, col. 281 A–C)
Manuel II, Emperor, *Dialogue with a Muslim*. E. Trapp, *Manuel II
    Palaiologos, Dialoge mit einem "Perser"* (Wiener byzantinische Studien, II:
    Vienna, 1966)
Manuel II, Emperor, *Letters. The Letters of Manuel II Palaeologus. Text,
    translation and notes*, ed. G. T. Dennis (Dumbarton Oaks Texts, IV
    [= *CFHB*, VIII]: Washington, D.C., 1977); ed. E. Legrand, *Lettres de
    l'empereur Manuel Paléologue* (Paris, 1893)
Matthew I, Patriarch, *Testament*. H. Hunger, 'Das Testament des
    Patriarchen Matthaios I (1397–1410)', *BZ*, LI (1958), pp. 288–309
Matthew of Ephesos, *Letters*. D. Reinsch, *Die Briefe des Matthaios von
    Ephesos im Codex Vindobonensis Theol. Gr. 174* (Berlin, 1974); S. I.
    Kourousis, Μανουὴλ-Ματθαῖος Γαβαλᾶς εἶτα Ματθαῖος Μητροπολίτης
    'Εφέσου (1271/2–1355/60), I (Athens, 1972)
Maximos Kavsokalyvites, *Vita*. F. Halkin, 'Deux Vies de S. Maxime le
    Kausokalybe ermite au Mont Athos (XIVe siècle)', *AB*, LIV (1936), pp.
    38–112
Metochites, Theodore, *Essays*. Ed. C. G. Müller and T. Kiessling, *Theodori
    Metochitae Miscellanea philosophica et historica* (Leipzig, 1821)
Metochites, Theodore, *Poems. Dichtungen des Grosslogotheten Theodoros
    Metochites*, ed. M. Treu (Potsdam Gymnasium Programme, 1890); R.
    Guilland, 'Les poésies inédites de Théodore Métochite', in Guilland,
    Etudes Byzantines (Paris, 1959), pp. 178–205
Nikephoros the Hesychast. Nicephorus monachus, Περὶ νήψεως καὶ
    φυλακῆς καρδίας, *MPG*, CXLVII, cols. 945–66; French trans., *Petite
    philocalie de la prière du cœur*, by J. Gouillard, 2nd edn (Paris, 1968)
Pachymeres, George, *History. De Michaele et Andronico Palaeologis*, ed. I.
    Bekker, 2 vols. (*CSHB*, 1835)
Pachymeres, George, *Quadrivium*. P. Tannery, *Quadrivium de Georges
    Pachymère* ου Σύνταγμα τῶν τεσσάρων μαθημάτων ἀριθμητικῆς,
    μουσικῆς, γεωμετρίας καὶ ἀστρονομίας (Studi e Testi, 94: Vatican City,
    1940)
Palamas, Gregory, *Opera*. Γρηγορίου τοῦ Παλαμᾶ Συγγράμματα, ed. P. K.
    Chrestou, 3 vols. (Thessalonike, 1962, 1966, 1970)
Palamas, Gregory. *Grégoire Palamas. Défense des saints hésychastes*, ed. J.

Meyendorff, 2 vols. (Spicilegium Sacrum Lovaniense, 30, 31 : Louvain, 1959; 2nd edn 1973)

Palamas, Gregory, *Homilies*. *MPG*, CLI, cols. 9–559

Philes, Manuel, *Poems*. E. Miller, *Manuelis Philae Carmina*, 2 vols. (Paris, 1855, 1857); Ae. Martini, *Manuelis Philae Carmina Inedita* (Naples, 1900)

Philotheos, Patriarch, *Historical Discourse on the Siege and Capture of Herakleia by the Latins*. Ed. C. Triantafillis and A. Grapputo, *Anecdota Graeca e codicibus manu scriptis Bibliothecae S. Marci*, I (Venice, 1874), pp. 1–33

Philotheos, Patriarch, *Letter to the citizens of Herakleia*. Ed. Triantafillis and Grapputo, *Anecdota Graeca*, I, pp. 35–46

Philotheos, Patriarch, *Life of Sabas*. Ed. A. Papadopoulos-Kerameus, Ἀνάλεκτα Ἱεροσολυμιτικῆς Σταχυολογίας, v (St Petersburg, 1888), pp. 190–359

Philotheos, Patriarch, *Encomium of Palamas*. *MPG*, CLI cols. 551–656

Philotheos, Patriarch, *Life of Isidore*. Ed. A. Papadopoulos-Kerameus, 'Žitija dvuch Vselenskich Patriarchov XIV v., svv. Afanasija I i Isidora I', *Zapiski istoriko-filolog. fakulteta Imperatorskago S.-Petersburgskago Universiteta*, LXXVI (1905), pp. 52–149

Philotheos, Patriarch, *Life of Germanos Hagiorites*. P. Joannou, 'Vie de S. Germain l'Hagiorite par son contemporain le patriarche Philothée de Constantinople', *AB*, LXX (1952), pp. 50–115

Philotheos of Selymbria, *Life of Makarios*. Ed. A. Papadopoulos-Kerameus, Ὁ ἐν Κωνσταντινουπόλει Ἑλληνικὸς Φιλολογικὸς Σύλλογος, XVII, Παράρτημα (Μαυρογορδάτειος Βιβλιοθήκη) [Ἀνέκδοτα Ἑλληνικά] (Constantinople, 1886), pp. 46–59

Planoudes, Maximos, *Letters*. M. Treu, *Maximi monachi Planudis epistulae* (Breslau, 1890)

Plethon, George Gemistos, *On the Laws*. C. Alexandre, *Pléthon, Traité des Lois* (Paris, 1858; reprinted Amsterdam, 1966)

Plethon, George Gemistos. Γεωργίου Γεμιστοῦ εἰς Μανουὴλ Παλαιολόγον περὶ τῶν ἐν Πελοποννήσῳ πραγμάτων, ed. Sp. Lambros, Παλαιολόγεια καὶ Πελοποννησιακά, III (Athens, 1926), pp. 246–65; Πλήθωνος συμβουλευτικὸς πρὸς τὸν δεσπότην Θεόδωρον περὶ τῆς Πελοποννήσου, ed. Lambros, *ibid.*, IV (Athens, 1930), pp. 113–35; *MPG*, CLX, cols. 821–40, 841–66

Pseudo-Kodinos, *De Officiis*. Ed. J. Verpeaux, *Pseudo-Kodinos, Traité des Offices* (Paris, 1966)

Romylos, St, *Vita*. F. Halkin, 'Un ermite des Balkans au XIVe siècle. La Vie grecque inédite de Saint Romylos', *B*, XXXI (1961) (*Hommage à Georges Ostrogorsky*), pp. 114–47

Sphrantzes, George, *Chronicon Minus*. Georgios Sphrantzes, *Memorii 1401–1477. În anexă Pseudo-Phrantzes: Macarie Melissenos, Cronica 1258–1481*, ed. V. Grecu (Bucharest, 1966)

Thomas Magister, Speeches. F. W. Lenz, *Fünf Reden Thomas Magisters*
  (Leiden, 1963)
Zoras, G. T. ed. Χρονικὸν περὶ τῶν Τούρκων Σουλτάνων (κατὰ τὸν
  Βαρβερινὸν ἑλληνικὸν κώδικα 111) (Athens, 1958)

Modern works

Ahrweiler, Hélène. 'L'histoire et la géographie de la région de Smyrne
  entre les deux occupations turques (1081–1317), particulièrement au
  XIIIe siècle', *Travaux et Mémoires*, 1 (1965), pp. 2–204
Ahrweiler, Hélène. *L'idéologie politique de l'empire byzantin* (Paris, 1975)
Alexander, P. J. 'Historiens byzantins et croyances eschatologiques', *Actes
  du XIIe Congrès International des Etudes Byzantines*, II (Belgrade, 1964),
  pp. 1–8
Altaner, B. 'Die Kentniss des Griechischen in den Missionsordnen
  während des 13. und 14. Jahrhunderts', *Zeitschrift für Kirchengeschichte*,
  LIII (1934), pp. 436–93
Anastos, M. 'Pletho's calendar and liturgy', *DOP*, IV (1948), pp. 183–305
Angelopoulos, A. A. Νικόλαος Καβάσιλας Χαμάετος. Ἡ ζωὴ καὶ τὸ ἔργον
  αὐτοῦ (᾿Ανάλεκτα Βλατάδων, 5: Thessalonike, 1970)
Arnakis, G. G. Οἱ πρῶτοι ᾿Οθωμανοί. Συμβολὴ εἰς τὸ πρόβλημα τῆς
  πτώσεως τοῦ ἑλληνισμοῦ τῆς Μικρᾶς ᾿Ασίας (1282–1337) (*Athens, 1947*)
Arnakis, G. G. 'Gregory Palamas among the Turks and documents of his
  capitivity as historical sources', *Speculum*, XXVI (1951), pp. 104–18
Art et Société à Byzance sous les Paléologues (Actes du Colloque…à Venise,
  septembre 1968 [Institut Hellénique d'études byzantines et
  post-byzantines de Venise, 4]: Venice, 1971)
Atiya, A. S. *The Crusade in the Later Middle Ages* (London, 1938)
Babinger, F. *Mahomet II le Conquérant et son temps (1432–1481)* (Paris,
  1954); English trans. by R. Manheim, ed. C. Hickman (Princeton, N.J.,
  1977)
Barker, J. W. *Manuel II Palaeologus (1391–1425). A Study in Late Byzantine
  Statesmanship* (New Brunswick, N.J., 1969)
Baynes, N. H. *Byzantine Studies and Other Essays* (London, 1955)
Beck, H.-G. *Theodoros Metochites. Die Krise des byzantinischen Weltbildes im
  14. Jahrhundert* (Munich, 1952)
Beck, H.-G. 'Die "Apologia pro vita sua" des Demetrios Kydones',
  Ostkirchliche Studien, I (1952), pp. 208–25, 264–82
Beck, H.-G. *Kirche und theologische Literatur im byzantinischen Reich*
  (Munich, 1959)
Beck, H.-G. 'Reichsidee und nationale Politik im spätbyzantinischen
  Staat', *BZ*, LIII (1960), pp. 86–94
Beck, H.-G. 'Humanismus und Palamismus', *Actes du XIIe Congrès
  International des Etudes Byzantines*, I (Belgrade, 1963), pp. 63–82

Bibliography

141

Beck, H.-G. 'Besonderheiten der Literatur in der Palaiologenzeit', Art et
Société à Byzance sous les Paléologues (Venice, 1971), pp. 41–52
Beck, H.-G. Geschichte der byzantinischen Volksliteratur (Munich, 1971)
Beck, H.-G. Ideen und Realitäten in Byzanz. Collected Studies (Variorum:
London, 1972)
Berger de Xivrey, J. Mémoire sur la vie et les ouvrages de l'empereur Manuel
Paléologue (Mémoires de l'Institut de France, Académie des Inscriptions
et Belles-Lettres, XIX: Paris, 1853)
Bosch, Ursula V. Kaiser Andronikos III. Palaiologos. Versuch einer
Darstellung der byzantinischen Geschichte in den Jahren 1321–1341
(Amsterdam, 1965)
Bratianu, G. I. Etudes byzantines d'histoire économique et sociale (Paris, 1938)
Bréhier, L. 'L'enseignement classique et l'enseignement religieux à
Byzance', Revue d'histoire et de philosophie religieuses, XXI (1941), pp.
34–69
Bréhier, L. Le monde byzantin, I: Vie et Mort de Byzance; II: Les Institutions
de l'empire byzantin; III: La Civilisation byzantine (Paris, 1969–70).
English trans. of vol. I, The Life and Death of Byzantium, by Margaret
Vaughan (Amsterdam–New York–London, 1977)
Brincken, v. den, Anna-Dorothee. Die "Nationes Christianorum
Orientalium" im Verständnis der lateinischen Historiographie von der Mitte
des 12. bis in die zweite Hälfte des 14. Jahrhunderts (Cologne–Vienna,
1973)
Cambridge Medieval History, IV: The Byzantine Empire. Part 1: Byzantium
and its Neighbours; Part 2: Government, Church and Civilisation. Ed. by
J. M. Hussey (Cambridge, 1966, 1967)
Cammelli, G. I Dotti bizantini e le origini dell'umanesimo, I: Manuele
Crisolora (Florence, 1941)
Chapman, C. Michel Paléologue, restaurateur de l'empire byzantin (Paris,
1926)
Charanis, P. 'Internal strife in Byzantium during the fourteenth century',
B, XV (1940–1), pp. 208–30
Charanis, P. 'The strife among the Palaeologi and the Ottoman Turks,
1370–1402', B, XVI (1942–3), pp. 286–314
Charanis, P. 'The monastic properties and the state in the Byzantine
Empire', DOP, IV (1948), pp. 51–118
Charanis, P. 'On the social structure and economic organisation of the
Byzantine Empire in the thirteenth century and later', BS, XII (1951),
pp. 94–153
Charanis, P. 'Economic factors in the decline of the Byzantine Empire',
Journal of Economic History, XIII (1953), pp. 412–24
Charanis, P. 'The monk as an element in Byzantine society', DOP, XXV
(1971), pp. 61–84
Charanis, P. Social, Economic and Political Life in the Byzantine Empire.
Collected Studies (Variorum: London, 1973)

Charanis, P. 'Cultural diversity and the breakdown of Byzantine power in Asia Minor', *DOP*, XXIX (1975), pp. 1–20

Constantelos, D. J. *Byzantine Philanthropy and Social Welfare* (New Brunswick, N.J., 1968)

Dade, E. *Versuch zur Wiedererrichtung der lateinischen Herrschaft in Konstantinopel im Rahmen der abendländischen Politik, 1261 bis etwa 1310* (Jena, 1938)

Darrouzès, J. 'Conférences sur la primauté du pape à Constantinople en 1357', *REB*, XIX (1961), pp. 76–109

Dennis, G. T. *The Reign of Manuel II Palaeologus in Thessalonica, 1382–1387* (*OCA*, 159: Rome, 1960)

Diehl, C. 'Sur quelques croyances byzantines sur la fin de Constantinople', *BZ*, XXX (1930), pp. 192–6

Dinić, M. 'The Balkans, 1018–1499', *Cambridge Medieval History*, IV, pt 1 (1966), Ch. XII

Dölger, F. 'Zur Bedeutung von *ΦΙΛΟΣΟΦΟΣ* und *ΦΙΛΟΣΟΦΙΑ* in byzantinischer Zeit', in Dölger, *Byzanz und die europäische Staatenwelt* (Ettal, 1953), pp. 197–208

Dölger, F. 'Politische und geistige Strömungen im sterbenden Byzanz', *JÖBG*, III (1954), pp. 3–18

Dräseke, J. 'Zum Philosophen Joseph', *Zeitschrift für wissenschaftliche Theologie*, XLII (1899), pp. 612–20

Ducellier, A. 'L'Islam et les Musulmans vues de Byzance au XIVe siècle', *Actes du XIVe Congrès International des Etudes Byzantines*, II (Bucharest, 1975), pp. 79–85

Ducellier, A. *Le Drame de Byzance. Idéal et échec d'une société chrétienne* (Paris, 1976)

Dujčev, I. *Medioevo Bizantino-Slavo*, 3 vols. (Rome, 1966–70)

Dujčev, I. 'Die Krise der spätbyzantinischen Gesellschaft und die türkische Eroberung des 14. Jahrhunderts', *Jahrbücher für Geschichte Ost Europas*, N.F., XXI (1973), pp. 481–92

Dujčev, I. 'Le grand tournant historique de l'an 1204', *ZRVI*, XVI (1975), pp. 63–8

Dujčev, I. 'La crise idéologique de 1203–1204 et ses répercussions sur la civilisation byzantine', *Cahiers de Travaux et de Conférences*, I (Ecole Pratique des Hautes Etudes, Sorbonne: Paris, 1976)

Evert-Kappesowa, Halina, 'La société byzantine et l'union de Lyon', *BS*, X (1949), pp. 28–41

Evert-Kappesowa, Halina. 'Une page des relations byzantino-latines. Le clergé byzantin et l'union de Lyon (1274–1282)', *BS*, XII (1952–3), pp. 68–92

Evert-Kappesowa, Halina. 'Le Tiare ou le Turban?', *BS*, XIV (1953), pp. 245–57

Evert-Kappesowa, Halina. 'Byzance et le Saint Siège à l'époque de l'union de Lyon', *BS*, XVI (1955), pp. 297–317

Evert-Kappesowa, Halina. 'La fin de l'union de Lyon', *BS*, XVII (1956), pp. 1–18

Every, G. *Misunderstandings between East and. West* (London, 1965; Richmond, Va., 1966)

Franchi, A. *Il Concilio II di Lione* (Studi e Testi francescane, 33: Naples, 1965)

Fuchs, F. *Die höheren Schulen von Konstantinopel im Mittelalter* (Leipzig, 1926)

Gay, J. *Le Pape Clément VI et les affaires d'Orient (1342–1352)* (Paris, 1904)

Geanakoplos, D. J. *Emperor Michael Palaeologus and the West, 1258–1282. A Study in Byzantine–Latin Relations* (Cambridge, Mass., 1959)

Geanakoplos, D. J. *Greek Scholars in Venice. Studies in the Dissemination of Greek Learning from Byzantium to Western Europe* (Cambridge, Mass., 1962); reprinted as *Byzantium and the Renaissance* (Hamden, Conn., 1972)

Geanakoplos, D. J. *Byzantine East and Latin West: Two Worlds of Christendom in Middle Ages and Renaissance* (Oxford, 1966)

Geanakoplos, D. J. *Interaction of the 'Sibling' Byzantine and Western Cultures in the Middle Ages and Italian Renaissance (330–1600)* (New Haven–London, 1976)

Geanakoplos, D. J. 'Bonaventura, the two Mendicant Orders, and the Greeks at the Council of Lyons (1274)', *Studies in Church History*, XIII (*The Orthodox Churches and the West*), ed. D. Baker (Oxford, 1976), pp. 169–81

Gibbons, H. A. *The Foundation of the Ottoman Empire. A History of the Osmanlis up to the death of Bayezid I, 1300–1403* (Oxford, 1916)

Gigante, M. 'Per l'interpretazione di Teodoro Metochites quale umanista bizantino', *SBN*, N.S. IV (XIV) (1967), pp. 11–25

Gill, J. *The Council of Florence* (Cambridge, 1959)

Gill, J. 'The year of the death of Mark Eugenicus', *BZ*, LII (1959), pp. 23–31

Gill, J. *Personalities of the Council of Florence and Other Essays* (Oxford, 1964)

Gill, J. 'East and west in the time of Bessarion: theology and religion', *Rivista di Studi Bizantini e Neoellenici*, N.S., V (XV) (1968), pp. 1–27

Gill, J. 'Emperor Andronicus II and Patriarch Athanasius I', *Byzantina*, II (1970), pp. 11–19

Gill, J. 'The Church union of the Council of Lyons (1274) portrayed in Greek documents', *OCP*, XL (1974), pp. 5–45

Gill, J. 'John Beccus, Patriarch of Constantinople 1275–1282', *Byzantina*, VII (1975), pp. 251–66

Gill, J. 'The sincerity of Bessarion the Unionist', *Journal of Theological Studies*, XXVI (1975), pp. 377–92

Gill, J. 'Was Bessarion a Conciliarist or a Unionist before the Council of Florence?', *Collectanea Byzantina* (*OCA*, 204: Rome, 1977), pp. 201–19

Gouillard, J. 'L'autoportrait d'un sage du XIVe siècle', *Actes du XIVe Congrès International des Etudes Byzantines*, II (Bucharest, 1975), pp. 103–8

Grecu, V. 'Pour une meilleure connaissance de l'historien Doukas', *Mémorial Louis Petit* (Paris, 1948), pp. 128–41

Grecu, V. 'Georgios Sphrantzes. Leben und Werk. Makarios Melissenos und sein Werk', *BS*, XXVI (1965), pp. 62–73

Grumel, V. *La Chronologie* (*Traité d'études byzantines*, ed. P. Lemerle, 1: Paris, 1958)

Guilland, R. *Essai sur Nicéphore Grégoras. L'homme et l'œuvre* (Paris, 1926)

Guilland, R. *Etudes Byzantines* (Paris, 1959)

Guilland, R. 'Moines de l'Athos, patriarches de Constantinople (Nicolas II, Isaïe, Isidore)', *EEBS*, XXXII (1963), pp. 40–59

Guilland, R. *Recherches sur les Institutions byzantines*, 2 vols. (Berliner Byzantinische Arbeiten, 35: Berlin, 1967)

Halecki, O. *Un Empereur de Byzance à Rome. Vingt ans de travail pour l'union des églises et pour la défense de l'empire d'Orient, 1355–1375* (Warsaw, 1930; reprinted London, 1972)

Halecki, O. *The Crusade of Varna. A discussion of controversial problems* (New York, 1943).

Hausherr, I. *La méthode d'oraison hésychaste* (*Orientalia Christiana*, IX, 2: Rome, 1927)

Hrochová, V. 'La révolte des Zélotes à Salonique et les communes italiennes', *BS*, XXII (1961), pp. 1–15

Hunger, H. 'Theodoros Metochites als Vorläufer des Humanismus in Byzanz', *BZ*, LV (1952), pp. 4–19

Hunger, H. 'Johannes Chortasmenos, ein byzantinischer Intellektueller der späten Palaiologenzeit', *Wiener Studien*, LXX (1957), pp. 153–63

Hunger, H. 'Das Testament des Patriarchen Matthaios I (1397–1410)', *BZ* LI (1958), pp. 288–309

Hunger, H. 'Der Ἠθικός des Theodoros Metochites', Πεπραγμένα Θ′ Διεθνοῦς Βυζαντινολογικοῦ Συνεδρίου, III (= *Hellenika*, Parartima IX: Thessalonike, 1958), pp. 141–58

Hunger, H. 'Von Wissenschaft und Kunst der frühen Palaiologenzeit. Mit einem Exkurs über die Kosmike Delosis Theodoros' II. Dukas Laskaris', *JÖBG*, VIII(1959), pp. 123–55

Hunger, H. 'Philanthropia. Eine griechische Wortprägung auf ihrem Wege von Aischylos bis Theodoros Metochites', *Anzeiger phil.-hist. Klasse Österreichische Akademie der Wissenschaften*, Nr. 100 (Graz–Vienna–Cologne, 1963), pp. 1–20

Hunger, H. *Prooimion. Elemente der byzantinischen Kaiseridee in den Arengen der Urkunden* (Wiener byzantinische Studien, 1: Vienna, 1964)

Hunger, H. *Reich der neuen Mitte. Der christliche Geist der byzantinischen Kultur* (Graz–Vienna–Cologne, 1965)

Hunger, H. 'Allzu Menschliches aus dem Privatleben eines Byzantiners. Tagebuchnotizen des Hypochonders Johannes Chortasmenos', *Polychronion. Festschrift Franz Dölger* (Munich, 1966), pp. 244–52

Hunger, H. *Johannes Chortasmenos (ca. 1370–ca. 1436/37). Briefe, Gedichte und kleine Schriften* (Wiener byzantinische Studien, VII: Vienna, 1969)

Hunger, H. 'On the imitation (mimesis) of Antiquity in Byzantine literature', *DOP*, XXIII/XXIV (1969–70), pp. 17–38

Hunger, H. *Byzantinische Grundlagenforschung. Gesammelte Aufsaetze* (Variorum: London, 1973)

Hunger, H. 'Klassizistische Tendenzen in der byzantinischen Literatur des 14. Jh.', *Actes du XIVe Congrès International des Etudes Byzantines*, I (Bucharest, 1974), pp. 139–51

Hunger, H. 'Thukydides bei Johannes Kantakuzenos. Beobachtungen zur Mimesis', *JÖB*, XXV (1976), pp. 181–93

Hunger, H. *Die Hochsprachliche Profane Literatur der Byzantiner*, 2 vols. (Munich, 1978)

Hussey, J. M. and Hart, T. A. 'Byzantine theological speculation and spirituality', *Cambridge Medieval History*, IV, Pt 2 (1967), Chapter XXVI

Inalcik, H. 'Ottoman methods of conquest', *Studia Islamica*, II (Paris, 1954), pp. 103–29

Inalcik, H. *The Ottoman Empire. The Classical Age, 1300–1600* (London, 1973)

Jireček, C. J. *Geschichte der Bulgaren* (Prague, 1876)

Jireček, C. J. *Geschichte der Serben*, 2 vols. (Gotha, 1911–18); rev. edn by J. Radonić, *Istorija Srba*, 2 vols. (Belgrade, 1952)

Jorga, N. 'Latins et grecs d'Orient et l'établissement des Turcs en Europe', *BZ*, XV (1906), pp. 179–222

Kaepelli, T. 'Deux nouveaux ouvrages de Fr Philippe Incontri de Péra, O. P.', *Archivum Fratrum Praedicatorum*, XXIII (1953), pp. 163–83

Karpozilos, A. D. 'Thomas Aquinas and the Byzantine East (De essentia et operatione)', *Ekklesiastikos Pharos*, LII (1970), pp. 129–47

Keller, A. 'Two Byzantine scholars and their reception in Italy', *Journal of the Warburg and Courtauld Institutes*, XX (1957), pp. 363–70

Khoury, A.-Th. *Les Théologiens byzantins et l'Islam. Textes et auteurs (VIIIe–XIIIe s.)* (Louvain–Paris, 1969)

Khoury, A.-Th. *Der theologische Streit der Byzantiner mit der Islam* (Paderborn, 1969)

Kourousis, S. I. Μανουὴλ-Ματθαῖος Γαβαλᾶς εἶτα Ματθαῖος Μητροπολίτης Ἐφέσου (1271/2–1355/60), I (Athens, 1972)

Kourousis, S. I. Ὁ λόγιος οἰκουμενικὸς πατριάρχης Ἰωάννης ΙΓ΄ ὁ Γλυκύς (Athens, 1975); reprinted from *EEBS*, XLI (1974), pp. 297–405

Krasavina, S. K. 'Mirovozzrenie i socialno-političeskie vzgljady vizantijskogo istorika Duki' [World outlook and socio-political opinions of the Byzantine historian Doukas], *VV*, XXXIV (1973), pp. 97–111

Krumbacher, K. *Geschichte der byzantinischen Litteratur von Justinian bis zum Ende des oströmischen Reiches (527–1453)*, 2nd edn (Munich, 1897)

Kyrou, A. A. *Βησσαρίων ὁ "Ελλην*, 2 vols. (Athens, 1947)

Laiou, Angeliki E. 'The provisioning of Constantinople during the winter of 1306–1307', *B*, xxxvii (1967), pp. 91–113

Laiou, Angeliki E. *Constantinople and the Latins. The Foreign Policy of Andronicus II 1282–1328* (Cambridge, Mass., 1972)

Laiou, Angeliki E. 'The Byzantine aristocracy in the Palaeologan period: a story of arrested development', *Viator*, iv (1973), pp. 131–51

Laiou-Thomadakis, Angeliki E. *Peasant Society in the Late Byzantine Empire. A Social and Demographic Study* (Princeton, N.J., 1977)

Langer, W. L. and Blake, R. P. 'The rise of the Ottoman Turks and its historical background', *American Historical Review*, xxxvii (1932), pp. 468–505

Laourdas, B. *Ἡ κλασσικὴ φιλολογία εἰς τὴν Θεσσαλονίκην κατὰ τὸν δέκατον τέταρτον αἰῶνα* (Thessalonike, 1960)

Laurent, V. 'La personalité de Jean d'Héraclée, oncle et précepteur de Nicéphore Grégoras', *Hellenika*, iii (1930), pp. 297–315

Laurent, V. 'La correspondance de Démétrius Cydonès', *EO*, xxx (1931), pp. 399–454

Laurent, V. 'La Vie de Jean, Métropolite d'Héraclée du Pont', *Archeion Pontou*, vi (1934), pp. 1–67

Laurent, V. 'Les grandes crises religieuses à Byzance. La fin du schisme arsénite', *Académie Roumaine. Bulletin de la section historique*, xxvi (Bucharest, 1945), pp. 225–313

Laurent, V. 'L'idée de guerre sainte et la tradition byzantine', *Revue historique du sud-est européen*, xxiii (1946), pp. 71–98

Laurent, V. 'Les droits de l'empereur en matière ecclésiastique. L'accord de 1380–1382', *REB*, xiii (1955), pp. 5–20

Laurent, V. 'La direction spirituelle à Byzance. La correspondance d'Irène-Eulogie Choumnaina Paléologine avec son second directeur', *REB*, xiv (1956), pp. 48–86

Laurent, V. 'Le trisépiscopat du Patriarche Matthieu Ier (1397–1410). Un grand procès canonique à Byzance au début du XVe siècle', *REB*, xxx (1972), pp. 5–166

Lemerle, P. *L'Emirat d'Aydin, Byzance et l'Occident. Recherches sur 'La geste d'Umur Pacha'* (Paris, 1957)

Lemerle, P. *Le premier humanisme byzantin. Notes et remarques sur l'enseignement et culture à Byzance des origines au Xe siècle* (Paris, 1971)

Loenertz, R.-J. 'Les missions dominicains en Orient au XIVe siècle', *Archivum Fratrum Praedicatorum*, ii (1932), pp. 2–83

Loenertz, R.-J. 'Les établissements Dominicains de Péra-Constantinople. Origines et fondations', *EO*, xxxiv (1935), pp. 332–49

Loenertz, R.-J. *La Société des Frères Pérégrinants. Etudes sur l'Orient*

Dominicain, I (Institutum historicum FF. Praedicatorum Romae: Dissertationes historicae, fasc. 7: Rome, 1937)

Loenertz, R.-J. 'Autour du Chronicon Maius attribué à Georges Phrantzès', *Miscellanea Giovanni Mercati*, III (Studi e Testi, 123: Vatican City, 1946), pp. 273–311

Loenertz, R.-J. 'Manuel Calécas, sa vie et ses œuvres d'après ses lettres et ses apologies inédites', *Archivum Fratrum Praedicatorum*, XVII (1947), pp. 195–207

Loenertz, R.-J. 'Fr Philippe de Bindo Incontri, O. P. du couvent de Péra, Inquisiteur en Orient', *Archivum Fratrum Praedicatorum*, XVIII (1948), pp. 265–80

Loenertz, R.-J. 'Pour la chronologie des œuvres de Joseph Bryennios', *REB*, VII (1949), pp. 12–32

Loenertz, R.-J. 'Théodore Métochite et son père', *Archivum Fratrum Praedicatorum*, XXIII (1953), pp. 184–94

Loenertz, R.-J. 'Ioannes de Fontibus Ord. Praedicatorum Epistula ad Abbatem et Conventum nescio cuius Constantinopolitani', *Archivum Fratrum Praedicatorum*, XXX (1960), pp. 163–95

Loenertz, R.-J. 'Démétrius Cydonès, I: De la naissance à l'année 1373', *OCP*, XXXVI (1970), pp. 47–72; 'II: De 1373 à 1375', *OCP*, XXXVII (1971), pp. 5–39

Loenertz, R.-J. *Byzantina et Franco-Graeca (Articles parus de 1935 à 1966 réédités avec la collaboration de Peter Schreiner)* (Storia e Letteratura: Raccolta di Studi e Testi, 118: Rome, 1970)

Loenertz, R.-J. 'La Société des Frères Pérégrinants de 1374 à 1475. Etudes sur l'Orient Dominicain, II', *Archivum Fratrum Praedicatorum*, XLV (1975), pp. 107–45

Longnon, J. *L'empire latin de Constantinople et la principauté de Morée* (Paris, 1949)

Lot-Borodine, Myrrha. *Un maître de la spiritualité byzantine au XIVe siècle. Nicolas Cabasilas* (Paris, 1958)

Lumpe, A. 'Abendland und Byzanz, III: Literatur und Sprache. A. Literatur. Abendländisches in Byzanz', *Reallexikon der Byzantinistik*, ed. P. Wirth, Reihe A, Bd. I. Heft 4 (Amsterdam, 1970), cols. 304–47

Maksimović, Lj. *Vizantijska provincijska uprava u doba Paleologa* (Byzantine provincial administration under the Palaiologi) (Vizantološki Institut, Posebna Izdania, 14: Belgrade, 1972)

Mango, C. 'Antique statuary and the Byzantine beholder', *DOP*, XVII (1963), pp. 55–75

Mango, C. 'Byzantinism and Romantic Hellenism' *Journal of the Warburg and Courtauld Institutes*, XXVIII (1965), pp. 29–43

Masai, F. *Pléthon et le platonisme de Mistra* (Paris, 1956)

Mathew, G. *Byzantine Aesthetics* (London, 1963)

Matschke, K. P. *Fortschritt und Reaktion in Byzanz im 14. Jahrhundert* (Berlin, 1971)

Mazal, O. *Die Prooimien der byzantinischen Patriarchenurkunden* (Byzantina
    Vindobonensia, VII: Vienna, 1974)
Medvedev, I. P. *Mistra. Očerki istorii i kultury pozdnevizantijskogo goroda*
    [Mistra. Essays on the history and culture of a late Byzantine town]
    (Leningrad, 1973)
Medvedev, I. P. *Vizantijskij Gumanism XIV–XV vv.* [Byzantine
    Humanism, fourteenth–fifteenth centuries] (Leningrad, 1976)
Mercati, G. *Notizie di Procoro e Demetrio Cidone, Manuele Caleca e Teodoro
    Meliteniota ad altri appunti per la storia della teologia e della letteratura
    bizantina del secolo XIV* (Studi e Testi, 56: Vatican City, 1931)
Meyendorff, J. 'Projets de concile oecuménique en 1367: Un dialogue
    inédit entre Jean Cantacuzène et le légat Paul', *DOP*, XIV (1960), pp.
    147–77
Meyendorff, J. *Introduction à l'étude de Grégoire Palamas* (Paris, 1959);
    English trans., *A Study of Gregory Palamas*, by G. Lawrence (London,
    1964)
Meyendorff, J. 'Grecs, Turcs et Juifs en Asie Mineure au XIVe siècle',
    Byzantinische Forschungen, I (1966), pp. 211–17
Meyendorff, J. 'Alexis and Roman: a study in Byzantine–Russian relations
    (1352–1354)', *BS*, XXVIII (1967), pp. 278–88
Meyendorff, J. 'Society and culture in the fourteenth century. Religious
    problems', *Actes du XIVe Congrès International des Etudes Byzantines*, I
    (Bucharest, 1974), pp. 51–65
Meyendorff, J. *Byzantine Hesychasm: historical, theological and social problems.
    Collected Studies* (Variorum: London, 1974)
Meyendorff, J. *Byzantine Theology. Historical Trends and Doctrinal Themes*
    (New York, 1974)
Meyendorff, J. 'Spiritual trends in Byzantium in the late thirteenth and
    early fourteenth centuries', *The Kariye Djami*, IV, ed. P. A. Underwood
    (New York, 1975)
Miller, T. S. 'The Plague in John VI Cantacuzenus and Thucydides',
    Greek, Roman and Byzantine Studies, XVIII (1976), pp. 385–95
Miller, W. *The Latins in the Levant. A History of Frankish Greece, 1204–1566*
    (London, 1908)
Miller, W. 'The last Athenian historian: Laonikos Chalkokondyles',
    Journal of Hellenic Studies, XLII (1922), pp. 36–49
Miller, W. 'The historians Doukas and Phrantzes', *Journal of Hellenic
    Studies*, XLVI, (1926), pp. 63–71
Mohler, L. *Kardinal Bessarion als Theologe, Humanist und Staatsmann*, 3 vols.
    (Paderborn, 1923–7; 1942)
Nicol, D. M. 'The Greeks and the union of the Churches: the
    preliminaries to the Second Council of Lyons, 1261–1274', *Medieval
    Studies presented to A. Gwynn, S. J.*, ed. J. A. Watt and others (Dublin,
    1961), pp. 454–80

Nicol, D. M. 'Constantine Akropolites. A prosopographical note', *DOP*, XIX (1965), pp. 249–56

Nicol, D. M. *The Byzantine Family of Kantakouzenos (Cantacuzenus) ca. 1100–1460. A genealogical and prosopographical study* (Dumbarton Oaks Studies, XI: Washington, D.C., 1968)

Nicol, D. M. 'Byzantine requests for an oecumenical council in the fourteenth century', *Annuarium Historiae Conciliorum*, I (Amsterdam, 1969), pp. 69–95

Nicol, D. M. 'The Byzantine Church and Hellenic learning in the fourteenth century', *Studies in Church History*, V, ed. G. J. Cuming (Leiden, 1969), pp. 23–57

Nicol, D. M. 'The Byzantine reaction to the Second Council of Lyons, 1274', *Studies in Church History*, VII, ed. G. J. Cuming and D. Baker (Cambridge, 1971), pp. 113–46

Nicol, D. M. 'A Byzantine emperor in England. Manuel II's visit to London in 1400–1401', *University of Birmingham Historical Journal*, XII, 2 (1971), pp. 204–25

Nicol, D. M. *The Last Centuries of Byzantium, 1261–1453* (London, 1972)

Nicol, D. M. *Byzantium: its ecclesiastical history and relations with the western world. Collected Studies* (Variorum: London, 1972)

Nicol, D. M. *Meteora. The Rock Monasteries of Thessaly* (London, 1963: 2nd, rev. edn. 1975)

Nicol, D. M. '*Kaisersalbung*. The unction of emperors in late Byzantine coronation ritual', *Byzantine and Modern Greek Studies*, II (1976), pp. 37–52

Nicol, D. M. 'The papal scandal', *Studies in Church History*, XIII (*The Orthodox Churches and the West*), ed. D. Baker (Oxford, 1976)

Nikolaou, T. S. *Αἱ περὶ πολιτείας καὶ δικαίου ἰδέαι τοῦ Γ. Πλήθωνος Γεμιστοῦ* (Thessalonike, 1974)

Norden, W. *Das Papsttum und Byzanz* (Berlin, 1903)

Obolensky, D. 'Byzantium, Kiev and Moscow: a study in ecclesiastical relations', *DOP*, XI (1957), pp. 21–78

Obolensky, D. *The Byzantine Commonwealth. Eastern Europe, 500–1453* (London, 1971)

Obolensky, D. *Byzantium and the Slavs. Collected Studies* (Variorum: London, 1971)

Obolensky, D. 'Nationalism in eastern Europe in the Middle Ages', *Transactions of the Royal Historical Society*, 5th ser., XXII (1972), pp. 1–16

Obolensky, D. 'A Byzantine Grand Embassy to Russia in 1400', *Byzantine and Modern Greek Studies*, IV (1978) (*Essays presented to Sir Steven Runciman*), pp. 123–32

Oeconomos, L. 'L'état intellectuel et moral des Byzantins vers le milieu du XIVe siècle d'après une page de Joseph Bryennios', *Mélanges Charles Diehl*, I (Paris, 1930), pp. 225–33

Ostrogorsky, G. *Pour l'histoire de la féodalité byzantine* (Brussels, 1954)

Ostrogorsky, G. 'Byzance, état tributaire de l'empire turc', *ZRVI*, v (1958), pp. 49–58

Ostrogorsky, G. *History of the Byzantine State*, trans. by Joan Hussey, 2nd edn (Oxford, 1968)

Ostrogorsky, G. 'Observations on the aristocracy in Byzantium', *DOP*, xxv (1971), pp. 1–32

Papadopoulos, S. G. Ἑλληνικαὶ μεταφράσεις θωμιστικῶν ἔργων. Φιλοθωμισταὶ καὶ ἀντιθωμισταὶ ἐν Βυζαντίῳ (Athens, 1967)

Papadopoulos, S. G. Συνάντησις ὀρθοδόξου καὶ σχολαστικῆς θεολογίας (ἐν τῷ προσώπῳ Καλλίστου Ἀγγελικούδη καὶ Θωμᾶ Ἀκινάτου) (Ἀνάλεκτα Βλατάδων, 4: Thessalonike, 1970)

Papadopoulos, S. G. 'St Thomas in Byzanz. Thomas-Rezeption und Thomas-Kritik in Byzanz zwischen 1345 und 1453', *Theologie und Philosophie*, xlix (1974), pp. 274–304

Papadopulos, A. Th. *Versuch einer Genealogie der Palaiologen, 1259–1453* (Munich, 1938; reprinted Amsterdam, 1962)

Pertusi, A. 'In margine alla questione dell'umanesimo bizantino: il pensiero politico del cardinale Bessarione e i suoi rapporti con il pensiero di Giorgio Gemisto Pletone', *Rivista di studi bizantini e neoellenici*, N.S., v (1968), pp. 95–104

Pingree, D. 'Gregory Chioniades and Palaeologan astronomy', *DOP*, xviii (1964), pp. 133–60

Pingree, D. 'The astrological school of John Abramius', *DOP* xxv (1971), pp. 189–215

Podskalsky, G. *Byzantinische Reichseschatologie. Die Periodisierung der Weltgeschichte in den 4 Grossreichen [Daniel 2 und 7] und den 1000 jährigen Friedensreiche [Apok. 20]* (Münchener Universitäts-Schriften, Philos. Fak., 9: Munich, 1972)

Podskalsky, G. 'Marginalien zur byzantinischen Reichseschatologie', *BZ*, lxvii (1974), pp. 351–8

Podskalsky, G. 'Die Rezeption der thomistischen Theologie bei Gennadios II. Scholarios (ca. 1403–1472)', *Theologie und Philosophie*, xlix (1974), pp. 350–73

Podskalsky, G. 'Der Fall Konstantinopels in der Sicht der Reichseschatologie und der Klagelieder', *Archiv für Kulturgeschichte*, lvii (1975), pp. 71–86

Podskalsky, G. *Theologie und Philosophie in Byzanz. Der Streit um die theologische Methodik in der spätbyzantinischen Geistesgeschichte (14./15. Jh.), seine systematischen Grundlagen und seine historische Entwicklung* (Byzantinisches Archiv, 15: Munich, 1977)

Rackl, M. 'Die griechische Übersetzung der Summa theologiae des hl. Thomas von Aquin', *BZ*, xxiv (1923–4), pp. 48–60

Raybaud, L.-P. *Le gouvernement et l'administration centrale de l'empire byzantin sous les premiers Paléologues (1258–1354)* (Paris, 1968)

Reynolds, L. D. and Wilson, N. G. *Scribes and Scholars. A Guide to the Transmission of Greek and Laṭin Literature*, 2nd edn (Oxford, 1974)

Roberg, B. *Die Union zwischen der griechischen und der lateinischen Kirche auf dem II. Konzil von Lyon (1274)* (Bonn, 1964)

Runciman, S. *A History of the Crusades*, III (Cambridge, 1954)

Runciman, S. *The Sicilian Vespers. A History of the Mediterranean World in the Late Thirteenth Century* (Cambridge, 1958)

Runciman, S. *The Fall of Constantinople 1453* (Cambridge, 1965)

Runciman, S. *The Great Church in Captivity. A Study of the Patriarchate of Constantinople from the Eve of the Turkish Conquest to the Greek War of Independence* (Cambridge, 1968)

Runciman, S. *The Last Byzantine Renaissance* (Cambridge, 1970)

Runciman, S. *The Orthodox Churches and the Secular State* (Auckland–Oxford, 1971)

Runciman, S. *Byzantine Style and Civilization* (Harmondsworth, 1975)

Runciman, S. *The Byzantine Theocracy* (Cambridge, 1977)

Sarton, G. *Introduction to the History of Science*, I–III (Baltimore, 1927–48)

Savramis, D. *Zur Soziologie des byzantinischen Mönchtums* (Leiden, 1962)

Schirò, G. 'Il paradosso di Nilo Cabasila', *SBN*, IX (1957), pp. 362–88

Schirò, G. 'Gregorio Palamas e la scienza profana', *Le Millénaire du Mont Athos 963–1963. Etudes et Mélanges*, II (Fondazione G. Cini-Editions de Chevetogne: Venice, 1964), pp. 81–96

Schmitt, W. O. 'Lateinische Literatur in Byzanz. Die Übersetzungen des Maximos Planudes und die moderne Forschung', *JÖBG*, XVII (1968), pp. 127–47

Schreiner, P. 'Zur Geschichte Philadelpheias im 14. Jahrhundert (1293–1390)', *OCP*, XXXV (1969), pp. 375–431

Setton, K. M. 'The Byzantine background to the Italian Renaissance', *Proceedings of the American Philosophical Society*, C, I (1956), pp. 1–76

Setton, K. M. 'The Latins in Greece and the Aegean from the Fourth Crusade to the end of the Middle Ages', *Cambridge Medieval History*, IV, Pt I (1966), Ch. IX

Setton, K. M. *Europe and the Levant in the Middle Ages and the Renaissance. Collected Studies* (Variorum: London, 1974)

Setton, K. M. *A History of the Crusades*, II: *The Later Crusades, 1189–1311*, ed. R. L. Wolff and H. W. Hazard (Philadelphia, 1962); III: *The Fourteenth and Fifteenth Centuries*, ed. H. W. Hazard (Madison, 1975)

Setton, K. M. *Catalan Domination of Athens 1311–1388* (Cambridge, Mass., 1948; 2nd, rev. edn, London, 1975)

Setton, K. M. *The Papacy and the Levant (1204–1511)*, I: *The Thirteenth and Fourteenth Centuries* (Philadelphia, 1976)

Ševčenko, I. 'Observations sur les recueils des *Discours* et des *Poèmes* de Th. Métochite et sur la Bibliothèque de Chora à Constantinople', *Scriptorium*, V (1951), pp. 279–88

Ševčenko, I. 'The imprisonment of Manuel Moschopulos in the year 1305 or 1306', *Speculum*, XXVII (1952), pp. 133–57

Ševčenko, I. 'The Zealot revolution and the supposed Genoese colony in Thessalonica', *Prosphora eis St Kyriakidin* (Thessalonike, 1953), pp. 603–17

Ševčenko, I. 'Intellectual repercussions of the Council of Florence', *Church History*, XXIV (1955), pp. 291–323

Ševčenko, I. 'Nicolas Cabasilas' "Anti-Zealot" Discourse: a reinterpretation', *DOP*, XI (1957), pp. 79–171

Ševčenko, I. 'Alexios Makrembolites and his "Dialogue between the Rich and the Poor"', *ZRVI*, VI (1960), pp. 187–228

Ševčenko, I. 'The decline of Byzantium seen through the eyes of its intellectuals', *DOP*, XV (1961), pp. 167–86

Ševčenko, I. *Etudes sur la Polémique entre Théodore Métochites et Nicéphore Choumnos. La vie intellectuelle et politique à Byzance sous les premiers Paléologues* (Brussels, 1962)

Ševčenko, I. 'Society and intellectual life in the fourteenth century', *Actes du XIVe Congrès International des Etudes Byzantines*, I (Bucharest, 1974), pp. 69–92

Ševčenko, I. 'Theodore Metochites, the Chora, and the intellectual trends of his time', *The Kariye Djami*, IV, ed. P. A. Underwood (New York, 1975), pp. 17–91

Sherrard, P. *The Greek East and the Latin West. A study in the Christian Tradition* (Oxford, 1959)

Stiernon, D. 'Bulletin sur le palamisme', *REB*, XXX (1972), pp. 231–341

Sykoutris, I. Περὶ τὸ σχίσμα τῶν Ἀρσενιατῶν, *Hellenika*, II (1929), pp. 267–332; III (1930), pp. 15–44

Tachiaos, A. N. Ἐπιδράσεις τοῦ ἡσυχασμοῦ εἰς τὴν ἐκκλησιαστικὴν πολιτικὴν ἐν Ῥωσίᾳ 1328–1406 (Thessalonike, 1962)

Taeschner, F. 'The Ottoman Turks to 1453', *Cambridge Medieval History*, IV, Pt 1 (1966), Ch. XIX

Tafrali, O. *Thessalonique au Quatorzième siècle* (Paris, 1913)

Talbot, Alice-Mary M. 'The Patriarch Athanasius (1289–1293; 1303–1309) and the Church', *DOP*, XXVII (1973), pp. 11–28

Tatakis, B. *La Philosophie byzantine* (*Histoire de la Philosophie*, ed. E. Bréhier, fasc. suppl. II: Paris, 1959)

Temperley, H. W. V. *History of Serbia* (London, 1917)

Thiriet, F. *La Romanie vénitienne au moyen âge* (Paris, 1959)

Thomson, J. 'Manuel Chrysoloras and the early Italian Renaissance', *Greek, Roman and Byzantine Studies*, VII (1966), pp. 63–82

Tinnefeld, F. 'Byzantinisch-Russische Kirchenpolitik im 14. Jahrhundert', *BZ*, LXVII (1974), pp. 359–84

Tomadakes, N. B. Ὁ Ἰωσὴφ Βρυέννιος καὶ ἡ Κρήτη κατὰ τὸ 1400 (Athens, 1947)

Tomadakes, N. B. Μελετήματα περὶ 'Ιωσὴφ Βρυεννίου, *EEBS*, xxviii (1958), pp. 1–33

Tomadakes, N. B. 'Ιωσὴφ Βρυεννίου δημηγορία περὶ τοῦ τῆς πόλεως ἀνακτίσματος (1415 μ. X.), *EEBS*, xxxvi (1968), pp. 1–15

Treu, M. 'Der Philosoph Joseph', *BZ*, viii (1899), pp. 1–64

Tsirpanlis, C. N. *Mark Eugenicus and the Council of Florence. A Historical Re-evaluation of his Personality* (Thessalonike, 1974)

Turner, C. J. G. 'Pages from the late Byzantine philosophy of history', *BZ*, lvii (1964), pp. 346–73

Turner, C. J. G. 'George-Gennadius Scholarius and the Union of Florence', *Journal of Theological Studies*, xviii (1967), pp. 83–103

Turner, C. J. G. 'The career of George-Gennadius Scholarius', *B*, xxxix (1969), pp. 420–55

Udalcova, Z. V. 'K voprosu o socialno-političeskich vzgljadach vizantijskogo istorika XV v. Kritovula', *VV*, xii (1957), pp. 172–97 [On the question of the socio-political views of the fifteenth-century Byzantine historian Kritoboulos]

Udalcova, Z. V. 'Filosofskie trudy Vissariona Nikejskogo i ego gumanističeskaja dejatelnost' v Italii', *VV*, xxxiv (1973), pp. 75–88 [The philosophical works of Bessarion of Nicaea and his humanist activity in Italy]

Udalcova, Z. V. 'Zizn' i dejatelnost' Vissariona Nikejskogo', *VV*, xxxvii (1976), pp. 74–97 [The life and activity of Bessarion of Nicaea]

Ullmann, W. 'A Greek Démarche on the Eve of the Council of Florence', *Journal of Ecclesiastical History*, xxvi (1975), pp. 337–52

Underwood, P. A., ed. *The Kariye Djami*, 4 vols. (Bollingen Series, lxx: New York, 1966–75)

Vakalopoulos, A. E. 'Ιστορία τῆς Θεσσαλονίκης 315 Π.Χ.–1912 (Thessalonike, 1947); English trans. by T. F. Carney (Institute for Balkan Studies: Thessalonike, 1963)

Vakalopoulos, A. E. *Origins of the Greek Nation, 1204–1461* (New Brunswick, N.J., 1970)

Vakalopoulos, A. E. 'Ιστορία τοῦ Νέου 'Ελληνισμοῦ, i, 2nd edn (Thessalonike, 1974)

Vasiliev, A. A. 'Putešestvie Vizantijskago Imperatora Manuila II Paleologa po zapadnoj Evrope (1399–1403 g.)' [The journey of the Byzantine Emperor Manuel II Palaiologos to western Europe in 1399–1403], *Žurnal ministerstva narodnago prosveščenija*, n.s., xxxix (1912), pp. 41–78, 260–304

Vasiliev, A. A. 'Il viaggio di Giovanni V Paleologo in Italia e l'unione di Roma', *SBN*, iii (1931), pp. 153–92

Vasiliev, A. A. 'Medieval ideas of the end of the world: West and East', *B*, xvi (1944), pp. 462–502

Vasiliev, A. A. *History of the Byzantine Empire, 324–1453* (Madison, 1952)

Verpeaux, J. *Nicéphore Choumnos homme d'état et humaniste byzantin* (*ca. 1250/1255–1327*) (Paris, 1959)

Vogel, K. 'Byzantine science', *Cambridge Medieval History*, iv, Pt 2 (1967), Ch. XXVIII

Vries, de, W. 'Die Päpste von Avignon und der christliche Osten', *OCP*, xxx (1964), pp. 85–128

Vryonis, S. 'Isidore Glabas and the Turkish Devshirme', *Speculum*, xxi (1956), pp. 433–43

Vryonis, S. 'The Byzantine legacy and Ottoman forms', *DOP*, xxiii–xxiv (1969–70), pp. 253–308

Vryonis, S. *The Decline of Medieval Hellenism in Asia Minor and the Process of Islamization from the Eleventh through the Fifteenth Century* (Berkeley–Los Angeles–London, 1971)

Vryonis, S. *Byzantium: Its Internal History and Relations with the Muslim World. Collected Studies* (Variorum: London, 1971)

Vryonis, S. 'Religious changes and patterns in the Balkans, fourteenth to sixteenth centuries', *Aspects of the Balkans* (The Hague, 1972), pp. 151–76

Vryonis, S. 'Nomadization and Islamization in Asia Minor', *DOP*, xxix (1975), pp. 41–71

Vryonis, S. 'Religious change and continuity in the Balkans and Anatolia from the fourteenth through the sixteenth centuries', *Islam and Cultural Change in the Middle Ages*, ed. S. Vryonis (Wiesbaden, 1975), pp. 127–40

Ware, K. 'The Jesus Prayer in St Gregory of Sinai', *Eastern Churches Review*, iv (1973), pp. 3–22

Weiss, G. *Joannes Kantakuzenos – Aristokrat, Staatsmann, Kaiser und Mönch – in der Gesellschaftsentwicklung von Byzanz im 14. Jahrhundert* (Wiesbaden, 1969)

Werner, E. 'Volkstümlicher Häretiker oder sozial-politische Reformer? Probleme der revolutionären Volksbewegung in Thessalonike 1342–1349', *Wissenschaftliche Zeitschrift Universität Leipzig*, viii (1958–9), pp. 45–83

Werner, E. *Die Geburt einer Grossmacht – Die Osmanen* (*1300 bis 1481*). *Ein Beitrag zur Genesis des türkischen Feudalismus* (Berlin, 1966)

Werner, E. 'Gesellschaft und Kultur im XIV. Jahrhundert: Sozial-ökonomischen Fragen', *Actes du XIVe Congrès International des Etudes Byzantines*, i (Bucharest, 1974), pp. 93–110

Wifstrand, A. *Laonikos Chalkokondyles, der letzte Athenen. Ein Vortrag* (Scripta Minora Soc. Hum. Litt. Lundensis, 1971/2, 2: Lund, 1972)

Wittek, P. *Das Fürstentum Mentesche. Studie zur Geschichte Westkleinasiens im 13.–15. Jh.* (Istanbul, 1934)

Wittek, P. *The Rise of the Ottoman Empire* (Royal Asiatic Society Monographs, 23: London, 1938)

Wittek, P. 'De la défaite d'Ankara à la prise de Constantinople (un demi-siècle d'histoire ottomane)', *Revue des Etudes Islamiques*, XII (1938), pp. 1–34

Wolff, R. L. 'The Latin Empire of Constantinople and the Franciscans', *Traditio*, II (1944), pp. 213–37

Wolff, R. L. *Studies in the Latin Empire of Constantinople. Collected Studies* (Variorum: London, 1976)

Zakythenos, D. A. *Crise monétaire et crise économique à Byzance du XIIIe au XVe siècle* (Athens, 1948)

Zakythenos, D. A. *Τὸ Βυζάντιον μεταξὺ 'Ανατολῆς καὶ Δύσεως*, EEBS, XXVIII (1958), pp. 367–400

Zakythenos, D. A. *Byzance: Etat-Société-Economie. Collected Studies* (Variorum: London, 1973)

Zakythenos, D. A. *Le Despotat grec de Morée (1262–1460)*, I: *Histoire politique* (Paris, 1932); II: *Vie et Institutions* (Athens, 1953); Edition revue et augmentée par Chryssa Maltézou, 2 vols. (Variorum: London, 1975)

INDEX

Adam, William, O.P., 91
Adrianople, 21, 24 n. 44, 120
Aesop, 54
Akindyńos, Gregory, 39–40
Akropolites, Constantine, 53
Akropolites, George, 29, 53, 118
Albanians, 41
Alexios I Komnenos, Emperor, 102 n. 16
Amarantine, sorceress, 102 n. 15
Ambrose, St, 81
Anatolia, 66, 73, 89, 109; *see also* Asia Minor
Andreas, Frater, O.P., 79 n. 36
Andronikos II Palaiologos, Emperor, 13, 18, 32, 34, 44, 64, 67 n. 3, 68 n. 6, 103, 118, 131
Andronikos III Palaiologos, Emperor, 10, 67 n. 3, 131
Andronikos IV Palaiologos, Emperor, 131
Angelikoudes, Kallistos, monk, 84
Anjou, *see* Charles I of
Ankara, 68 n. 6, 107
Anne of Savoy, Empress, 10, 76
annus mundi, 105
Anselm, St, 83
Antichrist, 105 n. 24, 123
Antonios IV, Patriarch, 4, 128, 133
Apokaukos, Alexios, 10
apophatic theology, 84–5, 110
apostasy, Christian, to Islam, 67–8, 89–90
Aquinas, *see* Thomas Aquinas, St
Arabs, 1, 6, 66, 72, 92, 107
Aratus, 54
Aristides, Aelius, 33, 118
Aristophanes, 33, 54
Aristotle, 6, 35, 48, 50, 55, 57, 62, 84, 101, 112, 113, 118
Armageddon, 104
Armenians, 91

Arsenios Autoreianos, Patriarch, 7–9, 133
Arsenites, 7–9, 19, 52
art, artists, Byzantine, 62–3, 130
Asia Minor, 1, 9, 66–8, 71, 73, 75, 86, 89, 107; *see also* Anatolia
askesis (discipline), 40, 61
Assyrians, 106
astrology, 47 n. 48, 100, 103
astronomy, 34, 48 n. 51, 49, 57, 58–9, 103, 118
ataraxia (tranquillity), 36
ataxia (disorder), 26
Athanasios of Alexandria, St, 29–30
Athanasios I, Patriarch, 12–14, 29–30, 31, 34, 41, 43, 45 n. 45, 61, 67, 89, 98, 99, 101 n. 11, 133
Athanasios of the Meteora, 42, 43 n. 37
Athens, 2, 23
Athos, Mount, 9, 10, 19, 28, 36, 37, 38, 39, 40, 41, 44, 57
Attic Greek, 23, 56
Auden, W. H., 85
Augustine, St, 55, 81, 98
Aydin, 71 n. 15

Bajezid I, Sultan, 107, 109 n. 32
Barlaam of Calabria, 38–9, 51 n. 58, 85 n. 58
Basil of Caesarea, St, 33, 49, 50, 116
Basil I, Grand Duke of Moscow, 4, 128
Basil, Bogomil leader, 102 n. 16
Bekkos, John, *see* John XI, Patriarch
Bektashi, dervish order, 90
Benedictines, 35
Bernard, Guillaume, de Gaillac, O.P., 78 n. 35
Bessarion, Bishop of Nicaea, Cardinal, 83, 111–12, 114 n. 41, 115, 117, 120, 128
Bithynia, 40, 66, 68, 69, 71, 72, 73